Recent Theories of Narrative

Recent Theories of Narrative

Wallace Martin

PN
212
.M37
1986

Cornell
University
Press

ITHACA

AND

LONDON

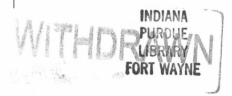

First published 1986 by Cornell University Press.

International Standard Book Number (cloth) 0-8014-1771-6
International Standard Book Number (paper) 0-8014-9355-2
Library of Congress Catalog Card Number 85-22401
Printed in the United States of America
*Librarians: Library of Congress cataloging information
appears on the last page of the book.*

*The paper in this book is acid-free and meets the guidelines for
permanence and durability of the Committee on Production Guidelines
for Book Longevity of the Council on Library Resources.*

Contents

5

Contents

Preface

The interest in theories of narrative that is evident in recent literary criticism is part of a broader movement—what Thomas Kuhn might call a "paradigm change"—in the humanities and social sciences. Since the nineteenth century, the methods of the natural sciences have served as a model for the rationalization of other disciplines. But during the past two decades that model has proved inadequate for an understanding of society and culture. The behaviorism that dominated psychology until recently has given way to an exploration of cognitive processes and purposive action. Philosophers of history have shown that narration is not just an impressionistic substitute for reliable statistics but a method of understanding the past that has its own rationale. Biologists, anthropologists, and sociologists have concluded that a study of mimetic behavior is as important as quantification in explaining animal development and social interaction. In philosophy the "theory of action," based on intentions, plans, and purposes, has proved relevant to emerging disciplines such as discourse analysis and artificial intelligence. Mimesis and narration have returned from their marginal status as aspects of "fiction" to inhabit the very center of other disciplines as modes of explanation necessary for an understanding of life.

We need not go to school to understand the importance of narrative in our lives. News of the world comes to us in the form of "stories" told from one or another point of view. The global drama unfolds every twenty-four hours—split up into multiple story lines that can be reintegrated only when they are understood from the perspective of an American (or Russian, or Nigerian), a Democrat (or Republican, or monarchist, or Marxist), a Protestant (or Catholic, or Jew, or Muslim).

7

Behind each of these differences there is a history, and a hope for the future. For each of us there is also a personal history, the narratives of our own lives, which enable us to construe what we are and where we're headed. If we were to revise that story by interpreting its events from a different point of view, much might change. That is why narrative, considered a form of entertainment when studied as literature, is a battleground when actualized in newspapers, biography, and history.

Viewed against this backdrop, my own discussion of narrative is relatively narrow. I have attempted to review theories of literary narration proposed by critics during the past two decades, with occasional reference to earlier theories and other disciplines. Even this circumscribed area is difficult to summarize in a single book. As Seymour Chatman notes in *Story and Discourse,* "libraries bulge with studies of specific genres" and aspects of narrative theory, but "there are few books in English on the subject of narrative in general." Increasing specialization results from the complexity of the problems revealed by previous literary research, as well as the introduction of analytic models drawn from other disciplines. When translations from French, German, and Russian are added to the writings of English and American theorists, the only alternative to few books on narrative in general might appear to be none at all.

Yet Chatman produced one, drawing together the results of structuralist studies during the fifteen years preceding its publication in 1978; and Dorrit Cohn's *Transparent Minds,* a comprehensive study of the presentation of consciousness in narrative, appeared the same year. Since then we have had translations of Gérard Genette's *Narrative Discourse,* and Franz Stanzel's *Theory of Narrative . . .* but already I am dwindling into bibliography, which belongs at the back of the book. My own attempt to encompass the subject differs from these books in two respects; it surveys a wider range of materials, and it juxtaposes them, rather than subsuming them in an integrated theory. Since the disadvantages of such broad and unsystematic treatment are apparent, it will require some justification; but first I will indicate what areas of narrative theory the following pages treat.

The introductory chapter begins with an account of the predominant theories of the novel in the years before 1960, glances back to their antecedents in the early part of the century, and then introduces the critics and trends to be discussed in subsequent chapters. The second and third concern the two issues that have been most crucial in the development of recent theories of narrative: the changes of perspective that result from studying narrative in general rather than the novel, and from viewing realism as a literary convention rather than as a trustworthy representation of life. The latter topic involves reference to what may prove to be the most important development in narrative theory during the next few years: its application to the study of history, biography, autobiography, and psychoanalysis. Chapter 4 discusses the attempts of structuralists and others to identify the conventions governing narrative sequences, whether fictional or factual. The most influential exponents of structural analysis— Roland Barthes, Genette, and Chatman—are the subject of chapter 5.

Between the story and the reader is the narrator, who controls what will be told and how it will be perceived. Point of view, which American and German critics consider the defining feature of narration, has taken on renewed importance in the past few years, and recent studies of the subject are the topic of chapter 6. In chapter 7, point of view is treated as one aspect of narrative communication from an author to readers who may or may not share the same assumptions and conventions of interpretation. Chapters 4 to 7 thus progress from abstract, "grammatical" models of narrative analysis to models based on convention and communication. The eighth chapter concerns the ways in which such narrative forms as parody and metafiction step outside theoretical frames of reference, and then returns to the basic questions that constitute the entire field of study: the specific characteristics of fiction and narrative.

To discuss literary theories without showing how they can be applied is difficult, if not useless, but to mention in passing how they apply to a wide range of works with which some readers may not be familiar is pointless. As an unsatisfactory compromise, I have applied the theories discussed to a series of stories on the traditional folk motif of "the lover's gift regained" and Katherine Mansfield's "Bliss" (these appear in the appendix), and to Ernest Hemingway's "The Short Happy Life of Francis Macomber" and *The Adventures of Huckleberry Finn*. Repeated analysis of the same examples makes it possible to compare and evaluate theories.

By means of the annotated bibliography and the figures interspersed in the text, I attempt to compensate for two of the shortcomings attendant on an effort to survey a vast field: inadequate representation of the theories discussed, and cursory treatment of the differences between them. The proliferation of technical terms in narrative theory does not result from carelessness or the needless coinage of new words to replace others already in circulation. The purposes, and hence the analytic frameworks of the theorists, differ;

they are not commensurate, and there is no way to reduce their ideas to a common vocabulary without effacing what is of particular value in each. In providing tabular comparisons of the terms they use, I have sometimes displaced their words toward a common frame of reference, but have more often highlighted their differences.

Attempting to catch the point and tone of each theorist, I would have them address each other; in some cases I make them proleptic commenters on theories that did not exist when they wrote. My intention in doing so is not to stir up trouble but to stimulate the curiosity of readers and steer them toward the essays and books I discuss. The disadvantages of such fragmentary treatment of complex theories are obvious. In defense of the method, I can offer only the following comments.

Within each theory, whether overtly or implicitly, there is the opposing voice of another theoretical perspective. The theorist has been incited into thought by the thought of another; the arena in which the two interact is the virtual space *between* theories that, in its entirety, makes up the context of criticism. The expository method that provides a complete and accurate account of a theory helps confirm its integrity and its isolation from others. Thus it reproduces the genial gesture of deference or dismissal through which critics avoid controversy, on the assumption that it is an ill-mannered and ill-tempered activity. But what could a theory be, other than a necessary step on the path to dialogue; and why would it be created, if not as a reply to another or an answer to a question? It is a sense of narrative theory as a whole, of the issues animating its lively debates and currently making it the most interesting area of literary criticism, that I hope to capture.

Among the trends not mentioned that would ideally have received at least cursory treatment are studies of themes and types, stylistics, unreliable narration, semiotics, and discourse and text analysis. These last are too technical for brief presentation. The same can be said of detailed structural analysis of narrative, introduced in the fourth chapter; but the writings of Jonathan Culler, Robert Scholes, and Chatman have already made them accessible to a wide audience. One of the most significant recent books on narrative, Fredric Jameson's *The Political Unconscious: Narrative as a Socially Symbolic Act,* does not lend itself to summary; not having discussed it, I recommend it to readers, along with William Dowling's *Jameson, Althusser, Marx: An Introduction to "The Political Unconscious."*

For supplying unpublished materials important to my work, I am indebted to Dorrit Cohn, Ann Harleman Stewart, and Richard Sheldon. A sabbatical leave granted by the University of Toledo provided time necessary for research and writing. Thomas Pavel and Lubomír Doležel kindly responded to requests for comments on portions of the manuscript; in an undertaking that provided endless possibilities for making mistakes, they have saved me from a few. Students contributed to such clarity as I have been able to attain by asking the right questions; I ended up asking some of them questions, and four (Nicholas Conrad, Deborah Resnick, Joseph Cothrell, and Johnson Nwabuwe) provided answers that I have used in the following pages. Those who have taught me most of what I know about narrative are the critics whose ideas make up the substance of this book. I can only offer them my gratitude and apologies for not having represented them more fully and accurately. Comments by readers for Cornell University Press have made the text better than it would otherwise have been; Kay Scheuer, senior manuscript editor, and Patricia Sterling provided meticulous editing. I am grateful to Claude Bremond for permission to reproduce the diagram from "Morphology of the Folktale" that appears in Figure 4b.

To minimize the clutter of documentation, I have eliminated footnotes. The sources for references in the text can be found in the bibliography, which is subdivided by chapter and section.

WALLACE MARTIN

Toldeo, Ohio

Recent Theories of Narrative

1

Introduction

During the past fifteen years, the theory of narrative has displaced the theory of the novel as a topic of central concern in literary study. The difference between the two is not simply one of generality—as if, having analyzed one species of narration, we went on to study others and then described the genus. By changing the definition of what is being studied, we change what we see; and when different definitions are used to chart the same territory, the results will differ, as do topographical, political, and demographic maps, each revealing one aspect of reality by virtue of disregarding all others. There is of course less agreement in literary criticism than in cartography. But the analogy does call attention to the fact that literary theories are created for different purposes, and their usefulness as well as their accuracy must be taken into account when comparing them. To understand the recent critical shift to an interest in narrative, it is helpful to look first at what problems the older and newer theories have attempted to solve.

Theories of the Novel, 1945–1960

The novel is now recognized as a major genre, the most representative literary product of European and American culture since the Romantic period. But as recently as three decades ago, it had not achieved this recognition and general acceptance. Traces of the marginal status assigned to the novel can still be found in college curricula whose historical sequences of courses in "literature" do not include prose narratives. The purposes and methods of critics of the novel af-

15

ter World War II were in large part determined by their desire to demonstrate the importance of the genre at a time when claims about literary merit were based on analysis of form. So long as discussions of the novel emphasized its subject matter and content, disregarding the formal issues that were then important in criticism and aesthetics, it would remain an uncanonized genre in literary study.

The New Critics, by fixing their attention on individual poems, had shown that claims about aesthetic value and meaning could be backed up by detailed analysis of form. One way to attain for the novel the esteem traditionally accorded to other genres would be to show that its techniques are as subtle and complex and its forms as significant as those of the epic, of drama, and of poetry. After World War II, a number of critics applied themselves to this task. In his essay "Technique as Discovery" (1947), Mark Schorer proposed a view of the novel that was soon to gain wide acceptance: "Modern criticism has shown us that to speak of content as such is not to speak of art at all, but of experience; and that it is only when we speak of the *achieved* content, the form, the work of art as a work of art, that we speak as critics. The difference between content, or experience, and achieved content, or art, is technique. When we speak of technique, then, we speak of nearly everything. . . . We are no longer able to regard as seriously intended criticism of poetry which does not assume these generalizations; but the case for fiction has not yet been established." Schorer's essay was reprinted in *Forms of Modern Fiction* (1948), a collection of essays in accord with his own view. In the second edition of that book (1959), William Van O'Connor, the editor, noted that "criticism of fiction, of the sort that had been devoted to poetry, was relatively rare" when the book was originally published; "since then, it has become a commonplace."

Schorer and most of his contemporaries disregarded or criticized the inherited technical vocabulary that treated the novel as a combination of plot, character, setting, and theme (terms that also apply to drama). The techniques specific to the novel involve the author's relation to the narrator, the narrator's relation to the story, and the ways in which they provide access to the minds of characters—matters of "point of view." If we assume that the author tries to achieve objective, realistic representation—free from intrusive commentary that would turn characters into puppets by judging them as soon as they are introduced, and credible by virtue of the ways in which we gain access to minds and events—then analysis of point of view becomes a means of understanding how form and content are fused in the novel. But form is not solely a matter of how the story is told; it can involve the structure of image, metaphor, and symbol that emerge from the action, and therefore the novel can be studied with methods that have been successfully applied to poetry. Joseph Frank's essay "Spatial Form in Modern Literature" (1945) was an influential example of such analysis, and he discussed two other topics that were to prove important in narrative theory: the treatment of time (an aesthetic as well as a representational concern), and the relationship between the novel and the structures of myth.

Analysis of point of view, images, and symbols converge in discussions of "the stream of consciousness," which Lawrence Bowling (1950) defined as "that narrative method by which the author attempts to give *a direct quotation of the mind*—not merely of the language area but of the whole consciousness." Books by Robert Humphrey (1954) and Melvin Friedman (1955) described stream-of- consciousness techniques and traced their history, respectively; in *The Psychological Novel, 1900–1950* (1955), Leon Edel treated the rendering of consciousness in the broader context of the symbolist novel, which, he said, requires us to read "prose fiction as if it were poetry" (207).

Ideally, a "theory of the novel" would contribute to our understanding of all novels, regardless of when they were written. But literary theories are seldom if ever ideal; their strengths and limitations arise from the practical problems they are intended to solve. In attempting to show that the novel repays theoretical study, critics found that recent novels provided the best evidence for their arguments. Modern novelists, from Gustave Flaubert and Henry James to the present, had discussed many of the techniques emphasized by the critics, and thus it was no coincidence that their works provided the best examples of narrative objectivity, artistic manipulation of point of view, the use of symbols or images as motifs, and subtle representations of consciousness.

A theory of the novel based on the critical tenets of a particular historical situation and emphasizing the literature of a particular period cannot escape certain limitations. Before the late nineteenth century, English and American novelists had not been particularly concerned with the formal refinements emphasized by some of their successors, and any description of the novel based on these techniques can lead to partial or prejudicial assessments of its earlier exemplars. Some postwar critics who emphasized the form of the novel tended to find fault with the methods used by novelists who either preceded or rejected this artistic tradition; others represented the history of the novel as an evolution from casual and careless methods to a perfected presentation of consciousness in the twentieth century.

The emphasis on the formal features of the novel after World War

II did not go unchallenged in its own time. Harry Levin (1963) suggested that it was in part a result of historical circumstances: during the depression of the 1930s, critics felt compelled to reduce literature to sociology; in the postwar period, "formal qualities are given careful attention, while once more the social aspect is slighted," possibly indicating a "retreat from the pressures of history itself." Concentration on form in the novel, said Lionel Trilling (1948), was a danger for both critic and novelist: "A conscious preoccupation with form at the present time is almost certain to lead the novelist, particularly the young novelist, into limitation. . . . Form suggests completeness and the ends tucked in; resolution is seen only as all contradictions equated, and although form thus understood has its manifest charm, it will not adequately serve the modern experience."

For these critics, the novel was distinguished from other genres by its content and subject matter—the representation of life in all its diversity. It was in fact by breaking away from conventional forms and imaginary situations that the novel came into existence; thus a freedom from formal constraints can be seen as its defining characteristic. The shift from anonymous repetition of traditional tales to original stories filled with circumstantial detail indicates why the novel is usually considered a "realistic" genre. The diversity of its techniques, from this perspective, results from the variety of experience itself. If form is identified with stylistic refinement, we must confess that "the novel is, as many have said of it, the least 'artistic' of genres," according to Trilling. But form can be conceived differently: "The novel achieves its best effects of art often when it has no concern with them, when it is fixed upon effects in morality, or when it is simply reporting what it conceives to be objective fact." F. R. Leavis (1948) agreed with Trilling. The great novelists of the English tradition, he said, were concerned with form, but in an ethical rather than an aesthetic sense. If we study the formal perfection of Jane Austen's *Emma*, for example, "we find that it can be appreciated only in terms of the moral preoccupations that characterize the novelist's peculiar interest in life."

Conceived as a representational genre shaped by human values, the novel attracts a wide range of commentary. The critic can see it as a record of the problems confronting individuals in a stable social structure, given their circumstances and class origin, or the problems they face when confronted with social change. The novel can serve a reportorial function, bringing into consciousness the varied human conditions that culture and literature had not previously considered important. It can record the human experience underlying and perhaps explaining the impersonal chronicles of historians. More generally, it can be conceived as the sphere in which illusion (in the form of inherited beliefs and ideologies, self-esteem, pretensions, romantic desire, the desire for possessions) meets reality (the social and economic conditions underlying these castles in the air). If "manners," the social customs that individuals manipulate to conceal and achieve their aims, are one focus of the novel, money is less obviously another, for it is the ground where self and society both define and confuse ethical and material values. The emphasis on representational truth and moral issues in this critical tradition are related to its educational goals: even when the novel is not didactic, it can be used to gain knowledge about life.

Most English and American critics hold that the novel originated in the eighteenth century, and a comprehensive theory of the genre should provide some explanation of why it appeared at that time. Critics who concentrated on its technical features argued that subjective points of view and the record of consciousness became important in literature when philosophy, political thought, and society began to emphasize the autonomy of the individual. For those who conceive the novel as a depiction of social reality, its appearance marks the emergence of the middle class as the shaping force of history, ending the period when literature portrayed all characters but the aristocracy as crude, comic, or unworthy of serious treatment. Irving Howe and Leslie Fiedler agreed with Philip Rahv, Levin, and Trilling that the bourgeoisie and its desire for material possessions constitute the mainspring of the novel, driving its characters and society toward our current condition. The novel is thus relevant to the diagnosis of social and cultural issues. Walter Allen (1955) and Ian Watt (1957) confirmed the view that the novel, characterized by realism, arose in the eighteenth century in response to changes in society, philosophy, and conceptions of history.

Earlier, I said that definitions of the novel imply a method of evaluation and a history of the genre. If defined through reference to technique, it is seen as evolving toward a perfection achieved in the twentieth century. When conceived as a representative record of human experience, the novel's history and achievements are viewed differently: the great novelists are the realists of the nineteenth and early twentieth centuries, from Jane Austen and Balzac to Thomas Mann. Two of the most important European critics of the twentieth century, Georg Lukács and Erich Auerbach, endorsed this view, which was the predominant one among American critics of the 1950s. Advocates of realism detected signs of decay in twentieth-century fiction; in the decade following World War II, a number of critics suggested that the "death of the novel" might be at hand, perhaps because the class structure which had furnished the novel with its subjects was being replaced by the "mass society" of postindustrial capitalism. For those who believed that the novel was an accurate reflection of its time, the "new American Gothic" and beat generation fiction, treating freakish or eccentric characters, could only be viewed as evidence of authorial decadence or read as an allegory of cultural disintegration.

Theories of the Novel in the Early Twentieth Century

This selective review of postwar theories of the novel—one group emphasizing form, the other emphasizing subject matter and content—is oversimplified; the articles by Bradford Booth and Norman Friedman listed in the bibliography provide more detailed accounts of critical trends during that period. But the views I have discussed were the predominant ones, and their opposition to each other can be traced back to the beginning of the century. During the 1920s and 1930s, Percy Lubbock and Joseph Warren Beach had emphasized the importance of technique in the "well-made novel," whereas E. M. Forster had advocated a less formal view of narrative methods. Lubbock and Beach continued a tradition founded by Henry James, whose discussions of point of view are among the first and best available. And James, who admired the technical mastery of Ivan Turgenev, had been opposed by H. G. Wells, who, in the tradition of Charles Dickens, saw the novel as "the vehicle of understanding, the instrument of self-examination, the parade of morals and the exchange of manners, the factory of customs, the criticism of laws and institutions and of social dogmas and ideas."

Theories are best understood in historical perspective, and despite their differences, American and English views of the novel during the first five decades of the century were based on a fairly stable set of assumptions. Underlying the opposition of form to subject matter and content is an agreement that these are the basic constituents of the novel. In one sense an interest in the representation of consciousness is antithetical to the view that the novel should represent social realities, but in a broader sense these positions are based on a shared opposition of subjectivity to objectivity. Despite their differences, advocates of both positions agree that accurate transcription, whether of mind or world, is desirable. Some critics tried to avoid or overcome these antitheses (as is evident in the quotations from Schorer and Leavis above), but no theoretically important methods of doing so were available until later, when the criticism of Lukács was translated into English, and Fredric Jameson extended Lukács's dialectical conception of form and content.

Within a broad framework of agreement and difference, there were significant changes in Anglo-American conceptions of the novel during this period. At the beginning of the century, the definition and hence the history of the novel were still matters of dispute, some critics holding that there had been no decisive change in the development of prose narrative since the medieval period, others arguing that the novel was a realistic genre—clearly distinguishable from its predecessors—that originated in the works of John Bunyan and/or Daniel Defoe, Samuel Richardson, and Henry Fielding. In books on the novel, advocates of the latter position would include a discussion of "romances" in order to show how the two differed. But once their view equating the novel with realism had gained general acceptance, discussion of romances declined. In criticism and college curricula, the immense range of prose narrative tended to be narrowed down to the novel and short story. Some major American writers, for example Hawthorne and Melville, do not fit comfortably into the confines of the realistic tradition, and they provided one impetus for the study of mythic and symbolic structures discussed above. Another noteworthy change in criticism was an increasing concentration on point of view as the primary technical device in narrative. Discussion of plot all but disappeared, despite the efforts of R. S. Crane and others to preserve it. The very conception of plot was associated with traditional tales and the stock devices of popular fiction; such formulae are unrealistic, and modern novelists usually avoid them.

Theories of Narrative: Frye, Booth, and French Structuralism

The first noteworthy challenge to this critical tradition redefined the issues involved by placing them in a more inclusive historical and theoretical perspective. In *Anatomy of Criticism* (1957), Northrop Frye took issue with the tendency to identify the realistic novel as the best or only form of prose fiction: "The literary historian who identifies fiction with the novel is greatly embarrassed by the length of time that the world managed to get along without the novel, and until he reaches his great deliverance in Defoe, his perspective is intolerably cramped. . . . Clearly, this novel-centered view of prose fiction is a Ptolemaic perspective which is now too complicated to be any longer workable, and some more relative and Copernican view must take its place" (303–4). In his view, the novel is but one species of the genus "fiction," the latter word originally having meant something made, not something false. By identifying the different conventions used in various types of fiction, the critic will, for example, avoid judging a romance (which involves stylized or idealized characters) by reference to methods of characterization that are appropriate to the realistic novel. In addition to the novel and romance, Frye identified two other species of fictional prose—the confession (autobiography) and anatomy (which presents "a vision of the world in terms of a single intellectual pattern")—and showed that the four kinds intermix, the novel often combining with the other three. The next chapter will treat Frye's taxonomy in more detail; at present, it is enough to say that his book marks an important stage in the transition from theories of the novel to theories of narrative.

Shortly after Frye introduced a broader perspective into discussions of the subject matter and conventions of fiction, Wayne Booth challenged the conceptions of narrative technique that had gained general acceptance in the preceding years. The first part of his book *The Rhetoric of Fiction* (1961) lists the precepts of this tradition—"true novels must be realistic"; "all authors should be objective"; true art should not cater to the tastes of the audience through its emotional or moral appeal—and argues that they are based on a false view of what fiction is and does. Taken together, these dogmas imply that the novel attains artistic value by cutting itself free from human values so that it can become a self-contained object of pure representation. But the novel is inevitably a "rhetorical" form in that it involves communication from an implied author to an audience of readers, and the varied methods it uses to secure effects cannot be understood apart from questions of tone, attitude, implicit evaluation, and variable degrees of attitudinal distance between implied author, narrator, characters, and reader. In the second and third parts of his book, Booth treats the uses of authorial commentary in fiction (usually considered an old-fashioned, clumsy intrusion) and its opposite, "impersonal narration." He argues that the latter, advocated by champions of the modern novel, is seldom achieved in practice, since an adept reader can detect signs of the author's attitude. When they have no clues about the author's opinion of what he presents, readers and critics are often at a loss to know what the story means or how to evaluate it. Frye had expanded the boundaries of fiction to show that the novel was one of its provinces; Booth removed some of the border markers that separated fiction as an art from ordinary methods of conveying meaning with language.

During the 1960s, several anthologies of writings on narrative theory since Henry James were published (see bibliography section 1.1); they contain a number of the essays and excerpts from books that I have mentioned. The following chapters treat trends in narrative theory beginning with Frye and Booth; themes from earlier criticism recur, but they often appear in a new light because of shifts in the ground of critical discussion during the intervening years. An attempt to describe briefly the welter of recent theory, which dwarfs that of the preceding decades in both quantity and complexity, will necessarily be partial, but it can serve to introduce the topics and critics that are discussed in subsequent chapters.

Two factors are in large part responsible for the changes that occurred after 1960. First, narrative theory became an international subject of study, whereas in the preceding period critics had usually remained within the limits of their own literary and scholarly traditions. Second, it became an interdisciplinary subject. We usually assume that rational knowledge is based on a single set of principles which, when applied to particular subjects of study, produce different theories and structural models. This assumption was crucial to the development of French structuralism in the 1960s and the theories of narrative that it produced. Structuralist critics conceived the study of literature as a subdivision of the "sciences of man" (what we would call the humanities and social sciences), and they used the most scientific of humanistic disciplines—linguistics—as the model or paradigm for the development of theories that would link literature, anthropology, and sociology together. Once freed of the notion that they should study only stories that are untrue and highly respected (the domain of traditional literature), critics realize that the anthropologist, folklorist, historian, and even the psychoanalyst and theologian are all concerned with narratives in one way or another. But differences in the purposes and materials of these disciplines make it difficult to see how they are interrelated.

The ways in which theories are dependent on the materials selected for study and on the objectives of the theorist are nowhere more evident than in the contrast between literary and anthropological approaches to narrative. Rather than original, realistic stories fixed in print, the anthropologist encounters dozens of oral tales, many of them only slightly different from one another. Often they involve magical events that have no obvious relationship to the "realities" of the society in which they are recounted. In almost every respect, the questions the anthropologist must try to answer are the opposite of those posed by the literary critic: not "why is this story unique?" but

23

"how and why is it so similar to others?"; not "what did this (identifiable) author mean?" but "what function does this (anonymous) collective myth serve when it is repeated on certain occasions?" For the critic, a single work is the locus of meaning; the anthropologist seldom treats less than several versions of a tale. The relationship between the narrative and everyday reality is obvious in one case, obscure in the other. Features such as point of view, characterization, description, and style—so important to the literary critic—scarcely exist in the oral tale. The critic's sophisticated methods of interpretation are of little help to the anthropologist. And the latter is committed, as a social scientist, to a conception of methodology which, though it may not necessarily be better than that used in literary study, is certainly more constraining.

Many features of French structuralist theories of narrative that may seem odd to the American reader result from the fact that they were inspired by anthropological methods and purposes. There had of course been many attempts to explain oral tales and myths before the publication of Claude Lévi-Strauss's "The Structural Study of Myth" (1955), but his approach to the problem marked a definite break with the conjectural methods of his predecessors. It was not just through this essay that Lévi-Strauss attracted the attention of literary critics. By showing how structural linguistics could be used as a model in the development of other human sciences, and by providing examples of how a collection of puzzling signs can be systematically analyzed to reveal an unconscious cultural content, he created the possibility of studying literature in a new way.

The anthropologist's methods of analyzing non-Western cultures can be applied to the myths, tales, and folklore of our own tradition. Popular, formulaic narrative kinds such as the detective novel, the modern romance, the western, and the soap opera, which literary critics seldom stoop to study, might yield interesting information about our society if their unconscious content could be recovered. For that matter, the literary critic could try to interpret his own society as if it were a foreign tribe, for we live amid a host of conventions (dress codes, menus, the rituals attached to sports, the sorts of names we give to horses or cats or boats) that appear to have no particular "meaning" but are as peculiar as many of the practices we consider "primitive." If the business of the critic is to interpret signs, our whole society could be the critic's text.

Roland Barthes, the most influential narrative theorist of the past twenty years, undertook a number of the projects I have just mentioned. He was more able than most of his contemporaries to extend and adapt the methods of anthropology and structural linguistics to the study of modern literature. Other French critics such as Claude Bremond and A.-J. Greimas based their narrative theories on earlier traditions and have only occasionally applied them to modern works. Lévi-Strauss's explanation of the narrative structure of myths is, in essence, a four-term formula that can include at most four actions and two characters; this is another example of the ways in which the kinds of stories analyzed (in his case, short ones) determine the structure of the theory used to explain them. Since Greimas and Bremond were interested in tales of greater length, they needed a more accommodating theory and found another model for narrative analysis in a work by the Russian folklorist Vladimir Propp, *Morphology of the Folktale* (1928).

Propp was one of several Russian scholars and critics who were important in the development of French structuralism. Though most of their publications appeared between 1914 and 1930, the Russian formalists and those they influenced (Propp and M. M. Bakhtin) were scarcely known in the West before the 1950s. Their importance has not yet received the general recognition it deserves, in part because of a lack of translations. The problem of constructing a truly comprehensive theory of narrative, one that could bridge the gap that the French structuralists encountered between the repetitive, formulaic structures of traditional literature and the original plots of the modern novel, was crucial to Victor Shklovsky. In his search for the underlying laws of literary structure, he studied the entire range of narrative kinds, from jokes and folklore to Laurence Sterne's *Tristram Shandy* and Twain's *Huckleberry Finn*. Shklovsky's name will appear frequently in the following pages; there is scarcely an aspect of narrative theory that he did not discuss.

Bakhtin is equally important. He rejected the formalist emphasis on literary technique at the expense of social and political factors in the study of the novel, but he considered the formalists worthy opponents and made good use of their insights. Three other members of the formalist group who wrote on narrative theory—Roman Jakobson, Boris Eichenbaum, and Boris Tomashevsky—also influenced the French critics of the 1960s. Jakobson had in fact helped Lévi-Strauss see how linguistic methods of analysis could be used in anthropology, and thus Russian thought converged on French criticism from two directions.

The history of recent criticism is so complex that it can only be conveyed through the use of narrative techniques, such as the preceding flashback to the Russian formalists in the middle of a discussion of

French structuralism. Soon after the publication in French of essays by the formalists in 1965, the structuralists began making use of their insights. The translator of the essays, Tzvetan Todorov, is the most systematic and comprehensive of the structuralist critics. His own writings on narrative show how Russian and French theories can be integrated; he also incorporates the insights of English and American critics, pointing out their relationship to Continental concerns. Such awareness of the Anglo-American tradition was not common among the structuralists, in part because its emphasis on point of view was not relevant to their interest in premodern narratives. But Gérard Genette, who treats point of view as equal in importance to narrative structure or plot, is familiar with point-of-view studies in English. Genette's influence on American criticism is evident in a book that uses the work of the structuralists as the basis of a comprehensive theory of narrative—Seymour Chatman's *Story and Discourse.*

The particular theories and terminology of structuralist critics are of less importance in this brief historical survey than their basic assumptions. For the traditional assertion that the novel is a realistic representation of life, they substitute the thesis that all stories are shaped by conventions and imagination. The novel is in their view but one relatively recent type of narrative. Their attempts to identify the conventions underying myths, folktales, science fiction, the fantastic, autobiography, and detective stories as well as the realistic novel, and to explain how language, society, and the mind have contributed to the formation of literary conventions, have raised more questions than they have answered. But this has proved to be the value of their criticism: it has suggested new areas of study and stimulated critics to develop alternative theories of the fundamental features of narration.

Recent Trends

The interdisciplinary and international character of narrative theory since 1970 is evident in American criticism. The most important writings of the French structuralists have appeared in English; Jonathan Culler, Robert Scholes, and others have published lucid summaries of structuralist thought; and the relevance to literary study of scholarship in other disciplines has achieved the recognition it deserves. Anthropologists and folklorists in England, Canada, and the United States have pursued lines of study suggested by Lévi-Strauss and Propp. In the philosophy of history, American scholars undertook investigation of history as a narrative mode before the subject had attracted the attention of structuralists. The application of new psychological and psychoanalytic models in narrative analysis, important in French criticism since the 1960s, has become common here and elsewhere. The structuralists were not the only instigators of these developments: linguistic studies of narrative conventions, which have produced important results in the past few years, began long before structuralism. Likewise, sociological and Marxist analyses of narrative have made use of structuralism but produce their most interesting results when challenging it.

A brief review of current trends in narrative theory will serve to introduce other topics examined in the following chapters. The most important of these has been the shift from formally defined linguistic models to communication models. The linguist and the critic who imitates him begin from our knowledge of what a noun and a sentence (or character and story) are; what they seek is a scientifically rigorous description of such structures. But literature is not really comparable to language in this analogy. We can call a sentence "grammatical" because we know what it means to say a sentence is ungrammatical, and we can explain the difference between clear and ambiguous meaning by pointing to structural and semantic features. No such categorical distinctions and systematic explanations are available in literature. There are many kinds of stories, little agreement about which ones are best, and less agreement about what they mean. Therefore, rather than trying to discover the formal structures on which all stories are based, the critic might better try to determine why and how we read stories as we do—asking not what they are in the abstract but determining what competence we intuitively exercise when reading them. Recent literary theories based on the communication model may treat the literary work as a rhetorical form that conveys meaning from implied author to reader (Wayne Booth's approach), or study the literary and cultural conventions that shape literary perception, as do structuralists and semioticians. "Reader-response criticism," a term used to describe such theories, is often intended to explain the effects of all types of literature; I shall discuss only those that attempt to account for our construal of narratives, the theory of the German critic Wolfgang Iser being one of the most important of these.

Another recent trend in both literary and narrative theory has been a renewed emphasis on problems of interpretation. Structuralists interested in analyzing narrative form and technique thought that it was possible to undertake such analysis without knowing beforehand exactly what stories mean. If general agreement about literary interpretation were a prerequisite for discussion of literary conventions, the latter would never begin, because the former will never be achieved. Those who hold that interpretation is the only purpose of reading are opposed to this purely formal analysis of literary structure. They may argue that it cannot tell us anything interesting or useful about literature; they may accuse the structuralist of the primal sin in criticism— the separation of form and content. But these are old arguments, and they leave unanswered the charge that interpretation is simply a matter of opinion. The most significant challenges to formal analysis have been those of interpreters who argue that narrative writing disrupts all codes and conventions that might give it unified form and meaning (J. Hillis Miller); or that form and meaning are always in a reciprocal relationship, creating and deforming each other (Frank Kermode).

While critics debate about theories, creative writers may produce new literary works that alter the very ground of the debate. The "death of the (realistic) novel," which attracted so much critical attention in America and France during the 1950s, coincided with the rebirth of narrative. The "new novel" in France (Alain Robbe-Grillet, Nathalie Sarraute), what has been called "fabulation" and "metafiction" in American fiction since the 1960s (John Barth, William Gass, Donald Barthelme, Richard Brautigan, Robert Coover), and South American writers such as Jorge Borges, Julio Cortázar, and Gabriel García Márquez simply cannot be discussed adequately if one uses the critical apparatus associated with realism. It may seem strange to refer to the influence of literature as a third trend in narrative theory, since critics should as a matter of course attempt to account for creative innovation. But some of the aforementioned novelists have themselves written penetrating essays challenging traditional attitudes toward fiction; their precepts and examples have shaped both French and American criticism. In the fiction of John Barth and others, innovation has taken the form of a revival of narrative techniques that go back to the origins of tale-telling.

The originality of recent fiction and narrative theory has drawn attention away from scholarly and historical studies that convey their insights in traditional terminology. As the example of John Barth shows, what appears to be new may simply be something that has been forgotten, and scholarship on the Greek romances, medieval literature, prose narratives of the seventeenth and eighteenth centuries, and non-Western tales provides evidence useful for any general theory of narrative. Historical studies and collections of pre-twentieth-century critical writings on prose fiction have shown that theories of narrative are not as recent a phenomenon as many critics previously thought. Scholars lend support to a conclusion implicitly drawn by theorists: the study of narrative cannot be limited to one period or one national literature. Throughout history, stories have wandered from one culture to another; and since the invention of printing, novels have so commonly been translated that there are few major novelists who have not been influenced by their foreign predecessors.

The preceding historical sketch of narrative theory in the twentieth century is oversimplified. Others may disagree with my estimate of which critics and trends have been most significant; the following pages include treatment of subjects not mentioned in this brief survey. The diagram in Figure 1a can serve as a rough guide to the differences between theories of narrative and the ways in which what a critic sees depends on the theory he uses. The early French structuralists emphasized axis (1) and occasionally treated the entire vertical column of which it is a part (in which case narrative is viewed as a record of social organization that can be analyzed formally). Axis (5) is discussed by semiologists and Marxist critics. The triangle (2) is the area in which the Russian formalists made their most important contributions to the study of narrative. Point-of-view criticism is represented by (3) and reader-response criticism by (4). I have not numbered other areas of the diagram, which have also been discussed by narrative theorists. Exclusive emphasis on one dimension of the diagram leads to the production of a theory that can and will be disputed by appeal to another dimension. "To understand narratives, we must study how they are understood by readers," say advocates of (4). "But readers are products of their sociocultural context, which determines what they see when they read" (5). "Society changes, and the total meaning of a literary work is the sum of the meanings it accumulates

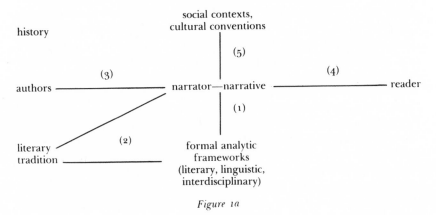

Figure 1a

through history." "But the history of literary traditions is largely independent of political and social history." Each statement, clarifying certain aspects of the narrative situation, is modified or radically altered by the introduction of another term from the diagram.

One further aspect of the diagram deserves mention. If we ask how the terms are related to each other—for example, how narratives are linked to literary traditions, and why readers bring certain expectations to narratives and tend to interpret them in similar ways—the answer must be that our shared understanding of conventions provides whatever stability there may be in these relationships. Readers have a large store of knowledge about stories and how to understand them, even if they have had little experience with "great" literature. Our familiarity with literary and cultural conventions is apparent when they are satirized, inverted, or parodied, as they frequently are in fiction and films: if we get the point, we recognize the departure from the norm. The violation of conventional expectations is as important as their observance in literary experience, and it has an important bearing on the relationship between literature and life. These topics are the subject of the last chapter.

It should by now be clear why the following chapters take the form of a discussion, or a series of arguments, concerning the nature of narrative. There is no single theory of the subject acceptable to a majority of those who have addressed it, and the unresolved differences among the critics cannot be either easily adjudicated or cavalierly dismissed. Ideally, perhaps, there would be one all-inclusive theory of narrative that would account for all stories ever told, from classical epics to science fiction, and all those that will be created in the future. But as the preceding survey shows, theories are intended to answer different sorts of questions, and when new kinds of narrative appear, critics are often forced to supplement or revise their explanations. Unlike "progressive" sciences, literary study has never succeeded in discarding old theories because they are demonstrably less adequate than those that replace them. It is a cumulative discipline to which new knowledge is added, but unfashionable ideas that have long been dormant may at any time prove their relevance to new critical concerns or creative methods. Literary theory flourishes when critics are engaged in dialogue and controversy, which prevent us from complacently assuming that we understand everything there is to know about literature. If recent theories of narrative are judged on the premise that only one of them can be true, they are likely to prove unsatisfactory. But if judged on the basis of the insights they can provide into particular narratives, their variety is an advantage, as I hope to show.

2

From Novel to Narrative

Kinds of Narrative

When he attempted to perceive and create some order in our methods of studying literature, Northrop Frye found that the vocabulary of criticism did not contain the conceptual distinctions he needed. "We have," he wrote in *Anatomy of Criticism* (1957), "no word for a work of prose fiction, so the word 'novel' does duty for everything, and thereby loses its only real meaning as the name of a genre. The . . . distinction between fiction and non-fiction, between books which are about things admitted not to be true and books which are about everything else, is apparently exhaustive enough for critics" (13–14). The consequences of such a rudimentary method of classification are evident in introductory literature textbooks, which usually consist of three sections: (lyric) poetry, drama, and fiction (which here means imaginary narrative in prose; verse narratives are in the "poetry" section). All three are considered creative or fictional in some sense; but the poems often appear to describe actual experiences, and the reason for excluding prose narratives about such experiences is not self-evident.

If critical theory in the 1950s had too few words for the classification of narratives, literary history had too many. An anthology of literature that is arranged chronologically will usually contain examples of the long narrative forms that preceded the novel—the epic and the romance. Short forms such as the humorous fabliau, the animal fable, the exemplum (an example with a moral), the Christian legend, and the folktale may be represented in selections from Chaucer's *Canterbury Tales*, which, like Boccaccio's *Decameron* and the *Thousand and One*

Nights, uses a "framework" to unify a number of short tales. Some narratives may remain unclassified (is Edmund Spenser's *Faerie Queene* a courtesy book, a romance, an epic, an allegory, or all four?). Other narrative kinds, such as the detective story, gothic fiction, and science fiction, are not represented in most anthologies. While all these names are useful in indicating what sort of story is involved, they are the haphazard products of history: narratives that are in many respects similar may have different names simply because they appeared at different times, and one name such as "romance" may include three or four kinds of story that have little in common. It is this gap between history without theory and an oversimplified theory that cannot account for literary history that Frye tried to fill in his classifications of narrative.

One difficulty presented by this welter of names for narratives is that the criteria used to distinguish them keep shifting. Sometimes the subject of a story will determine its name (as in the case of science fiction and the gothic); in other cases, a formal feature (verse or prose, long or short) is the defining characteristic; the work may even be classified on the basis of the reaction it evokes (comic, serious) or its method of creating meaning (as in the case of allegory and the exemplum). Frye was conscious of this problem, and solved it by redefining literary terms in accordance with one particular aspect of their meaning. In order to produce a coherent scheme that would give literary history some theoretical order, he classified "modes" of literature according to the nature of the worlds and characters they depicted (their subject matter).

One virtue of Frye's schema (see Figure 2a) is that it breaks down the artificial barriers that had separated verse from prose, oral from written, and short from long narratives, thus inhibiting discussion of what they had in common. Another advantage is that it reveals a general relationship between the course of history and changes in fiction. The progression from myth to irony corresponds roughly to the evolution from pre-Medieval Europe to the twentieth century. This same pattern can be discerned in classical literature, from Homer to Roman satire. Perhaps society and literature change in a cyclic rather than a linear pattern; if so, the imaginative strains of recent fiction may auger a return (with a difference) to myth.

Frye's historical theory is much clearer than history itself. Once a type of narrative has been preserved in writing, it can always be imitated later in Frye's cycle, as he himself points out; thus oral epics served as models for cultivated counterparts, and medieval romances were reborn in the Romantic period. Another complication of his the-

Mode	Defining characteristics	Narrative examples
Myth	Hero superior in *kind* to other men and their environment (a god)	"As a rule . . . outside the normal literary categories"; parts of the Bible and of epic poems are mythic
Romance	Hero superior in *degree* to others and to environment	Parts of classical and early European epics; romances; legends, folktales, märchen (fairy tales), ballads
High mimetic	Superior in degree to others, but not to environment	"Most epic," including *The Faerie Queene, Jerusalem Delivered, Paradise Lost*
Low mimetic	Superior neither to others nor to their environment	Realistic fiction (most novels and short stories)
Ironic	Protagonist inferior to ourselves in power or intelligence	Ironic novels and short stories— *Billy Budd,* Dostoievsky's *The Idiot,* Joyce's *Dubliners*

Figure 2a

ory is that while the subdivisions are clear, they identify certain tendencies in literature, not kinds of narrative, drama, and lyric. Parts of epic poems are spread across three modes. Perhaps this is inevitable because oral narratives may be modified and expanded over long periods, assimilating varied materials, and even written works can incorporate diversified fragments of the author's reading.

When he turns from literary history to a discussion of the kinds of literature, Frye provides a taxonomy that is more empirical. For the three categories drama, poetry, and fiction (an obviously faulty division, because fictional poetic narratives were common before the modern period), he substitutes three that are more precisely defined, on the basis of how they are presented to the audience. If acted before spectators, the work is a drama; for works originally spoken, sung, or chanted to listeners, Frye uses the word "epos"; if written to be read, he calls them "fiction." For those interested in narrative, this classification has disadvantages in that it separates stories that are delivered orally from those that are written. But the comparison of different theories to different maps (see Chapter 1) is relevant here: by disregarding some aspects of literature, Frye's theory of genres throws others into sharp relief. There is an important difference between oral and written narrative traditions. Scholars have studied the former in detail, but until recently they had not considered how writing and printing affect the production of stories "told" by an author who is

33

not present to a solitary reader. Second, by defining fiction as "something made for its own sake" rather than as something false that appears true, Frye can show that the novel and short story represent only one type of fiction, and that there are others equally deserving of attention.

Having defined genres on the basis of what he calls their "radical of presentation" (acted, spoken, or written), Frye identifies four species of fiction. It is not subject matter (the basis of his theory of modes) but the author's perspective on the subject that governs this classification. The author's gaze may be directed outward or inward—extroverted or introverted—producing a record of the world, or a vision of reality as transformed by the imagination. The subject may also be apprehended in personal or in intellectual terms. The combinations of these two dichotomies yield the classification of fiction shown in Figure 2b.

Frye says that "the forms of prose fiction are mixed, like racial strains in human beings, not separable like the sexes." Between the four primary types—novel, romance, anatomy, and confession—are four secondary ones produced when they combine. Two secondary forms that belong on the diagram do not appear there because of typographical limitations: the diagonal combinations of anatomy and romance (e.g., *Moby Dick*) and of novel and confession (fictional autobiography, such as Defoe's *Moll Flanders*). The center of the diagram is occupied by what Frye calls a "fifth and quintessential form," the encyclopaedic, which combines all the others. He does not explore the

	EXTROVERTED		INTROVERTED
PERSONAL	Novel (Defoe, Austen, James): "Deals with personality," defined society ↓	Novel + romance → (common; may be ironic—*Lord Jim*)	Romance (Emily ← Brontë, Hawthorne); stylized figures (hero, villain) ↓
	Novel + anatomy (thesis novels; *Tristram Shandy*) ↑	Encyclopedic forms (the Bible, other sacred books, *Finnegans Wake*)	Romance + confession (De Quincey, other romantic autobiography) ↑
INTELLECTUAL	Anatomy (Rabelais, → Swift): "Deals less with people than with mental attitudes"; can be entirely fantastic or moral, or contain "exhaustive erudition"	Anatomy + confession → (Carlyle's *Sartor Resartus,* Kierkegaard)	Confession (autobiography—St. Augustine, ← Rousseau); selects experiences to create integrated pattern

Figure 2b

34

question of why writing and reading should yield these types of literature, but his emphasis on the intellectual patterns found in the anatomy and the confession implies that they can be created and understood only when author and reader can repeatedly refer to a written record in a non-sequential fashion. The same is true of encyclopaedic forms. But the effect of writing on the novel and romance is less evident, in view of their close relationship to the oral tradition.

One question that critics have raised about Frye's method of classification involves not its shortcomings but the inevitability of its success. Like the four elements of medieval science, defined by reference to the dichotomies hot/cold and wet/dry, Frye's four species defined by two dichotomies cannot help but include all prose fiction, either as a "pure" type or as an intermediate mixture. In fact they can include all literature, which cannot escape being introverted or extroverted, personal or intellectual, and much writing not considered literary. What have we learned once the classification has been performed?

What we have learned, if I understand Frye correctly, is in part what we always knew. His characterizations of the novel and romance are close to the traditional ones. To our consciousness of the difference between them, he has added a convincing defense of the romance as a distinct kind which has its own conventions of idealization and should not be faulted for failing to attain realistic credibility. By naming the anatomy and the confession, he incorporates neglected areas of literature into our conception of prose and thus can provide insight into the sources and structures of works that contain mixtures of fact, imagination, and intellectual complexity. He implicitly calls attention to the fact that "narrative" is a certain mode of writing, and that a particular prose work such as a novel need not be narration from beginning to end; it can contain description, exposition, and dramatically rendered dialogue. His theory tends to shift the emphasis in discussion of fiction from evaluation by fixed standards to a more flexible assessment of how works differ in composition and meaning. Criticism of his theory must be considered in relation to the practical insights to which it gives rise.

In one respect Frye adheres to the critical tradition of his time: he sees the novel as a realistic genre that achieved its characteristic form in the eighteenth and nineteenth centuries. A different view of the novel's character and history appears in *The Nature of Narrative*, by Robert Scholes and Robert Kellogg (1966). They accept Frye's thesis that Western literature has undergone two cyclic evolutions from myth to realism and adopt some of his distinctions in naming narrative kinds. But they replace his two classifications (of modes and of

35

genres of prose fiction) with a unified theory and history of narrative. For Frye's linear sequence of historical modes, they substitute a "tree structure" that begins in the epic and then splits up into varied kinds. The epic itself, from our point of view, is a compound of myth, legend, history, folktale, and genealogy. But these categories are a product of later thought; they do not exist in preliterate cultures. "The epic story-teller is telling a traditional story. The primary impulse which moves him is not a historical one, nor a creative one; it is *re-creative*. He is retelling a traditional story, and therefore his primary allegiance is not to fact, not to truth, not to entertainment, but to the *mythos* itself—the story as preserved in the tradition" (12). From this "epic synthesis" two streams separate with the passage of time: the *empirical* and the *fictional*, which themselves subdivide as society develops more specialized activities and discourses. Later these strands recombine to produce new genres, one of which is the novel. "The novel is not the opposite of romance, as is usually maintained, but a product of the reunion of the empirical and fictional elements in narrative literature"(15).

I have summarized Scholes and Kellogg's theory in diagrammatic form (Figure 2c), listing the examples they give of various narrative kinds, most of which are taken from classical literature. Needless to say, such a reductive representation of their argument does not do it

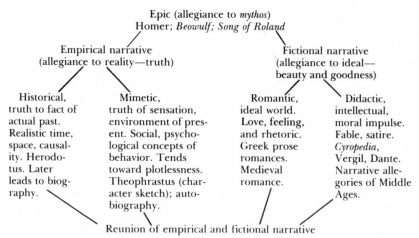

Epic (allegiance to *mythos*)
Homer; *Beowulf; Song of Roland*

Empirical narrative
(allegiance to reality—truth)

Fictional narrative
(allegiance to ideal—
beauty and goodness)

Historical, truth to fact of actual past. Realistic time, space, causality. Herodotus. Later leads to biography.

Mimetic, truth of sensation, environment of present. Social, psychological concepts of behavior. Tends toward plotlessness. Theophrastus (character sketch); autobiography.

Romantic, ideal world. Love, feeling, and rhetoric. Greek prose romances. Medieval romance.

Didactic, intellectual, moral impulse. Fable, satire. *Cyropedia*, Vergil, Dante. Narrative allegories of Middle Ages.

Reunion of empirical and fictional narrative

Late classical period: Petronius, *Satyricon*; "picaresque," the comic antitype of the romance; Apuleius, *Golden Ass*. "Confession" elements may appear in first-person forms. The 4 types—history, mimesis, romance, fable—begin to recombine again in late Middle Ages, eventually producing the novel.

Figure 2c

justice. As in the case of Frye, my brief discussion is intended to stimulate interest in their theory, not to serve as a substitute for it.

Frye excluded history and biography from his list of "fictions"; Scholes and Kellogg appropriately include them in the kinds of "narrative." This shift in theoretical perspective yields a different explanation of the social realism that Frye and others have always considered a defining feature of the novel. In the traditional account, romances gradually become more plausible and typical, increasing in realism until a new kind is born in eighteenth-century England. Scholes and Kellogg imply that the novel appears more abruptly through the lateral grafting of fact onto fiction. Their views are in accord with Continental accounts of the novel's history, which treat it as the modern counterpart of the epic, or argue that it originated in the Greek prose romance and was reborn in the Spanish picaresque and *Don Quixote*. The most unusual aspect of their theory is their claim that the novel is an "unstable compound," a shifting zone of mixed kinds with no fixed nature. Frye had said that novel and romance frequently combine; for Scholes and Kellogg, the novel does not exist except as a mixture. This conclusion verges on paradox, the essence of "the novel" being that it has no essential identity. If that is the case, the imperative governing the novel's development would be to become what it is not— that is, to be different from anything that looks like a normal novel. We shall encounter critics who explore the implications of this view.

In discussing oral narratives, Scholes and Kellogg summarize the results of recent scholarship and suggest further lines of study. Orally transmitted verse epics such as the *Iliad* and *Beowulf* have a number of features in common. Groups of words that fit the meter and rhythm of the work become formulas and are used repeatedly. About 90 percent of the *Iliad* and *Odyssey* consist of such formulae, which allow some freedom of choice when they are combined in larger units. At a higher structural level, groups of words and phrases are joined in conventional action patterns (motifs) such as "greeting a guest," which occurs several times in the *Odyssey*. The shape of a series of episodes or the whole work is often based on principles of repetition (e.g., three attempts necessary for success), parallelism (the characters and incidents in two episodes are similar, or opposite), and reversed repetition (the first incident corresponds to the last, the second to the next-to-last, etc.). These structural levels help the bard produce metrical lines, recount and connect incidents, and keep the overall course of the story in mind, while permitting creative changes and providing materials to fill in gaps caused by forgetfulness. The epic-romances of the late middle ages, *El Cid* and *Chanson de Roland,* are patterned on the same basic phrases and sequences of motifs or "narremes," as S. G. Nichols and Eugene Dorfman have demonstrated. This subject will be discussed further in chapter 4.

With the advent of writing, the nature of narrative changes dramatically. As Scholes and Kellogg point out, this change is not a single event but a process that extends over centuries. And writing/reading did not, until recently, replace the oral tradition; the two existed side by side, with a constant interchange of materials and methods. Nevertheless, the implications of writing become apparent once literacy is established, and it inevitably alters the kind of discourse a society uses: "When oral poetic narrative breaks down with the advent of literacy in the modern sense . . . the illustrative aspect of myth is developed in allegory and in discursive philosophical writing. The representational aspect of myth is then developed in history and other forms of empirical narrative" (28). Before, the only information that could survive transmission was formulaic and communal. Unique facts and fancies not locked in place by rhythmic structure or conventional action pattern would simply disappear in the course of oral repetition. Writing preserves the particular.

One effect of writing on narrative, Scholes and Kellogg suggest, is to create a new category that did not previously exist—the fictional. Once it exists, separated from the world's business of persuading, reasoning, and getting the facts straight, the writer of fictions need not attempt to create a new story. The skill required of those who produced the earliest stories that have survived was the skill to write, not to invent. The possibility of being original and attaching one's own name to the product would eventually be crucial, but the task facing the first transcribers was different. If they added "art" to the story, it would be art borrowed from oral skills—poetic or oratorical organization of language. If functioning as a scribe/scholar rather than an artist, the writer might add "interpretation" to the material copied, explaining what was obscure or supplementing it with other sources of information.

Though not immediate, the effects of writing on narration seem in retrospect inevitable. The most obvious of these, according to Scholes and Kellogg, is a movement away from traditional plots to plotlessness, the latter depending on writing for its transmission. Second, there is a tendency to add interpretation or commentary to the narrative (a skill learned by the scribe, as distinct from the singer or teller of tales; Eugène Vinaver describes this process in *The Rise of Romance*, chapter 2). Third, the possibility of writing and reading silently and privately, outside a conventional setting in which works are recited or acted, separates the rhetorical art from something called "prose" in a new sense, as Frye notes. The page is a site where different ways of talking, related to distinct cultural situations, can be juxtaposed. Some critics consider this an important aspect of the "mixed" nature of the novel. Finally, the "silent speech" of writing can serve as a model for unspoken thought in narrative—one of its distinctive features in comparison to other forms of literature. St. Augustine's astonishment when he saw St. Ambrose reading without speaking (something he had never before imagined possible) marks the importance of a change easily overlooked. Some critics argue that the very concept of "thinking for oneself" could not be widespread without practice in the use of language without speech—reading and writing.

The Romance-Novel Matrix: History, Psychology, and Stories of Life

The theories of Frye and of Scholes and Kellogg provide useful insights into narratives while showing why it is difficult to give a definitive answer to questions such as "what is the novel?" If we use the classic method of definition by genus and species (class and subclass), the choice of defining characteristics determines where a literary kind will appear in the conceptual grid we create. If we conceive of the genus as long narratives, we will classify novels with epics and romances. The first two differ from romance in that they are more realistic; epic and novel can be differentiated historically (ancient vs. modern), socially (heroic/aristocratic vs. bourgeois), perhaps philosophically (objective vs. subjective), as German critics have shown. If we decide that the novel is essentially a prose form, we will set it in opposition to verse epics and romances. Frye identifies the novel as a subclass of fictions in prose, some of which are not narratives. Scholes and Kellogg begin from narratives (whether true or false, in verse or in prose) and end up with a very different classification. All three admit that most works are "mixtures" of the abstract features on which they base their classifications.

Failure to reach agreement in defining words such as "fiction," "novel," and "romance" can lead to a reaction against the very attempt to distinguish narrative kinds. A more productive conclusion would be that definitions, especially those involving human activities, enable us to understand phenomena in particular contexts for particular purposes. The fact that human beings are perceived differently in psychology, anthropology, sociology, and medicine results not from failure to determine what we are essentially, but from the different interests of these disciplines.

Recent books on the origins of the novel exemplify the varied disciplinary interests that can be brought to bear on the definition of a literary kind. Frye and Scholes and Kellogg did not explain the emergence of particular genres in detail. For Frye, the evolution from oligarchic to proletarian societies, and the process of "displacement" whereby ideal, imaginary stories gradually become more plausibly realistic, serve as a minimal framework for understanding literary change. Philosophy and technology serve the same purpose for Scholes and Kellogg: narrative genres emerge with a distinction between the real and the imaginary, which is connected to the introduction of writing. In freeing us from a "novel-centered" view of narrative, they do not challenge the traditional account of the novel described in chapter 1: social and cultural historians provide a simple story of how the Reformation, empirical philosophy, and individualism produce the Protestant work ethic and the rise of the middle class, thus giving birth to the novel. Scholars and critics who analyze this narrative produced by historians find it inadequate. Rather than simply reflecting social changes that other disciplines explain, the novel may contain a more revealing record of how they came about and might even be a cause of social effects, insofar as its ways of constructing life stories become for us ways of projecting meaning on our own lives.

When the difference between romance and novel is conceived as one between ideal/imaginary and real/empirical accounts of experience, explanation of the contrast is often sought in psychology, philosophy, or the archetypalism of Frye and myth critics. René Girard integrated these explanations of the two genres with historical accounts of the rise of the novel in *Deceit, Desire, and the Novel* (1961). Members of traditional societies, including those of pre-Reformation Europe, pattern their lives on the role models provided by their culture. The loss of transcendent models—those of religion and myth—leads to imitation of heroes and heroines found in books. Don Quixote imitates the famous knight of romance, Amadis of Gaul; Madame Bovary imitates the heroines of the books she reads; Julien Sorel, in Stendhal's *The Red and the Black*, imitates a hero of history —Napoleon. We ourselves imitate individuals whom we admire. The current use in a positive sense of the phrase "role model" indicates how pervasive this phenomenon is. The idea of *selecting* a pattern to imitate, rather than having it imposed by the community, is related to the change from religious to secular society and the corresponding multiplication of potential patterns.

As Girard shows, these changes are recorded more clearly in literature than in other documents and disciplines. The idea of choosing a model to imitate conceals as insidious paradox. Freedom of choice is an expression of individuality; but the fact that we imitate another actually robs us of our self-identity. Our goals and desires are not really our own, but those of the Other—the role model. If we succeed in attaining them, we will probably find that they do not give us the satisfaction we imagined. Finding fault with ourselves or the object we have chosen, we recommence the deluded quest for "self"-satisfaction. This inescapable pattern underlies all modern narratives, if not our lives, since its death is the death of fiction and desire. Romance, in general, displays no self-conscious awareness of the pattern, especially when it depicts a concluding bliss of self-fulfillment. The novelistic impulse is to make the pattern of romantic delusion evident to those able to perceive it.

Like Girard, Marthe Robert thinks that a tension between the ideal and the real lies at the heart of modern narratives, but her method of explaining it in *Origins of the Novel* (1972) is more narrowly psychoanalytic. Freud's essays "Creative Writers and Daydreaming" and "Family Romances" are the basis of her theory. Storytellers, having been accused of indulging in idle fancies (this accusation was common in the seventeenth and eighteenth centuries), know that they are guilty as charged and attempt to produce more believable narratives. The result is not a substitution of truth for fiction but simply better-disguised fiction: "Fictional illusion can be achieved in two ways: either the author acts *as if* there were no such thing, and the book is then said to be realistic, naturalistic, or simply true to life; or else he can stress the *as if*, which is always his main ulterior motive, in which case it is called a work of fantasy, imagination, or subjectivity. . . . Thus there are two kinds of novel: one purporting to draw material from life . . . the other acknowledging quite openly that it is only a set of figures and forms. . . . Of the two, the first is of course the more deceptive, since it is wholly intent on concealing its tricks" (35).

This explanation of the development from fairy tales to novels is similar to Frye's theory of "displacement," but Robert sees it as a repetition of the stages of childhood development. The pre-Oedipal child, forced to share love with brothers and sisters, and disappointed by parents who prove less than perfect, imagines that he/she is a foundling whose real parents are royalty. But the fantasies of the pleasure principle are shattered by discovery of the facts of birth, and the child may feel like a lowly bastard who must struggle with the world (the reality principle) in order to attain a self-earned eminence. Stories written under the sway of the first stage of the Family Romance are all alike; the second stage produces stories endlessly different, crammed with "realistic" details of conflict and love, ambition and misfortune. The association of the novel with the rise of the middle class in the eighteenth century can thus be seen as the result of psychic as well as economic aspirations (what, in the end, is the real reason for wanting to rise in the world?).

English and American critics tend to see *Robinson Crusoe* as the first novel, whereas Continental critics accord *Don Quixote* that position. Robert's theory can accept both as typical. Psychologically, *Robinson Crusoe* is a transparent representation of the Family Romance (flight from the father, eventual worldly success), which is why it remains preeminently a children's book. *Don Quixote*, in which a dreambound foundling confronts tough-minded realists, shows us a more mature stage of psychic conflict. Romance and novel prove to be not opposites but expressions of the same underlying impulse.

Does "the Novel" Exist?

Revealing as they are, these explanations do not account for the differences between narratives and the ways that historical and literary factors shape their development. If we list the kinds of narrative available at various times since the Middle Ages, we find amazing diversity and continuous change. Collections of short prose tales, many taken from folk traditions, travel from one country to another, often supplemented by new materials that have reached Europe from Indian and Arabic sources. With the introduction of printing, the old poetic romances are reborn in short prose summaries that circulated widely. Jokes and short anecdotes are strung together as "jest biographies"; tales about rogues and their wanderings accumulate in the "picaresque" novel, closely related to criminal biographies that mix fact and fiction (Chandler). Translation of the Greek prose romances in the Renaissance leads to the creation of a new mode of romance in Italy, France, and England (Wolff). Almost every factual narrative— history, biography, autobiography, account of travels—generates an eponymous fictional counterpart (Mylne, 32–40; Adams).

The subclasses of these works are legion—the sentimental novel, the scandalous chronicle, the novel of manners, the biographical, historical, epistolary, allegorical, pastoral, and oriental novel; the *roman à clef* (real people represented with fictitious names), the *conte* (usually a philosophic story), and later the *Bildungsroman* (the development of a young man or woman). Needless to say, these "kinds" often mix. Another characteristic and perhaps crucial feature of prose narrative is that every noteworthy type evokes a parody of its materials and methods. Jonathan Swift (like his Greek predecessor Lucian) satirizes the improbable "true voyages" of his time, Fielding parodies Richardson, and Sterne's *Tristram Shandy* leaves the very idea of telling a story in shambles. The best way to discover for oneself the enduring relevance of such classifications and their tendency to provoke parody is to inspect the kinds of narrative available in a drugstore or small bookstore (more will be said about this later).

Just as theorists have been tempted to discover a clear conceptual pattern in the jumble of narratives they work with, so historians have tended to represent the "progress" from romance to novel as a much more orderly change than it was. Having decided that narratives belong in one of these two categories, we can find critical writings in the seventeenth and eighteenth centuries to confirm our opinion. In England, William Congreve (1691), Hugh Blair (1762), and Clara Reeve (1785) defined the two words about as we do, but most writers did not, and the generally accepted distinction between them dates from the nineteenth century. In France, there were attempts to distinguish the romantic *roman* from the realistic *nouvelle* (Segrais 1656), but in the end they failed. The word *roman*, in both French and German, remains the name of all long narratives that we categorize as novels or romances, and thus Anglo-American critics try to explain two distinct kinds of narrative where Continental critics see only one. (In fourteenth-century Italy the word *novella* meant a short tale, such as those in the *Decameron*; hence *novela* in Spanish, *nouvelle* in French, and "novel" meaning short story in seventeenth-century England. Our word "novella," like the German *Novelle*, refers to a short novel.)

Our tendency to look for an orderly "evolution" of narrative is itself evidence of how narratives work: we impose a pattern on the past so that we can tell a coherent story about it. As recent scholars have shown, most seventeenth- and eighteenth-century authors implicitly or explicitly *denied* that they were writing novels or romances. They entitled their works "histories," "lives," or "memoirs" to dissociate themselves from the frivolous, fanciful, improbable, sometimes immoral aspects of the former. In one form or another, the phrase "this is not a novel/romance/story" appeared frequently in prefaces. Richardson said that *Clarissa Harlowe* was not "a *light Novel*, or *transitory Ro-*

mance," but "a History of *Life* and *Manners.*" His assertion that this form needed a new name was repeated by his admirer Diderot (1761) and by one of the first important theorists of narrative, Friedrich von Blanckenburg (1774). Fielding defined his "kind of writing" as "comic romance," or "a comic epic poem in prose," but the title of the work containing this definition was *The History of the Adventures of Joseph Andrews* (1742), and critics referred to it as a new kind of history or biography. Thus literary history offers evidence in favor of the paradoxical conclusion of some theorists: "the novel" cannot be defined because its defining characteristic is to be unlike a novel.

One aspect of the paradox—the cunning or brazen attempts of authors to pass off their writings as true—will be discussed in the next chapter. Of immediate relevance to this one are recent theories of the novel that account for its unusual status by developing more complex models to describe it. They attempt to discover not what it is but how it works as a mode of communication in particular historical and cultural circumstances.

The Novel as Oppositional Discourse

Theories that define the novel as a paradoxical form involve a field–ground reversal: the abnormality of the novel, in relation to the system of literary genres, is accepted as its normal mode of existence. As a result, the novel is conceived of as an entity "that has no natural or positive existence," that "arises and rearises in different regional cultures at different times," and is not a distinct kind with a continuous history but a "succession" of works "bearing family resemblances to one another." These quotations are taken from Walter Reed's *An Exemplary History of the Novel* (24, 22, 56). What novels share, in Reed's view, is not certain characteristics, but a set of *relationships*—to other literary works, to the cultural situation in which they are produced, and to their readers. When culture and literature change, the novel changes with them; but such readjustments leave the total configuration unaltered, like an algebraic formula that is used with different sets of variables.

First, in relation to other literary works, the novel is an outsider, opposing itself to the rules that are characteristic of other genres and "poetics" (traditional literary theory). When the novel develops its own conventions, and critics begin to codify its rules, novelists set themselves in opposition to "the novel" by parody, by invention of new forms, or by incorporating and mixing together the "pure"

44

genres of the time. "The dialectical relation of the novel to literary tradition," according to Reed, "entails a conflict of rules, a competition among values, and a general lack of codified precedent for formal result" (49).

Second, in relation to society and sanctioned culture, the novel takes an oppositional stance. Spanish picaresque novels subjected "the literary humanism of the Renaissance to its first major critique" (13). Official cultural norms are often the intellectual embodiment of social and political relations. By depicting people and situations that have no place in accepted systems of value, the novel implicitly calls the latter into question. By asserting its place "not within the literary universe but within the 'real' world of non-literary discourse"—hence the "realism" of the novel—it lays bare the difference between brute fact and conventional ways of seeing.

Finally, the novel is defined by the problematic relation it creates with its audience—not a community of listeners hearing a bard, or one seeing a drama, but "a solitary, anonymous figure, scanning a bulk of printed pages. . . . The raison d'être of the novel is the ambiguity introduced into literature by the technology of the printed book" (25). As Reed shows, novelists were conscious of the fact that they were not addressing a particular social class. Some of them continued to employ conventions of address and attitude appropriate to a certain group, or to elicit the reader's allegiance "to some deeper power, higher ideal, or stronger fulfillment of desire," but works of this sort Reed would classify as romances. Novelists who realized that there was no set of social and literary conventions appropriate for the printed book created works for a new, socially displaced class increasingly aware of "their lack of identity as readers with the literature of the ruling class, or of the people" (35).

Reed's "history" of the novel is a series of "examples," none quite like the others but all of them showing how the novel's oppositional stance remains constant in a variety of social and literary circumstances. Thus he provides an alternative to traditional theories of the novel's origin, which Lennard Davis classifies as the evolutionary (romances, becoming gradually realistic, turn into novels), the osmotic (changes in society are absorbed by literature, and the novel appears), and the convergent (various types of narrative link together to create a new genre). Underlying all of these explanations is a fixed set of assumptions about how history, as a narrative, works. The most obvious of these, which will be discussed further in the next chapter, are that change is continuous and gradual; that causes immediately precede effects (the cause of event q is p, not some earlier event such as b or

45

h); that the cause of an event must be "like" the effect; that the world is made up of clearly defined entities such as "novel," "middle class," "realism"; that these entities can, like living things, be born or have an "origin" and then develop naturally; and that no genuinely new causes can appear that would disrupt this intelligible series.

These assumptions are taken from the physical and biological sciences. Reed and Lennard Davis (*Factual Fictions: The Origins of the English Novel*) assume that cultural products are not *given* entities, like atoms and plants, but *constituted* structures that exist only by virtue of human decisions concerning their nature and status. From their point of view, the failure of the seventeenth and eighteenth centuries to provide a clear definition of the novel was not a result of ignorance concerning its essential features; the conflicting opinions expressed during that period provide the only valid context and frame within which we can understand the phenomena involved. For Davis, as for Georges May and John Richetti, writers and readers of that period found themselves caught between the conflicting claims of secular reality—the realm of fact—and a religious-political "reality" that claimed wrongdoing would be punished in this life and the next. A narrative true to fact would be considered ethically "false" if the immoral or illegal acts it represented were not punished. One filled with improbabilities and coincidences might on the other hand be "true" to the laws of poetic justice, punishing the guilty. Given these circumstances, Davis argues, there was no clear distinction between true and false narratives, as we conceive it. News, newspapers, and fiction were one undifferentiated mass of narrative materials until, early in the eighteenth century, Acts of Parliament created legal definitions of news, libel, and (by implication) truth of historical fact. Though many would disagree with Davis's interesting thesis, he succeeds in showing that our categorical distinctions between truth and falsity, fact and fiction, literature and nonliterature, and ethics and aesthetics cannot simply be imposed on the narratives of earlier periods (cf. Nelson).

Formalist and Semiotic Theories of Narrative Kinds

In attempting to explain what narratives are and how they change, the theorists I have discussed emphasize different aspects of the diagram in the first chapter. For Frye, as for Scholes and Kellogg, the main forces shaping narrative are reality and imagination. Changes in the outer world cause changes in subject matter; the imaginary figures of romance—archetypal heroes, heroines, and villains—remain

46

remarkably constant through time. Marthe Robert would argue that more fundamental psychic forces are at work in narrative, that the development of the mind in childhood, not the outer world, determines what stories are told. May, Richetti, and Davis, on the other hand, think that the novel is an accurate register of social and political forces. Reed's theory is more complex in that it treats literary traditions as a third force, equal in importance to reality and the human imagination, but in his view the novel reacts against these traditions rather than being formed by them.

Scholes and Kellogg show how verbal formulas and action motifs serve as compositional elements in oral traditions, but they appear to keep literary form constant, rather than contributing to its differentiation and change. All of these theories assign the formal elements of narrative a marginal status and look to subject matter and content, man and his world, for explanations of literature. Is it then simply a reflection of reality, with no laws of its own, that must borrow its history from other disciplines?

In his writings between 1914 and 1925, Victor Shklovsky not only denied that this was the case but argued that *all* aspects of narrative, including the subjects treated, are "formal" elements that can be understood only through a study of the laws of linguistic and artistic construction. By this he did not mean that narratives have no function other than the creation of formal patterns. Because they differ so sharply from usual ways of speaking and seeing, literary devices "defamiliarize" reality, or make it seem strange, and as a result they renew our perception of what lies around us. Once we become familiar with estranging forms, however, they lose their shock value; we see them as formulas. It is then necessary for the artist to deform them, so as to make us see anew, and the history of narrative is a history of the elaboration, complication, simplification, and reversal of a few basic laws of literary structure.

Where other theorists see a rupture between oral and written narratives, Shklovsky sees formal continuity. The repetition and variation of short literary forms, transposed to the level of plot, become features of its construction. The pun and the riddle, involving enigmas or false solutions that impede recognition of the truth, are extended to provide the narrative structure of mystery stories and detective novels. Theorists have of course discussed plot structure, but they treat it as a formal element of narrative, not an explanation of its historical development. Three difficult questions face Shklovsky when he tries to rewrite the history of narrative in terms of its forms. How can the variety and succession of narrative subject matter be ex-

47

plained formally, when it is so obviously connected to changes in society? Does not the increasing realism of narrative constitute evidence against any theory such as his? And where could new materials and stories come from, creating the "defamiliarization" he considers so important, if not from reality itself?

Shklovsky argues that the realism of fiction is a product of technique, not of scientific observation of reality. The first stage in the renewal of perception through narrative is the exposure of literary conventions through parody. By laying bare the tricks of tale-telling, narrators show that stories are shams: compared to the real world, the characters are unbelievable, the events improbable. Subsequent writers are thus forced to create more believable fictions. The alternative to conventions is not a transcript of reality (for example, a videotape of someone's day), but better-concealed techniques. Every literary device must be "motivated," which means that the writer, beginning with the intention to create a story, must find plausibly realistic explanations of the techniques he or she uses.

There are three main methods of creating credible defamiliarization. The first involves finding plausible reasons for depicting unusual actions. Given the technical need to present readers with something unfamiliar, the plots in the earliest long prose narratives become understandable. Characters can stay in one place, as they do in drama, or move about. The latter choice is a technical possibility available in narrative; no wonder writers made use of it. Apart from single journeys from one place to another, what kinds of people might be engaged in fairly continuous movement, giving them plausible exposure to a variety of strange incidents? Merchants; those who are looking for someone or something; those fleeing from crime, family, or persecution; itinerant entertainers and frauds; the impoverished of no fixed address. Thus the selection of character types for extended travels is determined by the necessity to explain why they are traveling—a technical requirement—as well as the conditions of life in one or another century.

The lower-class drifter with no fixed address gives us the picaresque novel; those looking for someone or something are the people separated from family or loved ones in Greek romances, or the heroes of the Grail legend; the merchant or adventurer seeking his fortune is Sindbad the Sailor, or Robinson Crusoe; the traveler trying to return home or fleeing from impossible circumstances is Odysseus, Aeneas, Joseph Andrews, or Huck Finn. Groups of travelers can be fleeing from a plague or going on a pilgrimage, as in the *Decameron* or the *Canterbury Tales*. In these last two cases, the journey provides "motivation" not for unusual incidents but for putting together a group of people with time to kill, so that they can tell stories. Many early narratives are lengthened by the incorporation of tales that are not part of the main plot line, a technique that came to Europe from the Orient.

A second method of creating "motivated" defamiliarization involves the choice of characters. If they stay in one place, variety can be achieved by having them move through different realms and ranks of society. But this creates a new technical problem: how is it possible to make such social movement plausible? The answer is to make use of characters who ordinarily live in more than one social world— servants, for example—or aristocrats who have fallen on hard luck. Alternatively, a character can climb up through the ranks of society. A major shift in the history of narrative comes about when "character" itself becomes the sphere of variety and interest, substituting a varied inner world for the varied outer world of adventure stories. This development is evident in the *Bildungsroman*, in which the tribulations of growing up and finding a place in the ordinary world are in the head and the heart. Given unusual incidents, as in the earliest prose narratives, the character may be nothing but a "gray thread" that serves to tie them together, as Shklovsky said. If on the other hand the writer wants to defamiliarize the ordinary world, it must be seen through unusual eyes: hence the tendency to use outsiders, unusual or totally naive characters, clowns, madmen (Don Quixote), or people from non-Western cultures as observers who can shock us by showing that what we consider natural is in fact conventional or illogical.

A third source of "motivation" for narratives and new ideas for forms is the representation of social reality in nonfictional literature. As noted before, writers have often motivated their stories by presenting them as memoirs, biographies, histories, or letters. Shklovsky calls attention to the pervasiveness of this procedure by stating it as a law: "In the history of art, the legacy is transmitted not from father to son, but from uncle to nephew" (1923). By this he means that the source of innovation in the novel is not evolution from earlier novels, but incorporation of some minor or nonliterary kind of writing. This thesis accords perfectly with Davis's argument that the novel did not "evolve" out of the romance and that it has important connections with criminal biographies and the advent of newspapers. Published correspondence and manuals on how to write letters were of course the sources of the "epistolary novel," of which Richardson's *Pamela* is the best-known example.

Shklovsky would agree with Reed's conclusion that novelists always tend to avoid techniques and conventions that have been formulated for "the novel," but he would argue that defamiliarization, not social and cultural protest, is the cause of this constant renewal. His explanation of why narrative genres cannot be defined is even more radical than Reed's. Because verbal materials keep shifting across the boundaries of factual/fictional "kinds," they can only be identified in relation to a general "map of discourse" as it is laid out in a particular historical period. The "nonliterary" writing of one period may be defined as "literary" in another, and the appearance of a new kind may alter the content or character of others (Tynjanov). In our time, for example, when movies outdo novels in realism, the novel moves toward fantasy; when the movies take over fantasy, novelists are driven back to "factual" reporting and criminal biography (cf. Norman Mailer, Truman Capote).

Shklovsky's theory is persuasive, and I have found that it can produce new insights into the structure and history of the novel. Nevertheless, the thesis that everything in narrative is a matter of form seems "counter-intuitive." It may serve as a healthy corrective to theories asserting that fiction is simply a transcript of reality, but neither concept is adequate by itself. Once form, subject matter, and content (theme) are severed from each other, it is difficult to show how they interact and how they are integrated in different narrative kinds. Is it possible to explain the history of narrative without presenting it as a reflection of social history, or claiming that it is simply a succession of ingenious formal devices?

M. M. Bakhtin, the Russian critic whose writings were published (sometimes after long delays) between 1927 and 1979, attempted to answer this question. Rather than rejecting the theories of Shklovsky and the formalists, he used them as the starting point of a theory that transforms traditional ideas about form and content. Shklovsky's examples of defamiliarization and "laying bare" of conventional devices are often taken from parody and satire. Granting the significance of such devices, and pointing out that critics have always tended to discount the importance of "nonserious" genres, Bakhtin would ask exactly what is defamiliarized or exposed in parody. Shklovsky says that the artificiality of a literary or perceptual convention is revealed—in comparison to reality. But "reality" is nowhere present in the parody and cannot in any case be presented as a basis of comparison; narratives contain only words, not words and things. Parody, irony, and other forms of humor result not from a comparison of words and the world but from the disparity between two conflicting sets of *words*. We recognize language and literary conventions as pompous, insincere, or prejudiced when they appear next to another kind of language. Shklovsky says that narrative defamiliarizes the world; Bakhtin replies that it defamiliarizes different ways of talking about the world, each one pretending that it is transparent.

From this seemingly specialized argument about the nature of parody, important conclusions follow. Traditional theorists assume that narrators use words to represent or convey a picture of "reality" (factual or fictional) to an audience. But when a character speaks, the words are not a substitute for, or representation of, something else. The language of the character *is* the character, just as the words you and I speak *are* ourselves, in the eyes of others. The separation of form, subject, and content disappears when we recognize that all three are present—not "represented"—when we, and characters in a novel, speak to someone. Parody is a specialized case of an all-embracing phenomenon: the contrasts in language that are evident in any dialogue that involves people of different professions, classes, interests, ideologies, or points of view.

The history of narrative since Homer can be integrated with the history of civilization by conceiving both as a history of "languages." (Figure 2c will prove helpful in understanding this simplified account of Bakhtin's theory.) The epic, which usually refers to events distant in time from the bard and his audience, presents a unified language spoken by members of a unified, hierarchically ordered society. When classical Greek culture and language entered into dialogue with other cultures, it became apparent that different languages are not like different windows that let us see the same "reality"; each one refracts and colors the world in a particular way, depending on the knowledge, interests, and attitudes of its speakers. These differences became particularly evident to the Romans because their culture was bilingual and their empire polylingual. Furthermore, a single national language such as Greek inevitably developed different "speech communities," or different ways of speaking and thinking. Bakhtin refers to this internal differentiation of language as "heteroglossia." These different discourses are usually segregated from one another in life (the language of the law court, the legislature, the aristocracy, the merchant, the slave) and in literature (serious "high" genres, comic "low" genres, folktales, etc.). Broadly defined, "novelistic discourse" is any kind of speaking, acting, or writing that highlights the confrontation of different national languages or speech communities.

With minor variations, the theorists discussed in the preceding pages base their descriptions of narrative on extraliterary categories (powerful vs. weak person, introverted vs. extroverted, empirical vs. fictional, real vs. ideal, etc.) or on purely literary categories (Shklovsky). Bakhtin's idea of "discourses" cuts across these distinctions. The conflicts that characterize novelistic discourse can arise from (a) *implicit* contrasts between the language of a literary work and prevalent literary styles or modes of everyday speech; and (b) *explicit* contrasts between the discourses of different characters, or characters and author. Obviously, many works other than narratives can exemplify the mixture of discourses that Bakhtin calls "novelistic." His own essays on the history of the novel trace its origin to comic, satiric, and parodic plays and poems, as well as Socratic dialogues and folk literature. In the history of narrative itself, the most significant kinds of "heteroglossia" involve the potentially different discourses used by author and narrator, as compared to those of the characters presented and the audience to which the work is addressed.

From the polyglot and socially diversified world of the late classical period, according to Bakhtin, two stylistic lines of development emerged in narrative. In the first, found in some Greek romances, the author imposes a homogeneous, unified style on the diverse voices of heteroglossia and materials from various genres. This type of style, intended to unify different languages and points of view, is also exemplified in the medieval chivalric romance, and later in the historical and sentimental novel (seventeenth and eighteenth centuries). The second line of stylistic development lets the competing languages of heteroglossia—those of author, narrator, and characters—speak for themselves, not smoothing them out to express a single belief system and social standpoint. It is found in some classical prose narratives (Petronius), in Rabelais and Cervantes, in novels of "trial" and adventure (including the picaresque and the *Bildungsroman*), as well as in satirical and parodic works. The fool, clown, and rogue are important to Bakhtin not simply because they defamiliarize reality but because they lay bare the assumptions of socially approved "languages." The second line of stylistic development reaches its apex in works that let characters speak languages opposed to the author's point of view, yet link the different points of view together in mutual recognition (*The Dialogic Imagination*, 409).

This skeletal description of Bakhtin's theory does not take account of its evolution and complexity. I have not attempted to describe the alternative history of narrative that emerges from his essay "Forms of Time and Chronotope in the Novel." There he attempts to show that narratives can be classified on the basis of their "chronotopes" (from the Greek, time-space) and conceptions of causality. For example, some Greek romances present a hero and heroine who fall in love, undergo an incredible series of mishaps and separations, and are finally reunited. Their adventures can take place anywhere (the spatial element); the lengths of time involved are not realistically represented; chance and fate, rather than credible causality, govern this chronotope. Entirely different chronotopes characterize classical biography and autobiography; these eventually enter the novel. Form and content are fused in the chronotope. It is a unified way of conceiving and projecting a world, not a more or less successful attempt to discover the "true" concept governing reality.

Summary

The originality of Bakhtin's theory should not be allowed to obscure what he has in common with the critics previously discussed. His conclusion that narratives are usually generic mixtures is one he shares with Frye, Scholes, Kellogg, and Reed (who acknowledges his indebtedness to Bakhtin). German Romantic novelists, in particular Friedrich Schlegel, also emphasized the hybrid nature of the novel. The idea that Western narrative has undergone two parallel evolutions, one beginning with Homer and the other in the Middle Ages, is also one that Bakhtin shares with several critics. Scholes and Kellogg, Davis, Shklovsky, and Bakhtin call attention to the ways in which non-fictional writing can be absorbed into fictional narrative and alter its course of development. While Girard, Robert, Reed, and Davis seem to share a desire to distinguish the novel from other narrative forms, they refuse to do so categorically.

Different as they are, these theorists are convergent in their opposition to views that are still widely accepted. They hold that there is no such thing as "the novel," conceived as a clearly definable form that is somehow better than other types of narrative. On the whole, they reject the assertions that narratives are simply a reflection of social and psychogical reality, and that language and literary traditions have no independent force in shaping literary history. Some of them emphasize the importance of what might be called "conventional practice"—a zone lying somewhere between literature and life, or encompassing both—as a formative element in the genesis of narrative.

Theories of narrative are most interesting when they are put to use. By stripping the foregoing theories of the examples and detailed analyses that these critics offer to support them, I may have turned their ideas into bloodless abstractions. On the other hand, these critics refer to several hundred narratives, many of which are not commonly

53

read, and an analysis of a story we do not know cannot really serve us as evidence of a theory's validity. Critics quite naturally choose examples that will support their argument; even if we have read the work in question and find that it provides evidence in the critic's favor, it may not be representative of narrative in general. (Is *any* story really "typical"?)

If a theory really has anything to offer, we should be able to apply it to narratives we know and thereby discover things that we and others had not previously noticed. I have chosen *The Adventures of Huckleberry Finn* as one work that can be used to test theories of narrative. Is the discussion of narrative kinds of any relevance to the understanding of this masterpiece of American realism? Those familiar with the novel can answer the question for themselves; I will only mention some of the issues that strike me as important when comparing what critics have said about Mark Twain's novel with the theories discussed above.

Frye would lead us to conclude that *Huckleberry Finn* is an "ironic" as well as a "low mimetic" (realistic) work, and that rather than being a pure example of the novel, it contains an admixture of archetypal romance elements (the quest, death and rebirth) and traces of the anatomy. For Scholes and Kellogg, this novel is by definition a mixture of historical, mimetic, romantic, and didactic elements, not a purely empirical reflection of nineteenth-century America. In Girard's terms, Huck himself would be viewed as a character who cannot find any worthy role model in his society; interesting conclusions could follow from this premise. Robert's theory of fiction as a reflection of psychic development can explain both the structure of the book and its appeal for young readers. Reed could not find a better example of the novel as oppositional discourse; one chapter of his book is in fact devoted to Twain's *A Connecticut Yankee in King Arthur's Court*. The tension between empirical and moral "truth" that May, Richetti, and Davis find characteristic of eighteenth-century fiction is evident in Twain's work and in his career, as earlier critics have shown.

Shklovsky's theory of defamiliarization is remarkably similar to the one presented in Twain's essay "How to Write a Short Story"; they deserve comparison. Huck exemplifies the "naive" character who defamiliarizes the conventions and pretensions of his world by not understanding them. The novel itself has often been classified as "picaresque," and Shklovsky could show how Twain's technical problems and solutions (especially the one that occurs at the end of the sixteenth chapter) bring something new to the genre. Critics who want to see the novel as realistic find it hard to suppress their dissatisfaction with Twain's parodies of other novels in the first and last chapters.

Shklovsky would see such laying bare of novelistic devices as typical and perhaps important in relation to the literary context of Twain's time. The birth of realistic fiction in America, as elsewhere, involved a debunking of stock conventions and a grafting of nonliterary or uncanonized genres (e.g., the tall tale) onto the novel.

One of the notes that Twain inserted at the beginning of the book ("Persons attempting . . . to find a moral in [this narrative] will be banished; persons attempting to find a plot in it will be shot") suggests that he would endorse Shklovsky's idea of literature as formal deformation, not a way of stating a meaning or attaining aesthetic unity. But Twain's other note concerning the "painstaking" care he took in reproducing dialects can serve as the starting point for a Bakhtinian analysis of the novel. It represents not just American scenes and social classes but American languages—those of the poor white, the black, the rogue and the swindler, the religious revivalist, the hypocrite, the prim and proper—each charged with its own interests and values, all exposed as partial when set alongside the others. We *hear* the falseness of Huck's "conscience" in the very words it speaks; exposure of the linguistic inflections involved would require patient analysis. A better example of heteroglossia could hardly be found.

To assess the originality and usefulness of such responses to *Huckleberry Finn*, it would be necessary to develop them further and compare them to previous commentary on the novel, such as that found in the Norton Critical Edition and other similar collections. Mere identification of a genre does not, of course, take us very far in discussing how a story is made or what it means; this preliminary step simply helps us adjust our perception of the particular in relation to the great mass of narratives that have accumulated in the course of history. As Jameson says, generic categories are "ad hoc, experimental constructs, devised for a specific textual occasion and abandoned like so much scaffolding when the analysis has done its work. . . . Genre criticism thereby recovers its freedom and opens up a new space for the creative construction of experimental entities," hypothetical ways of seeing that reveal unnoticed aspects of narrative art (145).

A superficial yet informative assessment of the relevance of generic classification can be undertaken in a drugstore or supermarket. Most of the narrative kinds named in this chapter were in existence by the beginning of the nineteenth century. On the basis of the brief plot descriptions that are provided on the covers of most paperbacks, one can estimate what proportion of the popular books written today fall into traditional categories (historical novel, adventure novel, romance, detective novel, etc.). Traditional scholarship and recent theories help us see how conventional most novels really are. What is obviously different from one century or decade to the next is the materials of fiction—the scenes, events, careers, and physical environment of characters swept forward by social, political, and technological change. The relative importance of convention and reality in the shaping of narrative is the subject of the next chapter.

3

From Realism to Convention

Characteristics of Realism

No matter how it is defined, the novel occupies a special place in relation to other narrative kinds and our own experience. When critics characterize it as a mixture of genres, they show us not what the novel is but what it is not. Because it cannot be pinned down through verbal definition, many would argue that its essential ties are with experience and reality. That is why "the novel" and "realism" are often treated as interchangeable terms, especially by critics discussed in the first chapter. But what does it mean to say that the novel presents life as it really is? Once again we are plunged into questions of definition and, in addition, confronted with a paradox. Novels and short stories are generally distinguished from other literary kinds as "fiction," yet their distinguishing characteristic is their truth to reality.

In its least sophisticated but perhaps most important sense, I think "realism" refers to a certain kind of reading experience. If we believe (whether or not consciously) that a story might well have happened, we are absorbed in it in a special way. After discussing this sense of the term, I shall summarize what critics have said about two of its other meanings: "realism" as a period concept, best exemplified in the art and literature of the nineteenth century; and as a more general term designating a true reflection of the world, regardless of when the work was created. This brief treatment of a very complicated problem will serve as an introduction to formalist and structuralist theories that identify the conventions underlying realistic representation. The third and fourth sections of the chapter concern the question of whether narratives that we consider factual and true (history, for example) are also based on literary conventions. Having discovered that narratives which seem true to us are in fact highly conventional, some critics conclude that all representations of reality are equally arbitrary. The chapter ends with a short discussion of this issue.

Before it becomes a topic of theoretical analysis, our sense of the real in reading depends on intuitive discriminations and attitudes. Some people are addicted to detective stories, others to science fiction. Such personal preferences are not judgments about quality or value; in the end they involve the simple question of whether or not we want to lend our consciousness to a reading experience of a particular sort. Those who like identifiable kinds, such as the romance or western, are not bothered by the conventions they involve and in fact often resent deviation from them. In the context of reading, "realism" appears to be that broad area of narrative without any identifiable conventions, one in which literary artifice has disappeared and everything happens as it would in life. When we come across a well-worn situation or stock character in a detective story, we may be disappointed but usually recover our balance and keep reading. The appearance of a plot cliché in a realistic work has a different effect. It shatters the credibility we had not just lent but given to the story, and we may feel that the author has not simply made a mistake but betrayed our confidence. In the best realistic narratives, we are startled into awareness of the real: we would never have imagined the revelation that came just after we turned the page, but after it appears, we realize that it was inevitable—it captures a truth of experience that we knew, however dimly, all along.

Authors in the realistic tradition have been acutely aware of the importance that readers attach to credibility. I have quoted Richardson's assertion that *Clarissa* (1748) is not a romance or a novel, but a "history." He was unhappy with Bishop Warburton's preface to the work becasue it referred to the story as fiction. "I could wish that the *Air* of Genuineness had been kept up, tho' I want not the Letters be *thought* genuine . . . to avoid hurting that kind of Historical Faith which Fiction itself is generally read with, tho' we know it to be fiction" (letter to Warburton, 19 April, 1748). The French intellectual and novelist Diderot, one of the great skeptics of the time, was overwhelmed by the seeming truth of Richardson's novel. He tells how he began reading *Clarissa* several times in order to learn something about Richardson's techniques, but never succeeded in doing so because he always became personally involved in the work, thus losing his critical consciousness. Henry James insisted that the novelist must "regard himself as an historian and his narrative as history. . . . As a narrator of fictitious events he is nowhere; to insert into his attempts a backbone of logic, he must relate events that are assumed to be real" (248). James and Richardson speak not just as authors but as readers. If there is a difference between the novel and other kinds of narrative, it is related in crucial ways to the sense of actuality, or truth, or "realism," that readers obtain from a story. We believe it, yet we don't believe it, in a sincere and duplicitous manner.

The sense of what is believable, in fiction and in life, differs from one person to the next and from one age to another. Yet despite this variety, which helps explain why it is difficult to find a generally acceptable definition of realism, there is some regularity in the *attitudes* on which belief is based. They can be roughly classified as credulity, credence, and skepticism. When we are credulous, we yield ourselves to a story's seeming truth without any niggling suspicion or critical consciousness of its fictionality. In a more detached mood, we may find a story deserving of credence or credible (aptly defined in my dictionary as "worthy of belief or confidence"): when we are inclined to test it, it rings true. As skeptical readers, we will find our tough-minded attitude toward human illusions confirmed in many realistic novels. The skeptic's watchword, to friends and fictional characters, is "Be realistic!" He/she accuses the credulous reader of sentimentality; the latter replies that the skeptic knows the cost of everything and the value of nothing. All three of these readers, or attitudes, inhabit us at one time or another, even while reading a single book.

To call novels realistic is not simply to say that we experience them as real; the assertion implies that they do depict life as it is, not as it is conventionally represented in other narratives. But in literature, as in other spheres, agreement about the verbal definition of abstract terms such as "realism" and "convention" often breaks down when people apply them to concrete examples. Many critics argue that if "realism" is to have any meaning, it should be defined as a literary concept that is best exemplified in the nineteenth-century novel.

In their helpful analyses of realism as a period concept, which serve as the basis of my own discussion, René Wellek and George Becker agree that the choice of ordinary or typical subjects is the most important tenet of realism. But as they show, the very idea of "representative" subject matter is balanced uneasily between two extremes. The real, as opposed to the abstract, is concrete, individual, unique; in this sense, realism is opposed to the use of stock characters. In fiction, the particularized individual often provides an ironic perspective on the generally accepted values and behavior of other characters. Realism

59

in this sense provides a "systematic undermining and demystification, the secular 'decoding,'" of inherited assumptions about life (Jameson, 152; see also Levin). On the other hand, the real is that which is common rather than unique or atypical, and therefore some argue that realism is committed to maintaining a certain distance from particularity. An old philosophical dispute lies just beneath the surface of any definition of realism, and critical battles have erupted between advocates of particularity and generality. Georg Lukács is the most important of the critics who argue that these two concepts are fused in the "type," the character who embodies "the inseparable unity of the individual and universal."

Second, realism is characterized by "objectivity"—another term that is variously defined. In one dimension, it is the opposite of everything subjective or opinionated: the author should not let personal attitudes intervene in the representation of a narrative. Positively conceived, objectivity can mean that the author should suppress not only his/her personality but the narrating voice as well. Rather than being told what happened, the reader should be allowed to experience it directly, through dramatic presentation (for example, dialogue). Wayne Booth has discussed the pitfalls of this idea of objectivity, as I indicated in the first chapter. Lukács says that objectivity in this sense can degenerate into an uncontrolled, indiscriminate depiction of facts and incidents that lack the "real" form of life as we experience it (see his essay "Narrate or Describe?"). Irony and parody are useful when authors want to expose the delusions of characters whose behavior is patterned on inherited social or literary conventions. But pure irony, like detached, documentary transcription of real events, is not "objective" in Lukács's sense.

Third, realism involves a doctrine of natural causality, most easily defined through reference to its opposite—the chance, fate, and providence of romantic fiction. In a positive sense, natural causality involves inclusive presentation of all the factors that influence life; as Auerbach says, it shows individuals "embedded in a total reality, political, social, economic, which is concrete and constantly evolving." But once again, "realistic" causality can be construed in various ways. Many of life's incidents lack clearly identifiable causes, and our mania for understanding leads us to make up explanations where none are in fact possible. Some realists have specialized in the portrayal of life's complex randomness and man's deluded certainty that it is comprehensible. At the other extreme is the author who depicts the fate of individuals who are caught up in events beyond their control. In such cases, causality operates inexorably and believably, but many advocates of realism find this kind of work unsatisfactory.

In his penetrating survey of "realism" as a period concept, Marshall Brown shows that the varied meanings critics have attached to the concept of causality can be correlated with three conceptions of reality discussed by the German philosopher Hegel. The first stage is that in which people and objects seem to be random particulars that cannot be understood by examining their causes or consequences. It corresponds to narratives in which situations are vividly presented, but life as a whole seems unintelligible and uncontrollable. In the second stage, "reality" appears as an interconnected series of causal chains, weaving everything together in a necessary process. Narratives exemplifying this stage, according to Brown, may involve the "realism of class conflict, where the hero is both the agent and the chief victim of a historical change." But what appears necessary when viewed from a distance may seem accidental to those who experience it, because the clash of causality and human hope cannot be explained or disregarded. Hegel's third stage of reality is one in which the outer and the inner, the universal and individual, are fused, though this joining of opposites in the "realism of types" may not be fully understood by the characters themselves. The forces we see at work within a character are added to those we discern in nature and society. Brown sees this succession of causal realisms as leading from "the comic realism of details to the tragic realism of causal forces and the melodramatic realism of typological destinies."

In addition to the selection of typical subjects, objectivity, and an emphasis on causality, Wellek and Becker say that realism is characterized by a particular attitude toward the world. For Becker, it is a philosophical commitment to a scientific view of man and society, one opposed to idealism and traditional religious views. For Wellek, "didacticism is implied or concealed" in this commitment. It may seem contradictory to say that realism is objective and then add that it takes a particular philosophic or ethical stance, but the contradiction can be explained. The social criticism implicit in many realistic novels can be called didactic: they present life from one point of view, and others are possible. But the committed realist holds that this point of view is *true*, and that others are, if not false, at least seriously distorted. If we want to understand what was true of the nineteenth century, we should study not aristocrats, aesthetes, and nationalistic histories, but changes in society and the lives of the millions who were moving from the country to the city in response to the pressures of industrialism.

For a critic like Lukács, a genuinely realistic narrative does not borrow its form from literary tradition, but recovers it from the process of historical change; the plots and characters in realistic fiction show us what actually happened in history.

If realistic narratives are considered better than others because they are in fact true, and if realism is a period concept referring to works written since the nineteenth (or perhaps the eighteenth) century, one might ask why writers weren't able to tell the truth before that period. Advocates of realism would reply that the literature of earlier periods was true in the sense that it did depict the societies that produced it. As Levin says, "Epic, romance, and novel are the representatives of three successive states and styles of life: military, courtly, and mercantile." The beliefs, conventions, and lives of feudal aristocracies are represented in the romance. But the "truths" of that governing class, involving a social and literary stratification in which ordinary people were considered comic characters, to be depicted in a "low" style, are not the truths of our society. Realism is that which is true for us, in our time.

What started as a discussion of realism as a literary term must end as a debate about the relationship between history, literature, and reality. Most critics who identify realism with the nineteenth-century novel also think that capitalism was transforming society and class relations during that period. No wonder, then, that in the realistic novel we find "the collision of individual entities against one another, the clash of causality and contingency, the conflict between private intention or personal understanding and suprapersonal meaning," as Brown points out. He clarifies many of the dilemmas involved in the definition of realism by suggesting that the use of the word by writers and critics, beginning in the mid-nineteenth century, did not indicate that they had suddenly discovered what "reality" is. Rather, it was a sign of uncertainty or uneasiness, indicating that a tacit agreement concerning the nature of reality had disappeared. Discussion of realism begins when we are not confident about our understanding of reality (see Levine, 19–20). Differences of opinion are bound to result.

To identify realism as a historical phenomenon, it must be differentiated from the literature of another period. Brown distinguishes nineteenth-century realism, based on conflict and stylistic contrasts, from the more unified life and literature of the eighteenth century, which emphasized the word "truth." Ian Watt and others think that the social and ideological conflicts of the eighteenth century gave rise to realism, which was preceded by a relatively homogeneous literature and culture. Elizabeth Ermarth argues that the site of the unity that preceded realism was the Middle Ages. M. M. Bakhtin, as we have seen, locates the unity in the epic, which refers to a time before its composition; Jameson projects the unity into a utopian future, when social classes will have disappeared. In each case, we find that the explanation of realistic narratives is itself a narrative, telling how the world has gone from a unified past to a fragmented present, perhaps on its way to a unified future. We may conclude, as does Auerbach, that realism appears in all periods, whenever characters of all types can be treated seriously without being segregated by class and style and when all aspects of life are represented. This nonhistorical concept of realism obviously accords with the critical discussions in the preceding chapter that characterize the novel (and other types of narrative) as a mixture. But these concessions, which broaden and thus dilute the definition of realism, are not enough for the formalists and structuralists, most of whom simply deny that "realism" can be defined by reference to how truly it depicts reality.

Realism Viewed as a Convention

The overwhelming dominance of realistic narrative since the middle of the nineteenth century has led some novelists (Hawthorne, Robert Louis Stevenson, and Virginia Woolf among them) to feel that they must explain or defend their use of other modes. Once we grant that realism depicts life as it is, we have not only described but evaluated it. By contrast, other kinds of narrative must provide something else— fantasy, wish-fulfillment, conventional make-believe—which may be enjoyable, but only by virtue of being false. The traditional line of defense against this implicit charge was to assert that romance and the extraordinary give us access to truths that lie beyond the commonplace. As one recent critic puts it, "Great fiction transcends the quotidian, and is little concerned with banal destinies" (Guerard, 14). Nineteenth-century novelists who have been criticized for mixing realism and romance often did so consciously, as Edwin Eigner shows: they wanted to lead readers beyond the empirical and materialistic assumptions of realistic portrayal toward truths of philosophical idealism.

A second and more polemical way to challenge the claims of realists is to argue that realism is simply one convention among others. The positive terms used to define it are implicit negations of their opposites: realism is not selective, not idealized, not imaginary, not subjective, not dependent on fate or accidents, not stylized—in short, not

63

conventional. To admit that realism has any identifiable characteristics of a literary or verbal sort is to admit that it too is based on conventions, and thus to tamper with its claim to present reality without mediation.

In recent narrative theory, the second challenge to realism was initiated by the Russian formalists, who called attention to the fact that the meaning of the word has continuously shifted in the history of literature. Roman Jakobson, in an essay published in 1921, pointed out that each new generation of writers, in order to gain recognition, tends to assert that the works of its predecessors are improbable, artificial, stylized, not true to life. In our literary tradition, some Elizabethan narrators made this charge against writers of romances; the "modern" authors of the Restoration said that the ancients did not represent life as it is; likewise the eighteenth- and nineteenth-century novelists contrasted the "truth" of their stories with the conventionality of their predecessors. As Jakobson suggested and Ernest Gombrich later demonstrated, the same battle about realistic representation occurs in the visual arts: innovative painters first shock the public, then are accepted as "true to life," and later are challenged by upstarts who say that their realism is a convention. Northrop Frye says that if we make up a list of narratives from the Middle Ages to the present, "it is clear that each work is 'romantic' compared to its successors and 'realistic' compared to its predecessors" (49). The list he provides is selective—one could argue that this historical progression is by no means uniform—but in general it holds true.

The more or less continuous shift in the concept of realism (and its cognate terms "verisimilitude," the French *vraisemblance*, or simply "truth") seems to have come to a halt in the nineteenth century. The appearance of the *word* "realism" in literary contexts led to a crystallization of its meaning, according to Jakobson. Many now associate it with literary techniques characteristic of that century. Jakobson identifies two of these, which have been mentioned earlier: the inclusion of reportorial detail that is not essential to the movement of the story; and "motivation" of the action, which involves accounting for it in terms of natural causality. He illustrates the former with the following example: "If the hero of an eighteenth-century adventure novel encounters a passerby, it may be taken for granted that the latter is of importance to the hero or, at least, to the plot. But it is obligatory in Gogol or Tolstoy or Dostoievsky that the hero first meet an unimportant and (from the point of view of the story) superfluous passerby, and that their resulting conversation should have no bearing on the story" (44). This departure from the primary convention of literature, which prescribes that everything shall be meaningful, leads to the establishment of a new convention: inclusion of meaningless or random details characteristic of everyday life serves as evidence that the story "really happened."

"Motivation" is an essential feature of any realistic narrative. When puzzled by some aspect of a film or novel, wondering why a character acted in a certain way, we often try to imagine an explanation: perhaps she didn't try some alternative course of action because she felt the situation was hopeless, or she was distracted by her other problems. When we supply such missing links, we are doing essentially the same thing that the writer does in creating the story. Writers, as we learn from their notebooks and prefaces, often begin from an anecdote or scene that they find striking and then create an intricate web of character and circumstance that will "motivate" the scene or push it to a revealing conclusion. In their notebooks, we find them agonizing over motivation. The question is always—how can I make it plausible?

Tolstoy decided to create a character who would be killed in a battle. Even if he exists only to die, the character must first be created and endowed with traits that make him interesting; in this case, Tolstoy made him brilliant. "Motivation" requires that such characters be firmly woven into the texture of the novel as a whole, as Tolstoy indicated in a letter: "Since it is awkward to describe a character who in no way is connected with the novel, I decided to make this brilliant, young man the son of old Bolkonsky" (a character important in the chapters that follow the battle). This puppet, born only to die, took on a life of its own. Wars do cause pointless deaths, but they are doubly pointless if they simply illustrate, once again, the horror of war, and the character involved has stimulated but not satisfied our curiosity. "He began to interest me," Tolstoy wrote; "a role presented itself for him in the further course of the novel, and I had mercy on him, severely wounding him in the place of death." The character's survival led to events in the novel that Tolstoy had not originally planned, which themselves required further explanation. This process of motivation, which was well described by Victor Shklovsky and Boris Tomashevsky in the 1920s, is similar to what Frye calls "displacement." But in Frye's account of creation, the writer starts from a traditional, archetypal plot (such as is found in myths and romances), and then "displaces" it from its dreamlike unreality to make it plausible from a realistic point of view (134–40).

The process of motivation is well illustrated in three stories that appear in the appendix. The shortest version, recorded by a folklore collector in North Carolina, tells how a wife, when propositioned by her neighbor, demanded cash for her favors. The neighbor borrowed the money from her husband, paid her, and then told the husband he had returned the borrowed money to the wife—who had to admit the repayment and return the money to her husband. In Boccaccio's version of the story, we have authenticating detail: we learn the names of the characters and their occupations—for example, the husband is a rich merchant. But why, then, does the wife need money? Why can't she get it from her husband? On the assumption that the medieval merchant's wife would be under the eye of servants, how could a stranger gain private access to consummate the bargain? Geoffrey Chaucer's version answers all of these questions, while making the wife's actions more understandable, and he sets himself a more complicated task of motivation by making the other man a monk.

When taken together, the two characteristics of nineteenth-century realism described by Jakobson appear to be pulling in opposite directions. Inclusion of "inessential detail" involves the removal of the cause-effect relations of earlier narratives: encounters with strangers that used to be significant must be reduced to randomness. "Motivation" is the reverse of this process: it involves weaving details that were previously unimportant or unnoticed into causal chains. On the whole, the development of realistic narrative is a change from what Boris Tomashevsky (1925) called artistic and compositional motivation (character A meets B because the writer wants to use a traditional pattern and create a subsequent scene) to realistic motivation (A meets B for no particular reason, or because of something that happened earlier). Instead of being pulled toward its future, the story is pushed onward by its past. In either case, randomness and causality, inexplicable accident and inevitable destiny, must be balanced. This juxtaposition in realism is sometimes described as "silhouetting" (Brown).

No document is less "realistic"—in the nineteenth-century or conventional sense—than a newspaper, which records ordinary facts and sensational events simply because they happened, without any attempt to "motivate" them: "4 Killed, 24 Injured in Train Derailment"; "Inconsistency Laid to Foat's Ex-Mate" (a murder trial); "Woman Dies Trying to Save 2 Pets from Fire." How? Why? The creative writer can make these incomprehensible events real by fixing them in a web of circumstance. (Hawthorne's story "Wakefield" shows what he was able to do with a curious incident described in a newspaper, at the same time illustrating the process of motivation.)

Structuralist critics have shown that realistic motivation and inessential detail are but two of the conventions that lend credibility to narratives. The various kinds of verisimilitude and "naturalization" they identify in literature have been surveyed by Jonathan Culler in *Structuralist Poetics* (134–60). In the following account, I have relied on his classification of such conventions, modifying it slightly in order to emphasize its relevance to realism. The first and most basic kind of material important to the believability of fiction is simply "the real"— material that "requires no justification because it seems to derive directly from the structure of the world. We speak of people as having minds and bodies, as thinking, imagining, remembering, feeling pain . . . and do not have to justify such discourse by adducing philosophical arguments" (140). The whole range of facts and processes that are part of nature (smoke is a sign of combustion; once a laugh begins, we know it will eventually end) can enter into narrative as part of its irreducible factuality. Likewise, reference to particulars that are known to exist (Los Angeles, U.S. Route 101, smog) cannot be dismissed as fictions. A narrative saturated with such details, which are not always "inessential" in Jakobson's sense, declares its allegiance to the real.

The second category named by Culler is "cultural *vraisemblance*," which he defines as "a range of cultural stereotypes or accepted knowledge . . . which do not enjoy the same privileged status as elements of the first type, in that the culture itself recognizes them as generalizations." Expanding his conception, I would have it include two subclasses. The first consists of all the practices that make up our social world. Roland Barthes calls them "action sequences"; Roger Schank and Robert Abelson, drawing on psychology and philosophy in their work on artificial intelligence, call them "scripts" and "plans." We all know the series of events involved in thousands of different activities—going to a restaurant, taking a trip, frying an egg, greeting a friend, going to a movie. Such sequences, which are mixtures of causally necessary and socially conventional behavior, constitute a massive store of information about reality that a writer can evoke simply by mentioning one or two of their elements. In what Schank calls "instrumental scripts," the actions are prescribed. "Situational scripts" (such as going to a movie) often involve choices and contingencies; "personal scripts" and "plans," while arising from shared knowledge of goals and ways of achieving them, allow for a much wider range of alternative courses of action.

In order to understand the endless variety of human behavior, we rely on a second kind of accepted knowledge: the storehouse of cultural stereotypes, proverbial expressions, ethical maxims, and psychological rules of thumb that, as Culler says, we recognize as fallible generalizations. In their crudest form they are prejudices—about race, religion, nationality, and sex. When the features we want to understand are the product of personal choice—such as dress, hair style, and manner—we can assume that the meaning we infer is one that is intended. Particular bits of behavior in life or in a novel lead us to imagine a script or plan that would account for them. Though our automatic tendency to put people and their actions in categories often leads to mistaken judgments, there is hardly any alternative to doing so; we have no other way to construe them. Writers often evoke our tendency to generalize in order to confute it.

As Culler and Gérard Genette have shown, "cultural *vraisemblance*" was used in the eighteenth and early nineteenth centuries as a test of a narrative's truth: the audience found it believable if the characters conformed to the types and rules that were generally accepted. Proverbs and stereotypes reflect shared cultural attitudes, thus providing evidence that the writer represents the world as it is. The tale by Chaucer reproduced in the Appendix shows that these methods of insuring narrative credibility were employed in the fourteenth century. Among the maxims it includes are the following: if husbands have wives with expensive tastes, they had better pay the bills, or someone else will; a wife should say nothing ill of her husband; the chances of making a profit by going into business for yourself are slim; money is for the merchant what a plough is for a farmer. The wealth of customary actions and conventional scripts that are enacted in the tale (paying a visit to a friend; exchanging confidences; wishing someone a safe trip; an innuendo, a blush, an overfriendly embrace) both confirm the reader's confidence in the authenticity of the account and provide occasion to exercise interpretive skills we all possess.

Culler's third level of naturalization is that created by the conventions of literary genres. At first glance, realistic narratives appear to avoid them. Though they may be comic or tragic, they are seldom narrowly focused on such emotional effects, nor do they rely on the repertoire of characters and situations from which these effects were traditionally derived. But our impression of the naturalness of realism is in part a result of the fact that we have been used to it ever since we began reading. What is natural to us would appear conventional to someone from another age or culture. On first hearing of how Moses was left in a basket, Huck Finn is "in a sweat to find out all about him"; but on learning "that Moses had been dead a considerable long time," he loses interest, "because I don't take no stock in dead people." Isn't it even more foolish to take stock in people who never existed? Why is an inaccurate account in blank verse of the life of Richard the Second less "real" than a prose narrative about some imagined character?

Specific fictional techniques are among the most important conventions of realism. Some critics complain that the presence of an author who addresses the reader or admits that the characters are imaginary (Henry James called this "a terrible crime") is unrealistic. They would have no trace of the author in the text. But what appeal to truth or fact could determine which set of conventions—acknowledging that someone is telling a fictional tale, or concealing this fact—is more "real"? What we must be prepared to admit is that the conventions with which we feel most comfortable, far from being a detriment to a story's credibility, are the very features that naturalize it and thereby make it believable for us.

Fictionality and access to the consciousness of characters are the primary conventions on which realistic narrative is founded. There are others of a linguistic nature (for example, special uses of the past tense and of pronouns that blur the borders between author and character, between past and present) that will be discussed in a later chapter. Apart from the conventions that narratives share, however, there is a continuously shifting body of practices that are considered realistic in one period and unrealistic in another. These are most easily identifiable by reference to another kind of naturalization.

The fourth level is "the conventionally natural." By calling attention to devices used in other narratives and exposing their artificiality, the writer clears a space in which departures from convention will be taken as signs of authenticity. The idea that a story is worth telling if it illustrates a maxim and the allied assumption that stories should treat typical rather than unique characters (the criteria of cultural *vraisemblance*) are obvious targets of assault for later realists. Typical procedures for naturalization at this level are to contrast an event with those that normally occur in fiction ("you may think that X happened next, but it didn't; that sort of thing only happens in books") or to have a character comment that some event looks suspiciously like those in fiction. Huckleberry Finn begins his story by mentioning that he appears in a book "made by Mr. Mark Twain," which is on the whole true but contains "some stretchers." Like Cervantes, Twain naturalizes the character by juxtaposing him with the prior book in which he appears; Huck's dialect and bad spelling authenticate his discourse, in contrast to the proprieties of literary style. Chaucer uses one of the most effective of realistic devices: by presenting his tales as fictions narrated by real characters, he naturalizes the latter, and questions about the meaning of the tale can be reformulated as questions about the nature and motives of the teller.

Often we find characters in realistic novels who interpret the world through reliance on the conventions of the books they read. Tom Sawyer tries to recreate the imaginary chivalry he has discovered in Cervantes and Dumas; Madame Bovary tries to live the life described in romances. When tested by reality, these conventional worlds crumble, and we are brought back to the naturalized reality created by Twain and Flaubert. As Culler points out, a writer does not necessarily discredit his own imagined world by such comparisons; in displaying an awareness of conventions, he or she may create a more credible breadth of vision.

As the last example shows, an exposure of literary conventions spills over into a questioning of the conventional codes and beliefs that govern individual and group behavior. The first two pages of *Huckleberry Finn* reveal the artificiality of dress codes, good manners, the etiquette of eating, and religious beliefs from Huck's "unsivilized" point of view; the third page (in my edition) displays the superstitions and folk beliefs that he never questions, despite their implausibility. On the second level of naturalization, these pages are a concise encyclopedia of cultural *vraisemblance*: every detail evokes a repertoire of scripts and beliefs characteristic of Twain's time and surviving into our own. By evoking the fourth level, Twain shows that this repertoire is as conventional a construct as the narrative that depicts and deflates it.

Usually we can find a reason for a parody of literary conventions: the writer lays bare the artificial in order to establish a more natural alternative. Likewise, exposure of the folly or harmfulness of social practices is usually accompanied by some indication of how things might be different. There is, however, a fifth level of naturalization, according to Culler, in which alternative styles and points of view are not gathered together in a synthesis but simply left in suspension, without any indication of which are to be preferred. He names this level "parody and irony." Yet he says that in many cases the latter word is inappropriate; the writer does not clearly indicate how the reader is expected to react, and we are forced to supply the label "ironic" simply as a means of making the text comprehensible. To consider such texts realistic may seem odd, because they forestall not only choices between conventions but clear-cut distinctions between conventions and reality. In a sense, they return us to the first level of naturalization—the real—by showing that facts and actions, apart from a mind that understands and evaluates them, are meaningless (cf. Barthes, "The Reality Effect"). At the same time they reveal the most important convention of realism: we assume that life has meaning, while admitting that meaning is produced from human points of view. The choice in life and literature is not between conventional practices and a truth or reality lying outside them, but between different conventional practices that make meaning possible.

Narrative Conventions in History

Some feel that formalists and structuralists attempt to debunk realism because they are relativists, skeptics, or closet idealists. I think this conclusion both under- and overestimates their seriousness. In the early phases of both movements, there was a polemical tendency to shock stodgy professors and critics by making outlandish claims; it certainly succeeded. But in later writings, and in recent semiotics, the serious claims being made are that there is not something real in literature that can be *opposed to* convention and, furthermore, that social reality involves mutually understood regularities of behavior and interpretation that are inevitably conventional. To test these claims, it is useful to consider the traditional oppositions of fact and fiction, life and literature, real and imaginary, natural and conventional in relation to a third term: non-fictional writing. As critics since Plato and Aristotle have argued, literature's "truth" or "reality" can best be judged by comparing it not to life but to other modes of discourse such as philosophy and history. The latter belongs within the sphere of this discussion because, until the recent shift to quantitative methods in the discipline, history has usually been written in narrative form. In what ways is it similar to, and different from, realistic fiction? Admitting that there is a world of difference between real and imagined events, is this the only feature that distinguishes history from fiction? Do the narrative methods of historians, intended to identify true connections between events, differ in kind from those of novelists?

Until the end of the eighteenth century, history was considered part of "literature" in the broad sense and shared with fictional forms the heritage of classical rhetoric, from which it drew methods of organizing and presenting its subject matter (Gossman). Though the criteria used to distinguish fact from fiction have varied, the importance of the distinction has never been in doubt, and fiction has usually been the target of vituperation. But the question of whether or not an event took place can be separated from that of narrativity as such—the ways in which events are causally and temporally connected. Is the structure of a narrative in any way dependent on the truth of the events it recounts? Aristotle said that fictional narration is more philosophic/scientific than history because it concerns general truths: it deals with what usually happens rather than what actually happens, which often cannot be explained by reference to general laws. But of course the modern historian always tries to find an explanation of what happens, and writers of fiction have since the Renaissance deliberately included inexplicable facts or inessential details to validate their "realism" (Davis, 192–98, 215–16).

Having forsaken rhetoric in order to present the truth unadorned (Nelson, 40–41), historians had by the nineteenth century increased their distance from mere literature by emulating scientific methods. Yet history remained uneasily perched between the humanities and the social sciences, and a questioning of its scientific pretensions in the 1940s led to extensive discussion of its theoretical status. In America and England, the debate was touched off by Carl Hempel, who argued that historical explanation was not different in principle from scientific explanation, and that as a science, history had little knowledge to offer. In France, the "Annales" school held that narrative history was merely a recital of social and political change from the perspective of one or another ideology. These critiques prompted philosophers of history to re-examine the assumptions underlying historical narrative. Rather than attempting to summarize this debate (see von Wright, 10–32; Ricoeur, 91–120; White 1984), I shall simply point out some of the important similarities between fictional and historical narration that it brought to light.

At their points of origin, historical and fictional narratives appear to be entirely different. The novelist is free to reject inherited plots and start with what James called a "germ"—a scene or character to which anything imaginable can be added. The historian begins either from a fully saturated temporal series, each instant containing more events than can possibly be used and none of which can be altered; or—if studying a period from which few records survive—with a dearth of evidence and a prohibition against filling it with conjectures. Despite these differences, the two narrators face the same problem: that of showing how a situation at the beginning of a temporal series leads to a different situation at its end. The very possibility of identifying such a series depends upon the following presuppositions, as Arthur Danto and Hayden White have shown: (1) the events involved must all be relevant to one subject, such as a person, a region, or a nation; (2) they must also be unified in relation to some issue of human interest, which will explain why (3) the temporal series must begin and end where it does.

Given these conditions, the tasks of the historian and the realistic novelist begin to seem similar. Our conceptions of "one subject," "human interest," and "cause-effect relationships" are aspects of what Culler classifies as "the real" and "cultural *vraisemblance*." The idea that history can (and in fact must) be broken up into temporal units that have beginnings and ends seems trivially true, until someone points out that time and the physical sciences have no such boundaries; nature is indifferent to what culture calls the rise and fall of empires. The conventions of narrative, as identified by Danto and White, are not constraints on the historian and novelist; rather they create the possibility of narration. Without them, and confronted with a sheer mass of facts, the historian would have nowhere to begin. Knowing what is of human significance, the historian has a subject; knowing something of human thoughts, feelings, desires, the incredible variety of their manifestations, and the social structures that mediate them, he or she can form a hypothesis concerning why something happened as it did. This hypothesis determines which facts will be examined and how they will be put together. The novelist, who often depends heavily on realistic documentation, undertakes the same process. Louis Mink (1978) remarks that at present we have no standards or even suggestions for determining how the connections between events in fictional narratives might differ from those in history.

But surely, someone might reply, there is a clear difference between fact and fiction. There is, but philosophers of history have reduced it. Relying on a generally accepted axiom drawn from philosophy, they point out that a fact or event is such only "under a description," and that any phenomenon can be described in various ways, thus entering into different explanatory hypotheses. A preliminary decision concerning what unifies a particular stretch of history determines what it will include, and a change in temporal boundaries, constituting a different unity of subject and theme, will alter the connections between events (Danto, 167). The newspaper says that three people died in a car crash, two died in a riot, and about 10,000 are starving every month on another continent. Despite their temporal contiguity, these events cannot be joined together in a single history. They must be separated by theme and associated with particular modes of explanation before they make historical sense. (A medical examiner would provide a different account of the cause of death than would a policeman or political historian.) Simply to measure the size and note the placement of such stories in newspapers, correlating

73

them with geography, nationality, and political allegiances, would reveal a great deal about the interests that create historical significance.

In history, Hayden White says, the tail wags the dog; the conventions of narration determine whether or not an event under a description will be a "fact." Mink describes this change of perspective as follows: "Instead of the belief that there is a single story embracing the ensemble of human events, we believe that there are many stories, not only different stories about different events, but even different stories about the same events" (1978, 140). In *Metahistory*, White argues that historical works tend to exemplify recognizable literary plots (comic, tragic, romantic, satiric), and that the unity they attain is ultimately based on aesthetic and moral concerns. History and much realistic fiction also share certain linguistic conventions: the narrator never speaks in his own voice but simply records events, giving readers the impression that no subjective judgment or identifiable person has shaped the story being told.

Finally, there is an all-important feature of narration that is at once linguistic, temporal, and epistemological. Narratives concern the past. The earliest events recounted take on their meaning and act as causes *only* because of the later ones. Whereas most sciences involve prediction, narrative involves "retrodiction." It is the end of the temporal series—how things eventually turned out—that determines which event began it: we know it was a beginning because of the end. If a chance meeting or well-conceived plan comes to nothing, it was not a beginning, in fiction or fact. Thus history, fiction, and biography are based on a reversal of cause-effect relations. Knowing an effect, we go back in time to find its causes; the effect "causes" us to find "causes" (which are "effects" of our search). The present moment is teeming with causes and beginnings, but we cannot recognize them; at some end we will say, "Now I understand." And "if the future is open, the past cannot be utterly closed" (Danto, 196). The history of past causes, which is sealed off with the state of affairs described at the end of a historical account, will be reopened when we seek causes for what happened later. In any case, the history of the future, like that of the past, will be based on an ineradicable assumption that underlies all narrative and distinguishes it from natural science. We assume (because we know) that human action can alter the outcome of otherwise probable predictions. This conclusion (involving the concept of "boundary conditions") is one acceptable to analytic philosophers (von Wright, 64–68).

Given the conventions that history and fiction share as forms of narrative, it may be unnecessary to argue about the "realism" of the

74

novel, so long as we are willing to acknowledge that conventional practices do not separate us from reality but create it.

Narrative in Autobiography and Psychoanalysis

Realistic fiction is similar to history when it treats a large cast of characters and long stretches of time; when concentrating on a single protagonist, it approaches biography and autobiography. The story of a life is less speculative than that of a people, nation, or social class, since the latter are hypothetical entities (Ricoeur calls them "quasi-characters," insofar as the historian assumes that they have intentions and succeed or fail in their actions). In autobiography we find first-hand evidence about the connection between the two spheres of causation that historians must infer and novelists imagine: the outer and inner, action and intention. The unity of a person is neither hypothetical nor fictional. What does autobiography reveal about the nature of narrative? To answer this question, I rely on Georges Gusdorf and Roy Pascal, who identified essential features of the genre that have been treated in greater detail by subsequent critics.

Autobiographers are as fallible as other human beings. They often present themselves in the best possible light, suppressing some facts, failing to recognize the significance of others, and forgetting incidents that biographers can show were important. Such shortcomings deserve study, but they are not the defining features of the form. We all display the same sort of partiality to ourselves in writing and in conversation. Of greater interest are the elements of autobiography that issue from the basic conditions of its creation: someone describes the personal significance of past experiences from the perspective of the present. This definition of the genre distinguishes it from the memoir (usually a record of events of public interest, such as a statesman's career), the reminiscence (a record of personal relationships and memories, without emphasis on the self), and the journal or diary (in which the immediate record of experience is not altered by later reflection).

An autobiography is typically a story of how a life came to be what it was, or a self became what it is. Looking back, the writer discovers that some events had consequences not expected at the time; others yield their meaning only when contemplated in the act of writing. Even the least self-reflective of autobiographers records changes in the self as it passes from childhood to adolescence and maturity. More radical changes of outlook, such as a conversion experience (St. Augustine)

75

or a change of political commitment (Arthur Koestler) can completely alter the meaning of events when they are viewed in retrospect. In some cases, the autobiographer does not set out to describe a self that he or she already knows but to discover one that, despite its changes, has been implicit from the beginning, awaiting an act of self-recognition that will draw all of the past together in the "I" of the present.

There are, then, two variables in autobiography that can keep it from presenting an unchanging picture of the writer's life. The significance of the events may change when they are viewed in retrospect; and the self that describes the events may have changed since they were first experienced. We tend to think of "truth" as knowledge that is not subject to change; this is one reason that mathematics and science have, since Plato, occupied a privileged position in relation to other kinds of knowledge. Autobiography exemplifies fundamental features of narration that unite it with history and fiction, while separating it from the sciences. In narrative, truth is time-dependent. As Ricoeur says (52–87), three temporal periods are necessary to make up a story, whether true or false. The first is the beginning state, when human beings find themselves in a situation that they want to change or simply to understand. This is the time of "prefiguration": given our knowledge of social practices and human inclinations, we can envisage what is likely to happen next and plan to intervene, if that seems wise, to affect the outcome. The second time is that of action, or "figuration": we try to do, or understand, as events unroll. Finally, there is "refiguration": we look back at what happened, tracing the lines that led to the outcome, discovering why plans did not succeed, how extraneous forces intervened, or how successful actions led to unanticipated results.

The three temporal moments that are necessary for the creation of narrative bring with them the possibility that the significance of events may change when they are viewed in retrospect. Further, it is axiomatic that what appears as success from one perspective may be a failure or defeat when seen through different eyes. Finally, the change of commitment may occur within a "self" as a result of later knowledge or a conversion experience that radically alters the pattern in which life develops. Since autobiographies are one of the main sources of our knowledge about such changes, the historical conditions that give birth to the genre deserve investigation.

In the eighteenth century, as Genette and Culler note, characters in novels were considered "realistic" if their thoughts and feelings were appropriate to their position in life (age, sex, and class). Eccentric psychological responses could at that time be ascribed to forces outside the self, which the church might attempt to exorcise, or to wayward impulses that should be subjected to Christian discipline. What is the source of impulses that cannot be explained by self-interest, moral maxims, or generalizations based on stereotypes? If we confess that these impulses exist but ascribe them to the self rather than to its temporary possession by spirits or devils, the self becomes a problematic source of causation, rather than a site that may be transversed by alien forces.

At the end of the eighteenth and beginning of the nineteenth century, autobiography, the autobiographical novel, realism, and modern history all emerge together. The relationship between past and present is no longer explained by cyclic repetition and eternal laws but by particular chains of events that lead toward an uncertain future. Likewise, the individual acquires a particular self—not a fixed, abstract identity, such as that which Descartes and Locke were sure they possessed, but a fluctuating collection of perceptions, thoughts, and intentions that either had no identifiable center (as Hume argued in 1738) or attained one only through a process of self-formation. At the end of the eighteenth century, Restif de la Bretonne said that novels lacked verisimilitude because the characters they portrayed were not subject to the sudden, contradictory changes of feeling that he knew from his own experience (Pascal, 54; see also Spacks). Thenceforth, novelists increasingly recorded the varied moments of the psychic life, sending characters on individual paths toward self-discovery. To conclude, as Jakobson and the earlier structuralists did, that these changes are simply a result of changing conventions of literary realism, is to underestimate their importance.

If my "self" is unique, it cannot be fully understood by reference to social and religious norms; if it is to undergo development (rather than simply being disciplined to conform to ethical patterns), it imposes on me a burden of responsibility as well as a possibility of fulfillment. If I have trouble constituting a self that can cope with my immediate circumstances, I may seek help from a psychologist or psychiatrist.

Psychoanalysis might be described as the art of eliciting autobiographies from people and helping rewrite them, through recovery of omitted episodes and clarification of connections, so that the patient can accept and live comfortably with the resultant story (Schafer). Two psychoanalytic conclusions about narrative are of general significance. The first, which is in accord with a point made by philosophers of history, is that the meaning of an event can be radically dependent on what happens later. It may be true to say it was meaningless and inconsequential when it occurred, and also true to say it later became all-important. If such statements are not contradictory, they make "facts" time-dependent. One instance of such time-dependency is the guilt that results from early sexual experiences, even though these occurred before there was any understanding of sex (and hence meant nothing); in light of later knowledge, the incidents are reinterpreted and become so painful that they are repressed (Laplanche, 38–42). The second conclusion is an extension of the first. A crucial experience in a patient's life—which the psychoanalyst may only with difficulty succeed in eliciting—may not even have occurred; but this does not alter its crucial importance. In view of the retrospective character of all narrative and the inseparability of the self from its story, the event is a necessary hypothesis for understanding, regardless of whether it is factual or fictional (Brooks; Laplanche, 31–47; Culler).

Conclusions drawn from psychoanalysis cannot simply be transferred to criticism, on the assumption that authors and readers are that special class of neurotics who have learned how to cope. But the points that analysts and critics of autobiography make about self-narration are theoretical, and of general applicability. If we concede that the "I" of the present can differ from its previous manifestations, and that early experiences now have a different meaning than they did when they occurred, we tacitly accept a split in ourselves between a self who acts and an other who reflects, judges, and composes. The dilemmas that result from this split are often represented in fiction. Mansfield's "Bliss" (reproduced in the Appendix) shows how a potentially transforming desire is thwarted, leaving the self in disarray. In "The Short Happy Life of Francis Macomber," Hemingway depicts a decisive change of consciousness that transforms a middle-aged adolescent into a mature man. One distinctive feature of modern fictional narrative is that the writer can assume the positions of autobiographer and psychoanalyst at the same time, entering the minds of characters to present their thoughts and feelings and then stepping outside to show how they are viewed by others.

When finished writing, the autobiographer is composed and, on his or her own terms, comprehensible. Whether the motive was self-justification, explanation of a conversion experience, or self-knowledge (discovery of what one is), the product must be understandable as a narrative. We may conclude that the "I" so composed is a fiction but must concede that it exists as a fact. In any case, recent writers on history and autobiography have alerted us to the importance of narrative conventions in the most factual genres, and we can no longer speak of reality and realism without considering how the world is altered and created when it is put into words.

78

Conventions and Reality

In their emphasis on the conventional nature of realism, some recent theorists seem to imply that there is no reason to consider one fictional narrative more realistic than another, since we have no absolute
standard that would enable us to assess the accuracy of different conventions. Likewise, since history and biography are always narrated
from one or another ideological perspective, it can be argued that
what they present as reality is in fact an arbitrary (conventional) view
of it. Having described these theories, I want to mention some alternative interpretations of the evidence they provide concerning the relationship of narratives to reality.

While it is true that the conventions of realism change from one period to the next, this does not necessarily justify the conclusion that
"realism" is a purely relative term. When one set of literary conventions is compared with another, there is obviously no basis for deciding which is "truer." But readers do not decide whether or not a literary work is true to life by comparing it only to other literary works.
That is why David Lodge defines realism as "the representation of experience in a manner which approximates closely to description of
similar experience in non-literary texts of the same culture" (25).
Nonfictional writing registers and sets the standards for how experience is described in words. Admittedly, the kinds of discourse used to
describe reality also change—in part because social reality and social
relations change. But such changes are not themselves purely "conventional," if that term is taken to mean that they are arbitrary and
hence inexplicable. They become more understandable if we consider
them as a product of "consensus."

Elizabeth Ermarth argues that the realism of the nineteenth-
century novel results from its recognition that no single perspective is
adequate for the representation of reality. Novelists of that period
often employ omniscient narrators who allow us to see events from
different points of view. Recognizing that each character claims to be
uniquely in possession of the truth (one might say that they employ
different "conventions of realism"), the writer depicts them in all their
variety. The underlying assumption of this method is that reality can
be known only through consensus—the expression and mediation of
different perspectives as they are revealed by the passage of time.

As I noted earlier, many critics think that the conventions of realism established in the nineteenth century have not changed much
since then, though they find evidence of their evolution in previous
periods. From the point of view of a formalist such as Jakobson, this
stability of the concept is not only inexplicable; it is contrary to his the-

ory of literary change. If Lodge and Ermarth are right, the defining features of realism should be sought in social structures and discourses, not in literary conventions. It is, after all, readers who decide what is and is not realistic, and their attitudes are a product of the realities they experience.

The critic who is committed to the notion that literature and history are never anything but conventional forms, without any essential relationship to reality, is not convinced by this argument. "You have shown that realism is not simply a literary convention," such a critic might reply, "but revealed a deeper weakness in your argument by doing so. For you have been forced to admit that realism is a *social* convention. Societies and ideologies change. What is now considered real in Leningrad would have been thought absurd when it was named Petrograd." Examples from anthropology, physics, and philosophy can be adduced to strengthen this position.

At this point the discussion enters the no-man's-land between critical theory and philosophy, where many have pursued it. The conventionalists, who for some years appeared to be winning the argument, now seem to be losing ground. The articles by Hilary Putnam, Menachim Brinker, and Nelson Goodman listed in the bibliography are excellent introductions to recent discussions of the subject. Marxist critics provide an incisive critique of critical ideologies that find nothing but conventions in literature. Leaving this subject to the curiosity of readers, I turn in the following chapter to a problem raised in this one: the ways in which the temporal progression of narrative determines its structures.

4

Narrative Structure:
Preliminary Problems

I f the structures underlying fictional narratives are identical to those that organize history, biography, newspaper stories, and our sense of pattern in our own lives, the question of how they are constituted takes on renewed interest. The literary term for narrative structure is of course "plot," and most of what the critical tradition tells us about it is derived from Aristotle's *Poetics*. We know that a ✓ plot is formed from a combination of temporal succession and causal-￼ ity. As E. M. Forster put it, "'The king died and then the queen died' is a story. 'The king died, and then the queen died of grief' is a plot." We also know that plots are unified, moving from a stable beginning through complications to another point of equilibrium at the end. In its most conventional representation, derived from the German critic Gustav Freytag, a "normal" plot is depicted as an inverted V,

or more accurately by a variant of that diagram:

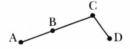

in which AB represents the exposition, B the introduction of the conflict, BC the "rising action," complication, or development of the conflict, C the climax, or turn of the action, CD the dénouement, or resolution of the conflict. While there is no reason to regard this pattern as an absolute necessity, like many other conventions it became conventional because great numbers of people over many years learned by trial and error that it was effective; one ought not to forsake it, therefore. . . . This can't go on much longer; it can go on forever.

Satisfying as it is, this conception of plot has one serious weakness: it doesn't describe most plots. The preceding quotation is taken from John Barth's "Lost in the Funhouse," a story that is, among other things, a parody of this normative description, as the last sentence indicates. Few narratives of any length display the tight-knit unity that Aristotle found in some plays. He had noted that the epic contained a greater variety of incident than drama, and conceded that narrative thus attained "mass and dignity" and "grandeur of effect." But in the end he preferred drama because it conformed to his conception of unified action. Similarly, Edgar Allan Poe argued that the short tale is the perfect narrative form because it can be read at one sitting and thus attain a "unity of effect or impression" that cannot be conveyed by longer forms. By the beginning of the twentieth century, most critics admitted that the tidy plot structure advocated by Aristotle and his followers could not be imposed upon that loose, baggy monster called the novel. Therefore, though it did remain relevant to short stories, discussion of narrative structure waned.

For a revival of interest in the subject, we are indebted to folklorists and anthropologists—in particular Vladimir Propp and Claude Lévi-Strauss. The results they obtained from precise analysis of short tales were so striking that literary critics undertook the more ambitious task of discovering the structural principles in longer narratives. However, it is now apparent that formal analysis of narration involves difficulties far greater than those that confront linguists who attempt to discover the principles underlying sentence structure.

Before surveying the varied theories of narrative structure produced in the past twenty years, I shall indicate why some critics consider this project a pointless one. Critics who occupy the middle ground in this argument see obvious connections between narrative patterns and the ways in which we conceive beginnings and endings in life, time, and history. Discussion of these positions is followed by the heart of the chapter (or, depending on one's view, its gristle and bone): the description of several formal methods of narrative analysis.

Modern theories of narrative fall into three groups, depending on whether they treat narrative as a sequence of events, a discourse produced by a narrator, or a verbal artifact that is organized and endowed with meaning by its readers. This chapter emphasizes the first group (plot in the traditional sense); theories of narrative "discourse" ("point of view") and of reading are examined later.

"Open Form" and Its Predecessors

Before undertaking a search for principles of narrative structure, we should consider the evidence, serious and satirical, that such an enterprise is futile. Although popular fiction remains formulaic, novels and short stories have for a century tended increasingly not just to deviate from traditional formulae but to deride them, and there is little hope of discovering an underlying set of structural principles in texts that so obviously confute our zeal for regularity. Some critics argue that the modern writer attempts to create a unique, personal imaginary order, as opposed to those shared by communities of readers. Alan Friedman and others find in the modern novel a rejection of both collective and individual order in the interests of "open form," which precludes narrative closure and its attendant certainties about meaning. At its extreme, modern narrative may even reject its own intelligibility as a means of taking on existence as an object: it becomes a text, an opaque collection of words that do not refer to any other world, real or imaginary. Such is the "writable" text described by Barthes, as opposed to the "readable" narratives of the past.

In order to explain the disappearance of traditional plots, these critics create a historical narrative that begins with stable social and literary conventions, develops through a phase of conflict and crisis, and ends with a kind of permanent openness or lack of resolution. Except for the ending, this is a traditional plot; and it testifies to the power, if not the inescapability, of the very conventions that it challenges.

A thoroughgoing repudiation of traditional conceptions of plot would reject even this historical scheme and attempt to show that narratives have never really been characterized by the unity of action and meaning that critics find in them. One kind of evidence for this view can be found in traditional novels. The narrator of Sir Walter Scott's *Old Mortality* (1816) wants to leave his tale dangling without closure; when forced by a reader to supply an ending, he says that the protagonists "did live long and happily, and begot sons and daughters." If a writer can knit up (or, as Aristotle would have it, unravel) a story with ease—through death, marriage, homecoming, economic success or failure, discovery of one's parents, or escape from delusion—the unity supplied by endings would appear to be no more than a technical trick. And since authors seem able to alter endings at will, without changing the events that lead up to them (Dickens's *Great Expectations* is the most notorious of many examples), the idea that narration involves a structural integration from beginning to end would seem to be at best dubious. Those who find a historical progression from closed to open endings can do so only by disregarding the wonderfully chaotic novels of the German romantics, Sterne's *Tristram Shandy*, the intricate interlacings of rambling medieval narratives (Vinaver), and the labyrinthine structures of Eastern epics and collections of tales.

To counterbalance Aristotle's assertion that plots begin at the beginning, one can cite another classic authority, Horace, who says that epics should begin *in medias res*, in the middle of things. Many narrators follow this advice, supplying details about the characters and anterior situation after starting a story. Though it seems obvious that narratives should end as soon as the main conflict is over, such closure is rare except in short stories and novellas. Novels tend to ramble and often end arbitrarily.

As Shklovsky points out, picaresque and adventure novels are by nature interminable, consisting of one episode after another. The technical device most commonly used to end them is a change of time scale: the last chapter is an epilogue that covers many years, providing an after-history for the characters. Epilogues may appear to lack closure in the strict sense: rather than stopping the story and tying up all loose ends, they allow it to drift into the future. But these endings serve another purpose: they graft the novel, which when read is apart from life, back onto the real time of history, joining it and the reader to our world. Many of the tales studied by anthropologists end the same way: they happen in prehistory, or myth time, and conclude with the arrival of "the People"—ourselves and our ordinary world (Kermode; see also Torgovnik). But closure in the novel, by epilogue or other means, is seldom so definite that it cannot be reopened in a subsequent novel involving the same characters (a series of novels thus linked together is known as a *roman fleuve*).

The shift toward "open" endings in the late nineteenth century can be construed as a technical innovation, produced by the continuing literary impetus to secure new effects by breaking with conventions. Shklovsky identifies some of the methods used in the short story to evade traditional closure—for example, finishing a story with a description (of the sky, the weather, the season) or a commonplace remark. He calls these "negative" or "degree zero" endings and says that they are effective precisely because of their contrast with the "inflected" endings that earlier stories lead us to expect.

J. Hillis Miller (1978) argues that our inability to define beginnings and endings is not just a formal problem that might be solved by constructing a better theory: "No narrative can show either its beginning or its ending. It always begins and ends still *in medias res*, presupposing as a future anterior some parts of itself outside itself." The very words we use to describe plot are infected by contradiction: the use of both "tieing up" and "unraveling" to describe endings is not an accidental looseness of usage but an inherent undecidability in language and thought. D. A. Miller suggests a less apocalyptic way of viewing the issue. The "narratable" is a "disequilibrium, suspense, and general insufficiency from which a given narrative appears to arise"; the "non-narratable" is the "state of quiescence assumed by a novel before the beginning and supposedly recovered by it at the end." The two terms are not symmetrically opposed to each other, because a final stasis would not simply be a fulfillment of desire, a stable life, or complete knowledge; it would imply that the narratable, and all impulses to move into the future, are wayward deviations from total rigidity. Thus the narrator could truly end only by rejecting the very impetus to narrate in the first place. The dialectic of desire and satisfaction cannot be stopped, even by traditional novelists, and those who realize this (D. A. Miller's examples are Stendhal and André Gide) reject closure.

Endings and Beginnings in Life, Literature, and Myth

Faced with these arguments, we can concede that they may be half right. More than that we need not concede, simply because all evidence that beginnings and endings don't exist presupposes that we have some notion of what these words mean and how they are applied. D. A. Miller remarks that attempts to evade closure would be impossible if there were no closure to evade; to oppose it is to admit and even to reconfirm its existence. And J. Hillis Miller, in another explanation of his position (1974), argues that our conceptions of narrative and history depend on a shared set of assumptions about causality, unity, origin, and end that is characteristic of Western thought. He shows that characters in realistic novels, like the rest of us, usually act in accordance with these assumptions. If the novelist attempts to show how fallacious they are, readers often miss the point and impose the traditional conception of beginnings and ends, goals and results, on texts that would undermine it.

Attempts to break away from this tradition—to produce open-ended narratives—attract the attention of critics who recuperate and naturalize them by explaining their concealed unity. As Paul Valéry said, "There is no discourse so obscure, no tale so odd or remark so incoherent that it cannot be given a meaning." Even if a philosopher succeeded in convincing the world that all talk and thought of beginnings and ends is a delusion, the source of the delusion, its universality, and its mode of operation would remain to be explained. Therefore a survey of how critics account for the human propensity to constitute structured narratives is in order.

The best starting point for such a survey is Frank Kermode's *The Sense of an Ending*, a book that explores both the persistence of traditional narrative patterns and skepticism about them. The most inclusive and important of such patterns in our culture has of course been the Bible, which encompasses all time, from beginning to apocalyptic end, in a coherent divine plan. Nineteenth-century science shattered confidence in that story; yet as Kermode shows, the modes of thought that in the end find ways to construe order from the beginning persist in our ideas about history, life, and fiction.

Why do we break up the evenly spaced ticks of the clock (which are themselves an imposition of order on a continuum) into tick-tock? Kermode cites a psychological study indicating that we inevitably tend to create such patterns, and by doing so we come to apprehend the interval between tick and tock, while losing track of the following one (tock to the next tick). Regardless of whether this tendency is innate or acquired, it seems to persist at all levels of act and thought. Making sense of things in time involves a wide range of common words—plan, fail, decide, achieve, succeed, cause, opportunity, accident (the list is endless)—that cannot be eliminated from the language; as J. Hillis Miller says they entail a network of assumptions about the relation of beginning to end.

Kermode's example reveals the fundamental features of time and narration. As an undifferentiated flow of successive events, time does not even exist. For the events to be "successive," some concept must be positioned outside the flow that will enable us to compare them. The word "tick" yields such a concept: two ticks are abstractly the same, and we can create the idea of time flowing in a direction only because their (atemporal) identity is repeated. This repetition without difference, however, gives rise to a time that returns to its starting point—a cycle, or circle, on a clock or in one turn of the world. To give time a linear progression, we must have repetition of the same with a difference. "Tick" and "tock" yield it: one difference in sound shows that something has changed (the words "tick" and "gong" would not work).

86

But what is it that has changed? As Kermode implies, in this case the change is simply one that humans impose on the world, a way of thinking and perceiving. Forster's example is closer to our experience. In "the king died and then the queen died of grief," the change is not merely imagined; an altered state of the world, resulting from causes and effects, enters to turn time into narrative or plot. To temporality and causality we must add a third factor if our inventory of the conditions necessary for narrative is to be complete. As philosophers of history show (see the third section of chapter 3, "Narrative Conventions in History"), it is human interest that determines whether events and causes fit together in a plot with beginning and end. For chemistry and zoology, "grief" is not a cause; for our society the death of kings and queens, as opposed to less exalted deaths, is not as compelling a subject of interest as it once was. The shapes of narrative are then instances of general cultural assumptions and values—what we consider important, trivial, fortunate, tragic, good, evil, and what impels movement from one to the other.

Kermode and others trace the survival of Christian conceptions of time in our thinking about historical periods, crises, and the rise and fall of civilizations. Paternal authority in religion and the family is mirrored in the succession of kings, ruling by divine right. Atomic war is our secular substitute for apocalypse. As the Western world loses its devotion to the biblical plot of life, death, and rebirth, it finds earthly substitutes for God and a divine plan: empire and nation become objects of devotion, or a paradise at the end of history is conceived, in human terms, as a classless society. The continuity of genealogical succession from one generation to the next can serve as an earthly counterpart for theological conceptions of time; it structures the plots of many nineteenth-century novels (Patricia Tobin).

While acknowledging the importance of these socially sanctioned ways of conceiving time, Edward Said argues that the emergence of the novel—an "original" story about a unique character—involved new views of time and the self. He opposes "origins," which imply a collective, religiously sanctioned view of time, to novelistic "beginnings," which mark the start of an individual, secular career or narrative pattern. Authors assume authority to compete with the Creator. In the end they may choose or be forced to concede that they have created illusions, that society's view of origin, generation, decay, and end is the true one. Or, asserting their individuality, they may cut themselves off from the procreative enterprise of life, condemning their characters and themselves to textual self-creation, a celibate and sterile existence. But Said's account in *Beginnings* of how narratives have departed from traditional patterns is balanced by his emphasis on their persistence, despite all attempts to escape from them.

Perhaps our sense of a cyclic return that unites beginning and end comes from nature—days, seasons, and years, which provide a model for conceptions of human death and rebirth. Northrop Frye sees the major narratives or "myths" of literature as broken arcs in the circle of the seasons: spring is comedy; summer is romance; autumn, tragedy; and winter, irony and satire. The idea that most narratives are variations on a few basic, universal plots is one that Frye shares with the writers of three other books that appeared at about the same time as his *Anatomy of Criticism* (1957), and during the next decade many American critics attempted to show that these "archetypal" myths formed the substructure of modern narratives. A brief description of this theory will indicate why it proved useful, and why the next generation of critics rejected it.

In *The Hero with a Thousand Faces* (1949), Joseph Campbell argues that myths, folktales, and even dreams taken from a variety of cultures display the same essential pattern, which he names the "monomyth." The universality of the narrative incidents emphasized by Campbell had attracted the attention of earlier scholars (F. M. Cornford, Jessie L. Weston, and of course James Frazer in *The Golden Bough*). His skeletal summary of the story, which he diagrammatically represents as a circle from "departure" to "return," is as follows:

> The mythological hero, setting forth from his commonday hut or castle, is lured, carried away, or else voluntarily proceeds, to the threshold of the adventure. There he encounters a shadow presence that guards the passage. The hero may defeat or conciliate this power and go alive into the kingdom of the dark . . . or be slain by the opponent and descend into death (dismemberment, crucifixion). Beyond the threshold, then, the hero journeys through a world of unfamiliar yet strangely intimate forces, some of which severely threaten him (tests), some of which give magical aid (helpers). When he arrives at the nadir of the mythological round, he undergoes a supreme ordeal and gains his reward. The triumph may be represented as the hero's sexual union with the goddess-mother of the world (sacred marriage). . . . The final work is that of the return. . . . The hero re-emerges from the kingdom of dread (return, resurrection). The boon that he brings restores the world (elixir). [Campbell, 245–46]

A somewhat different "typical" myth was reconstructed by Lord Raglan in *The Hero* (his book and Campbell's were both republished in

1956; the former first appeared in 1936). Campbell is a visionary, whereas Raglan set out to debunk many purportedly historical facts by showing they are actually traditional in origin. Even in recent history one can find examples of rather commonplace events that have been transformed, in the course of oral transmission, into archetypal stories; such changes offer further evidence that there are narrative patterns, innate or acquired, that shape our perception of experience. Raglan's account of a universal plot—which, like Campbell, he finds in Eastern as well as Western cultures—involves a hero of royal birth conceived in unusual circumstances and reputed to be the son of a god. Escaping an attempt to kill him at birth, he is reared in another country by foster parents and then, like Campbell's hero, goes on a journey (in this case, to a land of which he will eventually be king). Having won a combat with a king, giant, or dragon, he marries a princess (the substitute for Campbell's goddess-mother). Both versions then involve a flight or departure. Here they diverge, Raglan's ending in tragedy rather than triumph (174–75). Campbell's story looks like a fairy tale, whereas Raglan's looks like a retelling of Oedipus, but the range of parallels they find in other narratives is astonishing. Some of the best evidence for their theories, apart from reading their books, can be garnered by sitting back and asking what narratives we know also fit into these patterns (Star Wars? *Huckleberry Finn?* the Gospels and the story of Moses? Superman?).

The pervasiveness of this pattern is strikingly confirmed in Propp's *Morphology of the Folktale* (1928; first English translation, 1958). Carefully analyzing one hundred tales, Propp concluded that they all consisted of thirty-one "functions." In order to emphasize the similarities of his account to those of Raglan and Campbell, I have skipped over the first seven functions (since they are, in Propp's words, "the *preparatory part* of the tale"), and omitted four of the remaining twenty-four:

The villain causes harm or injury to a member of the family or one member of a family either lacks something or desires to have something. Misfortune or lack is made known; the hero is approached with a request or command; he is allowed to go or he is dispatched. The seeker agrees to or decides upon counteraction. The hero leaves home. The hero is tested, interrogated, attacked, etc., which prepares the way for his receiving either a magical agent or helper. The hero reacts to the actions of the future donor. The hero acquires the use of a magical agent. . . . The hero and the villain join in direct combat. The hero is branded. The villain is defeated. The initial misfortune or lack is liquidated. The hero returns. The hero is pursued. Rescue of the hero from pursuit. The hero, unrec-

89

ognized, arrives home or in another country. . . . A difficult task is proposed to the hero. The task is resolved. The hero is recognized. . . . The villain is punished. The hero is married and ascends the throne. [Propp 1928, 30–63. Ellipses indicate omitted functions; all other text omitted]

This plot ends with marriage; in the preceding two, marriage occurs near the middle. It is worth noting that all three versions involve *two* major tests or conflicts, not one, as we might expect from intuitive conceptions of plot unity. Given the universality of this basic story and the near impossibility that it spread to remote corners of the globe through migration or oral transmission (neither of which would in itself account for the story's survival), one can understand the desire to see whether modern narratives can be interpreted as realistic versions or "displacements" (Frye's term) of age-old myths.

Though not chosen for this purpose, the two modern stories I use as examples in this book, Hemingway's "The Short Happy Life of Francis Macomber" and Katherine Mansfield's "Bliss," might plausibly fit into the scheme of the monomyth. Both stories involve tests that the modern hero and heroine succeed in passing, thus attaining a new state of consciousness. The "other kingdom" of fairy tales becomes modern Africa, or a magical garden. The hunter Robert Wilson (in Hemingway's story) and the friend Pearl (in "Bliss") are the "helper" figures who "initiate" the protagonists, whose trials involve big game hunting or sexual competition, rather than confrontation with the traditional villain. You may be able to discover more precise correspondences than those I suggest. Identification of universal narrative patterns would seem to tell us not just about literature but about the nature of the mind and/or universal features of culture.

Structural Analysis of Narrative Sequences

Though it appeals to many, the attempt to discover a single plot with a deep meaning in all the world's stories has been repudiated by those who seek a rigorous analysis of narrative structures. Beginning from a fairy tale or monomyth, and lacking any particular criteria for deciding whether other stories are "really" a version of it at some ultimate level, one can usually find the similarities one seeks. The only limit to the success of the method is the ingenuity of the critic. Barbara Herrnstein Smith calls attention to studies that have identified hundreds of tales as variations of the Cinderella story, and mentions a critic who thinks all of Dickens's novels are "basically" versions of Cinderella. Others claim that Cinderella is simply a surface manifestation of an underlying story of "psychosexual development," or "an allegory of Christian redemption." The objection of structuralist critics to these conclusions is not that they are wrong but simply that there is no way to determine whether they are right or wrong—which is to imply that they can be produced forever without hope of definitive result. A similar complaint can be made about other forms of archetypal, symbolic, and psychoanalytic interpretation.

A search for the origins of plot structure in primeval myths is different from a study of plot itself, just as knowledge of what a word originally meant in Latin or Sanskrit differs from awareness of its current meaning. Aristotle, who lived when seasonal myths were an integral part of culture, said that plots depict *human* actions, and the basic features of such acts served as elements of his analysis of plot. Structuralist and semiotic critics are the successors (if not the followers) of Aristotle. They are not satisfied with analogical or metaphorical explanations of narrative structure. To say that comedy is like spring, or that a nineteenth-century novel is like parent and offspring, is to leave unanswered the question of why these things are like each other and what conceptual relationships they involve.

Whereas American criticism tended to follow the critical paths of Frye and Campbell, French criticism followed the one suggested by Propp. Despite the apparent similarity of their conclusions, Propp's methods were entirely different from Frye's and Campbell's. His passion was for scientific precision, as the word "morphology" in his title indicates. Eschewing their far-ranging search for themes and meanings, Propp tried to describe and classify the surface level of a limited corpus—what actually happens in the stories—and to reduce if not eliminate subjective interpretations that could distort his search for abstract forms. Even more valuable than the results he obtained, from the point of view of French structuralists, were his discussions of theory and method, which served as a starting point for a new type of narrative analysis and at the same time established some of its limitations.

Propp's predecessors had developed varied classifications of tales on the basis of their subject matter ("tales with fantastic content, tales of everyday life, animal tales") or themes ("about those unjustly persecuted, about the hero-fool, about three brothers"). A glance at these lists shows that they violate the basic principles of classification, since they are not based on clear-cut conceptual distinctions. But what is the purpose of niggling precision in literary analysis? "Does it matter," said the critics of his time, and many today, "how we isolate basic elements, how we classify a tale, and whether we study it according to motifs and themes?" Propp answers such critics with an analogy that was to prove very important for French structuralists: "Is it possible to speak about the life of a language without knowing anything about the parts of speech, i.e., about certain groups of words arranged according to the laws of their changes? A living language is a concrete fact—grammar is its abstract substratum. These substrata lie at the basis of a great many phenomena of life, and it is precisely to this that science turns its attention. Not a single concrete fact can be explained without the study of these abstract bases" (1928, 15).

The most obvious elements of a tale are the characters or actants, on the basis of which one can develop any number of classifications— tales about wolves, foxes, birds; about orphans, daughters, kings, witches, etc. (the inconsistencies of this list, from a logical point of view, should be apparent). But to classify tales on the basis of such "concrete facts" obscures the structural similarities we intuitively recognize in comparing them. I have included in the appendix two stories that we recognize as having "the same plot": a married woman responds to a sexual proposition with a request for money; the man borrows money from the husband, gives it to the wife in exchange for her favors, and then tells the husband that the wife has received repayment of the loan. In various versions of the story, the man is a German, a neighbor, a monk, and a goldsmith. While a classification that used categories such as "foreigners" and "clergy" might reveal a great deal about social attitudes in particular times and places, it would conceal the structural similarities that Propp wanted to identify. We recognize that the tales have "the same plot," but what precisely do we mean by this, in conceptual terms?

Propp's solution to the problem, one that has far-reaching consequences in the study of language and literature, was to identify function and context—that is, *relations* between elements, rather than elements themselves—as the basic units of narration. A linguistic example will make the difference clear. Given the word "bit" alone, there is no way to 'e'ermine what it means or for that matter whether it is a noun, a verb, or an adjective. When placed in a sentence, however, its potential for meaning, within a wide range of possibilities, is actualized and determined by its function in the context. (Dog bit man. Actor got bit part. Eight bits make one buck, or one byte.)

Likewise, to say that a story is about a monk, or about a monk who has sexual relations with an unmarried or married woman, can be very misleading to those who are studying not religious history or popular prejudice but the structure of narratives. From Propp's point of view, the monk, like the word "bit," gets its meaning when it is put into one of the available slots in a sequential structure—a sentence or narrative. Function determines meaning. This implies, first of all, that verbs or actions are more structurally significant than nouns or characters. To use his examples, it means that in "a tsar gives an eagle to a hero," "an old man gives Sucenko a horse," and "a princess gives Ivan a ring," the giving is more important for narrative analysis than the people or objects involved. Second, it implies that even this abstract structure (A gives B to C) is not a unit or motif with a single meaning, because the function and hence the meaning of the giving will depend on its context—the purpose it serves in the story as a whole. In our exemplary tale, there is obviously a difference of function between the husband giving the money to the man, and the man giving money to the wife.

The importance of Propp's identification of the "function" as the basic element of a tale becomes clear through a comparison of his theory with those of Campbell and Raglan. In order to determine what it means to say that different stories have the same plot, all three assumed that "the same plot" means "the same essential events in the same order." But there is always a danger that our search for regularities of this sort will lead us to distort the evidence. This is of course the besetting flaw of most attempts to use scientific methods in the humanities and social sciences. The analyst sets out in search of a single form that will explain varied phenomena; having found one that, with a bit of stretching, will account for many examples, he either discards those that don't fit or says that there is some fault in the examples, not in the explanation he has created; and thus instead of theories that explain what exists, we get theories—imposed by critics—in the form of "norms" from which the evidence deviates.

Campbell and Raglan succeeded in finding the same plot in different stories by listing only the events that the stories had in common, discarding the others. They did not develop any criterion other than repetition for selecting events to be listed. Obviously, we can make stories appear more similar than they actually are by omitting all features that make them different. Propp was more rigorous in two respects. His definition of "function" provided a clear basis for identification of narrative units, and he listed every one that appeared in the tales he studied. He found thirty-one functions, which always appeared in the same order, though not all appeared in every tale.

But if Campbell and Raglan can be accused of creating a single plot by eliminating unique incidents, Propp might be faulted for including them. If he finds an event that appears in only two or three of the hundred tales he studied, he can simply insert it in his master plot; its absence from the others is explained by his rules. When we read his sequence of functions, it appears to tell not one story but two or three. The first function that I quoted (number eight on his list) indicates that a villain causes harm *or* a member of the family lacks or desires something. Functions nine and ten involve alternative paths of development and different kinds of "hero" as a result of the split that occurred in function eight. Propp might have solved this problem by deciding that he was dealing not with one type of tale, but with two or three (Liberman, xxxi; see also the discussion of the problem in Apo). But such a decision, he knew, would be unscientific; the analyst must try to explain all the evidence, not just divide it up into categories so as to segregate examples that are hard to deal with.

Having criticized these three theorists, I must admit that they provide a useful and perhaps inevitable starting point for any analysis of narrative structure. Since we can recount briefly what happened in a story or movie when asked to do so, or recognize the same plot in different versions of a story (though Barbara Herrnstein Smith warns us to be careful about this), there is good reason to suspect that a plot, like a sentence, has a structure we intuitively apprehend. As in other analytic studies, we must work back and forth between theory and practice, changing our methods as we learn. The fruitfulness of Propp's theory is demonstrated in the writings of others who followed in his path. The French critics Claude Bremond and A.-J. Greimas are among those who used his insights as the basis of more encompassing theories. Rather than summarizing their methods and results (which are well analyzed by Culler, Scholes, Budniakiewicz, and Hendricks), I shall discuss the conceptual choices available to those who think that the essential form of a narrative is to be found in the sequence of its actions.

A story, like a sentence, seems to have a structure; we usually know whether one or the other is complete on the basis of our previous experience. If a linguist were to use the methods of Propp, Campbell, and Raglan, s/he would first sort the sentences into groups that appeared to be similar and then look for the same sequence of parts of speech in each group. Various classifications might result (all sentences are active or passive; simple, compound, or complex; declarative, interrogatory, imperative, etc.). Another school of linguists might well argue that this method is faulty, in that we should be looking for a single structure underlying all sentences. One method of doing so would be to try to create a series of rules capable of generating all the sequences of words that we recognize as grammatical and complete. A critic of both these approaches could argue that sounds and grammatical forms do not in themselves create a sentence; it exists only to convey meaning. An adequate grammar should explain why varied strings of words can have the same meaning, showing how different surface structures can be produced from a single deep structure, and why a single sentence can have different meanings. These second and third approaches to the problem of sentence structure have served as models for the analysis of plot.

A comparison of the action sequence described by Propp with the stories by Boccaccio and Chaucer (see the Appendix) reveals that Propp's scheme is "corpus specific": it does not apply to other types of tales (see Bremond 1982; Bremond and Verrier 1984). Instead of trying to find a single sequence in many stories, the theorist can create an abstract structure that might be made concrete in various ways, assigning different descriptions to different stories, just as linguists do when dealing with different types of sentences. Analysts of narrative, like linguists, sometimes use visual models that provide a clear representation of a theory and suggest by analogy how it can be developed (Ann Harleman Stewart). They have represented sentences and stories with two sorts of "tree structures." One type branches down from the top, splitting up first into main units (for example, "noun phrase" and "verb phrase," or "event," "conjunction," "event") and then into the particular words or incidents that make up the abstract units. Gerald Prince is one of those who have used this kind of diagram. He defines a "minimal story" as consisting of a state of affairs, followed by an action, which causes another state of affairs that is the inverse of the first. Others who use this model take the "episode" as the basic unit of a story, breaking it down into "event" and "reaction," or "motivation" and "response," which in turn yield subunits, on down to the concrete sequence of words and actions involved (Colby; Rummelhart).

Another method of using a tree structure to describe various types of stories is to exploit what appears to be a flaw in Propp's theory, turning it into a theoretical virtue. He found that the main action of the tales he studied begin with harm *or* lack (desire for something). Why not admit that alternative possibilities exist at each point in the tale—since they obviously do and are important in creating suspense—and then depict the story as the actualization of one particular pathway through the choices involved? The character can attempt to recover from the harm or accept it, seek revenge or not seek it, and the like. At each point there are two possibilities: the character acts or does not act, and succeeds or fails (Bremond 1973). In our exemplary story, a man propositions a married woman, who can refuse or accept; she makes a counterproposal, asking for money; he can decide not to give her the money, or to do so; if the latter, he may try to borrow the money and succeed or fail . . . etc. Different plot types emerge from other choices in this maze of possibilities (the woman refuses once, refuses twice . . .; one or the other resorts to deception— the man pretending to be her absent husband one night, or the wife having another woman in her room for the assignation).

A variation on the tree structure is a diagram that branches out as events occur; then, as later events complete the chains opened by earlier ones, the chains converge. Figure 4a gives a rough example of such analysis, applied to our kernel story.

It should be apparent that this representation (a "flowchart" tree) is a refinement of Propp's linear sequence. It provides connecting lines between events that are obviously related to each other, such as "departure" and "return" in his sequence ("contract" and "contract complete" in this one). Representation of these connections makes the relation between the main plot line and subordinate sequences more evident. The whole plot opens from an initial problem and closes with its resolution.

Two other methods of representing multiple plot lines deserve mention. Propp used the traditional method of making parallel horizontal lines, one for each action sequence. A line continues so long as

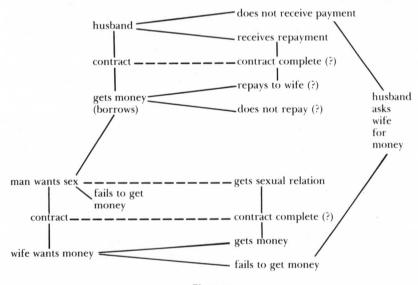

Figure 4a

the sequence is being presented in the story and stops when the story shifts to another sequence. Lévi-Strauss (1955) went a step further: when he found action sequences in different parts of a tale that seemed parallel in structure, he shifted the later ones under the first, in order to examine their structural similarities. In Chaucer's version of our kernel tale, "husband borrows money—repays" would be placed underneath "monk borrows money—repays" (Martin and Conrad).

When plot is conceived, in very broad terms, as leading from harm or lack to a satisfactory state, or from satisfactory to unsatisfactory (from bad to good fortune, or vice versa, according to Aristotle; modern theorists use different terminology), the "flowchart" we have just constructed can be reduced to a "circuit" diagram—a square, circle, or diamond (Stewart). Figure 4b shows four examples, one taken from linguistics. One of these diagrams branches out and then closes in a linear fashion. The other three return to their starting points, thus representing not just a temporal progression but a conceptual or thematic unity.

These three models—tree structures, flowchart trees, and circuits—solve several of the problems associated with Propp's method. They make it possible to describe almost any narrative and do not encourage the critic to look for a single pattern in plots that are in fact different. But when critics create theories that enable us to describe any story whatsoever, we encounter another problem. As the foregoing examples show, there are many different methods and vocabularies that enable us to label the parts of a narrative. We can use the words event, function, episode, motif, state, kernel, or action to describe the situation and what happens (these and others have been used); we can create abstract terms for the characters (actant, subject, object, helper) that may help prevent us from making subjective judgments about them. But having done so, and created meticulous descriptions or diagrams of stories, what have we achieved?

What is lacking, in any method that substitutes a sequence of abstract terms for the concrete actions of a story, is an explanation of how the actions interlock with each other to create a plot, and how formal patterns are related to the story's content. Propp and his successors have been accused of disregarding content in their search for form (hence the perjorative use of the word "formalist" by Lévi-Strauss 1960) but that criticism is not entirely just. Propp's functions and actants (harm, villain) do have semantic content; having emphasized form in his early writings, he and others have since shown that the order of events in stories can be related to a deeper mythological

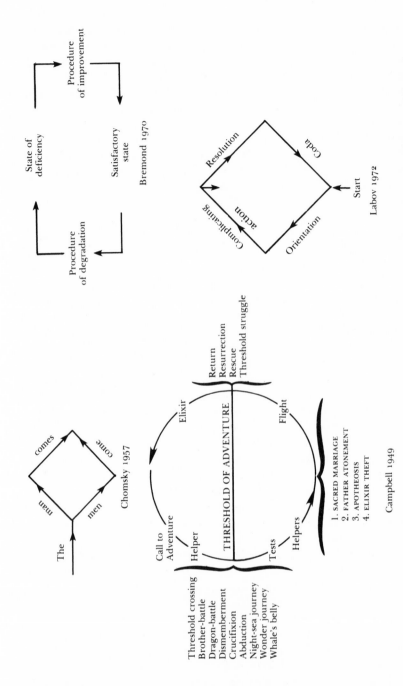

Figure 4b. These diagrams are reproduced from the works noted by permission of their publishers, listed in the Bibliography.

theory (Propp 1946). When analyzing realistic narratives rather than oral tales and myths, theorists find that conventional patterns of social behavior provide a pattern of meaning that organizes the temporal progress of plots.

Some connections between narrative actions are of a quasi-logical order, as Propp and his successors noted. Departure implies return; a promise or contract implies an intention to fulfill it; a desire to achieve a goal results in an attempt to do so. On the surface level, many narratives proceed along the lines of the action sequences or "scripts" described by Barthes, Culler, and Schank (see "Realism Viewed as a Convention," chapter 3). More than half of the tale by Chaucer (in the Appendix) is a chronological progression based on the conventional sequences "having a guest stay overnight" and "getting up in the morning and having breakfast"; Mansfield's "Bliss" (also in the Appendix) is a story about a dinner party (preparation; greeting the guests; eating; talking after dinner; saying goodbye), in which every episode unfolds in accordance with a social formula. Some critics hold that narrative can best be studied as a special area within much broader fields: the philosophy of action and discourse analysis (van Dijk). In general, the more realistic a narrative is, the most closely it adheres to the sequential structuring provided by social practices.

These attempts to explain the "surface structure" of narratives— the sequence of actions, or syntagmatic dimension—show that Propp's model can be improved through recourse to semiotics and allied disciplines. An entirely different approach to the problem (the third and last in my list of three) is to assume that the diverse surface structures of stories are generated from a smaller set of "deep structures" that can be actualized, as a temporal succession, in various ways. This is the approach of Lévi-Strauss (1955), which is sometimes compared to the "transformational grammar" of Noam Chomsky. Lévi-Strauss posits the existence of an abstract structure, an equation, in which the variables are universal cultural oppositions (for example life/death, or heaven/earth) and symbols that mediate between the opposed terms. Depending on the culture and its environment, these variables will take on different values in the surface structure of the culture's myths.

These deep structures are timeless, in a sense; they generate the rules and lawlike regularities of human behavior that impel us to move from the beginnings to the endings described by Campbell, Kermode and others. In a state of equilibrium—let's assume a world of good fortune, in which all desires are satisfied—time and change would scarcely exist. (That is why Karl Marx said that history, and perhaps narrative, will end when there is a classless society.) Narration starts when that world is thrown out of kilter, or there is a need to explain the world's origin and structure. It ends when the initiating need or desire finds its corresponding satisfaction.

Through its conventions and laws, society maintains a framework of procedures for human interactions, such as making agreements or contracts, exchanging information, and achieving goals despite obstacles. A single aim, such as the desire to enter into a sexual relationship, can be realized in various ways in narratives. Some theorists conceive narrative deep structure as a set of basic functions and actants: for example, "sender–communication, contract or transfer–receiver" and "subject–contest or confrontation–opponent/object" (Greimas). In order to show how these patterns are actualized, the theorist must develop a set of rules or transformations that account for the relations between the atemporal deep structure and the chronological surface structure.

While temporal succession and causal connection are necessary links in narrative sequences, they are not in themselves sufficient to explain any plot that is likely to prove interesting to us, as Aristotle pointed out. Even in the sciences, there are two types of causality— the probable and the necessary. Necessity (which we may call "fate" if we don't understand it) is opposed to pure chance or accident, and the probable to the improbable. By themselves, these connections might explain the "plot" of a scientific study, but not of a narrative. Aristotle held that concepts of good and bad character and fortune are required in plots with human interest, and such value judgments are connected to social rules—prohibition and obligation.

This preliminary list of links necessary for the construction of a plot helps account for Propp's list of functions ("interdiction," "harm," "villain defeated") and for other recent theories of narrative structure. Lubomír Doležel suggests that narrative structure may best be analyzed through the use of modal logics—in particular, the alethic (possibility, impossibility, necessity), the deontic (permission, prohibition, obligation), the axiological (goodness, badness, indifference), and the epistemic (knowledge, ignorance, and belief). To these "narrative modalities" it might be necessary to add other terms, and some account of desires in relation to plans and goals. The result would be a theory of "possible worlds"—how things happen in real and imaginary circumstances.

In attempting to correlate descriptions of narrative sequences with an underlying structure of human actions, the analyst has a means of testing the adequacy of a theory. The linguistic example used earlier makes this clear: to determine the formal status of the word "bit" in a sentence, we need to understand its meaning, and vice versa. But unlike the linguist, the narrative analyst finds it difficult to escape from circular reasoning. There is general agreement about what "bit" means in various contexts, but little agreement about the interpretation of stories. Once we decide that a story exemplifies a particular action or theme, we will quite naturally construe the events (the surface level) in a particular fashion, though another reader might understand the theme and hence the action differently.

Some theorists claim that they do not interpret but simply describe and name the actions in the stories they analyze. But even to assign a name to an action is, in a sense, to interpret it. One formal analysis of the tale by Boccaccio represents it as follows: the man desires to be in sexual relation with the wife, and she asks him to pay her; he conceals his actions, and she thinks she has been paid; but then it is revealed that he didn't pay. Yet the formal method that yields this analysis also contains terms that would allow us to describe the story as one in which the wife transgressed and was punished for her actions (Todorov). Too often the pattern that even the most scientific of critics "discover" in a story is one that their interpretation put into it in the first place.

Other analysts hold that deep narrative structures are in fact patterns of meaning, not actions, and attempt to avoid subjectivity by imposing rigorous formal constraints on the process of interpretation and the relation between deep and surface structures. Advocates of this method often state themes as equations involving logical terms such as "a" and "not a": married, unmarried; paying, not paying, etc. The best-known advocates of this approach are Lévi-Strauss and Greimas.

A third method of avoiding circularity or subjectivity in exploring the relationship between plot and theme is to assume that every experienced reader is a competent interpreter, to collect all available interpretations of a narrative, and to try to discover what they have in common. Perhaps a sequence of actions can be correlated with a single but very general thematic substructure that branches out into particular interpretations. Alternatively, one could assume that a story, like an ambiguous sentence, has two or more distinct deep structures, depending on how one construes it. One other approach to the problem deserves mention. Aristotle analyzed plot through reliance on what the modern theorist would call "narrative modalities"—probability, accident, knowledge (recognition) or ignorance, good and bad. He attempted to correlate these not with theme or meaning, about which opinions varied in his day as they do in ours, but with emotional responses that are relatively uniform in the entire audience of a dramatic performance. This method might prove useful in the study of obviously comic and tragic narratives, but the variety of emotions experienced by solitary readers is too great to make it generally applicable.

Uses and Abuses of Structural Analysis

Having discussed three types of analysis based on models derived from linguistics, I shall call a halt to this superficial survey in the hope of persuading you that something can be learned from it. Many who are fascinated with narration find this whole topic boring. There is obviously something of human importance in the writings of Kermode, Frye, Said, and Miller when they discuss how our sense of beginnings and endings is shaped by more general conceptions of life, society, and the universe. But a passion for dissecting stories in order to reduce them to formulae remains alien, if not incomprehensible, to most readers of fiction.

There are others who think, as Propp did, that we may make genuine discoveries about narrative structure, comparable in importance to those that resulted from applying scientific methods to the study of language. In reply to the charge that they reduce stories and meanings to formulae, they say that they do so in order to identify the conventions that make it possible for stories and life to have meaning. Rather than rejecting this claim, on the basis of some categorical distinction between the sciences and humanities, I think we should allow the theorists to present their case and see whether they can tell us anything that is both scientific and interesting.

Most of the theories I have discussed were developed to explain oral traditions (or, in the case of Aristotle, plays that were based on a small group of stories). A comparison of tales taken from a particular society shows that while details vary, the plot structures are often similar and can be reduced to a series of motifs, as indicated in chapter 2. In reply to the question of what constitutes a motif, Propp answered, "A *function*, regardless of who or what performs it." His conclusions have proved useful to many who have studied oral literature, but they become questionable when applied to written narratives.

With the advent of writing, authors can preserve differences of action and detail that are lost or subject to variation in oral retelling. We can see how writing affects storytelling in our exemplary tale. Surviving oral versions are brief. Boccaccio's is somewhat longer and more particularized. Chaucer's is so rich in detail that there is reason to ask whether it can be said to have "the same plot" as earlier versions. When authors add new turns to traditional materials and attempt to produce stories never told before, the hypothesis that all of them have one basic structure becomes less plausible.

When they attempt to generalize Propp's results by assuming that tales from different cultures have the same structure, theorists encounter opposition from within their own ranks. One group, which would include Shklovsky, Campbell, and Lévi-Strauss, thinks that by studying narratives, we can learn something about the human mind apart from its social conditions. Another school insists that their significance varies from one culture and situation to another. The anthropologist Dell Hymes and Kermode (1969) have discussed a Chinook Indian story that simply makes no sense to those not knowing the cultural and social practices involved. In tape-recording oral tales, anthropologists have sometimes thought they were finished and started to pack up their equipment, only to be told there was more to come; so much for our intuitive sense of an ending. In some cultures a tale can take on different meanings depending on the circumstances in which it is recounted. The moral that the armchair theorist should derive from these examples is that literary history and anthropology have as much claim to be part of a science of literature as do abstract terms and formulae.

Another lesson to be learned from attempts to show what all stories have in common is that to the extent they succeed, they usually blur distinctions and thus make it impossible, within the theory, to show how and why stories are different. If the theorist gives up this search for narrative universals and tries to show how different plots are related to different meanings, s/he encounters another set of problems. The relationship between grammar and meaning is fairly clear in natural languages. Knowing the meaning of a sentence, we can explain its grammatical structure, and vice versa. Chomsky and others were able to identify the structures underlying ambiguous sentences (one expression, more than one content) because they understood the structure of unambiguous sentences. But ambiguity is the norm, not the exception, in tales that attract the attention of literary critics. That is why there is so much disagreement about how they should be interpreted. Structural analysis of narrative would ideally be able to show how a single surface structure (sequence of events) could be related to as many deep structures as there are interpretations of the tale. Narrative analysts have tended to overlook surface ambiguities and to assign one structural description to stories that have more than one meaning.

An example may help clarify this point. To show that beginnings and endings in narrative are governed by social practices, some theorists assume that contracts must be completed *or* broken, as a result of which there is gain *or* loss (transfer, acquisition, or retention of objects, etc.). As Figure 4a shows, our tale violates that assumption. Did the man repay the husband? Yes—but in a sense no. Did he pay the wife? If she returns the money to her husband, the answer is no, not ultimately. If we say the man got something for nothing, is it entirely fair to say that the woman got nothing for something? In sexual relations, gain and loss depend entirely on the attitudes and motives of the participants, which few theorists account for in their formulae. If we insist on strict accounting principles in our narrative equations, we may conclude (as one of my students did) that the possibility of sexual activity without monetary compensation reveals "the surplus of sex"; in economic terms, if the supply is not restricted, the price will drop.

One interpreter of the original tale was Chaucer, who changed the ending, producing new problems for the theorist. In his version, the merchant asks his wife about the money at a particularly delicate—or perhaps indelicate—moment. In the past he had not given her all the money that she wanted; on this occasion, she is not giving him all the satisfaction he desires after his lengthy absence. Irritated, he asks whether she received the money from the monk. Yes, she replies, but I didn't know it was repayment of a loan. I spent it on clothes. So now I'm in debt to you, and "I wol nat paye yow but abedde." The question now confronting the theorist is this: can her proposal concerning repayment be accepted, or must we charge the husband with a loss because of violation of a contract?

Attempts to show that narrative structures are governed by social practices and conventions lead me to suspect that plots cannot be explained *within* the rules of a society because they are *about* those rules. In Chaucer's version of the tale, the legal and moral codes that tell us husband and wife are "one person" (for such purposes as incurring and repaying debts) come into conflict with the fact that marriage has traditionally been a contractual arrangement of two persons that involves an exchange of sex and money. And any loss or gain involving the exchanges between husband, wife, and monk must be considered in relation to the larger economic framework of the tale. As a result of borrowing money and going on a business trip, the merchant makes a handsome profit, which he will balance against the loss to his wife.

Formal analysis takes us beyond formalism to the economic history of Chaucer's time. This line of thought leads to the hypothesis that every interesting story is an ambiguous *deviation* from the "well-formed narratives" of everyday life. But until narrative theory, discourse analysis, and semiotics produce more complete accounts of how we usually describe past actions, such a hypothesis is difficult to sustain.

My criticism of the theories I have discussed (with what zest and ease the critic proves others are wrong!) would not have been possible without reliance on the very methods of analysis I find fault with. For until theorists developed precise tools for labeling and interrelating events, the question of whether or not stories close in some formal fashion could not even be posed precisely. What we require of a theory, as philosopher Karl Popper shows, is not necessarily that it be true but that it be falsifiable. To propose a literary theory that is arguably false is a triumph over muddle-headedness: to the extent that we see its errors clearly, a theory contains clues about how to find the truth we seek. As Bacon said, "Truth emerges more readily from error than from confusion."

To understand formalist and structuralist theories of narrative, it is necessary to study and attempt to apply them. In addition to creating the most influential of such theories, Propp and Lévi-Strauss have commented on each other's work (see Propp 1966); they provide the best starting point for anyone interested in this branch of narrative theory. (One caution to intrepid venturers into this field: Lévi-Strauss will be misunderstood, as he has been by many commentators, if one does not know that the "-1" in reproductions of his famous formula should be placed *above the line*; it is an exponent, not a subtraction, and it refers to a mathematical figure known as the Klein group.)

To those who say that this type of analysis has always failed, the structuralist replies that the alternative to inadequate or reductive theories is not none at all but better ones. Intensive research in this area has been under way for only twenty years, and recent critics have overcome some of the limitations of the theories I have discussed. One such limitation is that they tend to reduce narratives to a static, atemporal deep structure and thus cannot account for the tensions and reversals of situation that make us want to find out what happens next. In a simple yet revealing application of set theory, the Russian critics O. G. Revzina and I. I. Revzin show how relationships and roles in a story can change as it departs from and returns to a stable situation. Another critic, John Holloway, has used set theory in a different solution to the problem. In his discussion of the *Decameron*, he suggests that as we progress through a story, each new situation is construed as a revised configuration of the entire sequence up to that point (a set of sets), leading to revised expectations concerning the outcome. By explaining structure from the reader's point of view, Holloway accounts for the dynamic element of narrative development and shows that meaning is something we produce, not a product we try to acquire.

This quest for a rigorous theory of narrative must end without closure. Some argue that it should never have been undertaken because the quarry doesn't exist: narrative is not based on, nor can it be reduced to, theoretical structures. Others keep on searching. Their task would be easier if they knew exactly what the quarry in question will look like when they find it. But of course that will depend entirely on how they imagine it in the first place. If there is a moral to be drawn from this inconclusive tale, it is that theories are as revealing, misleading, reductive, or constructive as the people who create and use them.

5

Narrative Structure:
A Comparison of Methods

Varieties of Narrative Theory

The previous chapter was based on the assumption that there is a bare-boned entity called plot that remains the same regardless of whether it is fleshed out in words or on celluloid. Such was Aristotle's assumption: the essence of the story can remain constant despite changes in the medium (print, dramatic presentation) or manner (direct quotation, summary) of representation. Plot analysis is the comparative anatomy of narrative theory: it shows us the structural features shared by similar stories. Perhaps we study the skeleton because that is all that remains when oral tales are printed in a book. What is lost is the complexity of the teller's interaction with the audience, which anthropologists have only recently started to restore. The living creatures we know — narratives created and disseminated through writing — are preserved on the page, and they require a different kind of study, one that can show how their movement springs from our ways of reading them.

Before describing some theories of modern narrative, I want to treat two issues that have divided critics since the classical period and that lead to different kinds of narrative analysis. The first concerns the question of whether we can reconstruct an essential series of events that a narrative can be said to "represent." The Russian formalists distinguished the raw materials of the story (the *fabula*) from the procedures used to convey them (the *syuzhet*). The materials are an abstract "constant" in fiction-making; the words and techniques used can vary. There are obvious reasons for this distinction. We can't discuss the "how" of storytelling without assuming a stable "what" that can be presented in various ways.

Drawing on the formalists, French structuralists created a distinction between "story" and "discourse." They defined these terms in various ways (see Figure 5a). For Gérard Genette, "story" is made up of the pre-verbal materials in their chronological order and thus corresponds to one formalist definition of "fabula." Genette's "discourse" contains all the features that the writer adds to the story, especially changes of time sequence, the presentation of the consciousness of the characters, and the narrator's relation to the story and the audience. Nearly the same definitions are used in Seymour Chatman's *Story and Discourse.*

One advantage of these terms is that they are useful in identifying

---

Aspects of Narration: Formalist and Structuralist Terminology

Fabula/syuzhet: Russian formalist terms translated as "fable" or "story"/"subject" or "plot." A secondhand description of the story line would convey the *fabula* (the pre-literary materials). The *syuzhet*—the narrative as told or written—incorporates the procedures, devices, and thematic emphases of the literary text. In Tomashevsky, these terms correspond closely to Genette's "story" and "discourse" (see below). For a more detailed account, see Todorov (1973).

Histoire/discours: In French, *histoire* menas both "story" and "history." Benveniste pointed out that French has two systems of past tense verbs—one for *histoire* (written narration of past events), the other for discourse (oral utterance assuming a speaker and hearer). Written forms such as memoirs, correspondence, and plays use the tense-system of discourse. English lacks this differentiation of past tenses, though fictional narration generally uses special tense forms (see chapter 6). French critics altered Benveniste's distinction in significant ways, as noted in the following entries. In the most general sense, all narrative is discourse, insofar as it is addressed to an audience or reader. Booth calls this aspect of narrative communication "the rhetoric of fiction." In the limited sense, discourse consists of only those remarks that are specifically addressed to the reader (commentary, interpretation, judgment concerning the action). Since sentences that are not "scene" (dramatic presentation) or "summary" (narrative in the usual sense) have until now been without a name, there are obvious advantages in using "discourse" in the narrow sense to name them. See also Scholes, 111-12.

Histoire/récit/narration: Story/narrative/narrating (Genette 1972). The "story" consists of the events, in temporal and causal order, before they are put in words. The "narrative" is the written words, which Genette also calls "narrative discourse." "Narrating" involves the relations between the speaker/writer (the narrative "voice") and the audience/reader. All changes the narrator makes in the pre-verbal story materials are aspects of "discourse," in his terminology.

Story/discourse: For Chatman, "story" includes the events, characters, and setting, as well as their arrangement (an aspect of "discourse" for Genette). Chatman's "discourse" is "the means by which the content [what happens] is communicated." Although film, narration, and ballet employ different "media," they all use the same "discourse" (form of expression), from his point of view.

Figure 5a

and describing certain techniques of narration. But the conceptual clarity gained by distinguishing fabula from syuzhet, and story from discourse, is achieved at a certain price: it implies that what the narrator is *really* telling is a chronological story—one that the reader tries to reconstruct in the right temporal order—and that the elements of narration are deviations from a simple tale that existed beforehand. The result is a powerful method of dissecting narrative, but it pays scant heed to the narrator's structural reintegration of the materials in larger units of action and theme. That is why some theorists hold that there is no reason, in principle or in fact, to reconstruct a hypothetical chronological "story" from which the written narrative deviates (Smith).

A second basic issue dividing theorists is related to the previous one in that it also concerns assumptions about the "essence" of a narrative. As indicated in the comment about Aristotle, abstractions such as syuzhet and story seem to imply that the same actions can be represented in various media. Again, this is in one sense obviously true, but when honed to a sharp edge by theorists, it leads to questionable dissections. It is useful if not essential to point out that characters can be presented differently—visually or verbally—and that what they say can be enacted/quoted ("scene" or "mimesis") or rephrased by a narrator ("summary" or "diegesis"—the latter words being those used by Plato and Aristotle). The gist is the same, despite changes in the manner. But the distinction becomes invidious when it is assumed that dramatic presentation, because it is closer to reality, is somehow better than narration. The theorist who takes drama and film as the norm concludes that the narrator must add descriptions and explanations, which are in themselves undesirable, to supplement the lack of concrete, visual presentation. Some twentieth-century critics have argued that narration should be as "dramatic" as possible, substituting scene for summary and suppressing signs of the narrator's presence (cf. chapter 1).

If we assume that narrative is the norm and drama the deviation, we get a different view of their relationship and relative advantages. While drama can present scenes and actions economically, it cannot summarize and thus blend in stretches of time not worth enacting; hence its choppy structure. Unlike a book, a play or film can't be picked up and set down at will. The pauses for intermission are imposed on us, and the span of human attention is such that performances can seldom entertain us for more than three hours. The distinguishing feature of narrative—access to the thoughts and feelings of characters, as Blanckenburg noted in 1774—is simply missing in drama, unless it is clumsily introduced. Further, drama is usually tied to the lockstep progression of clock and calendar, whereas narrative can treat the human reality of time, dipping into memory for the past when it is relevant to the present, and imagining the future. Admittedly, narration is thrust into an absolute past, in which everything has already happened, whereas a play or movie can pretend (so long as we accept the pretense) that it is happening in our "now." But this is small compensation for what is lost in a medium that can show us everything but tell us nothing. The dramatist is absent, leaving us to infer meaning from an illusion; the narrator, on the other hand, can take the responsible choice of speaking to us directly.

In practice, of course, these lines are blurred: the dramatist may use a narrator (as in *Glass Menagerie*) or address the audience ("parabasis" in classical drama); soliloquies are an accepted convention for the expression of thoughts; flashbacks or dream sequences are not uncommon. Some consider mimesis preferable because of its concrete detail and immediacy; others like to consume plays as a written form so that they will not be distracted by the odd details introduced by an actor's appearance or a director's ingenuities. But the basic differences remain important, and my prejudicial comparison of the two is intended to redress a balance that has too often been tilted in favor of the dramatic. Perhaps they seem more similar than they are because when we compare them (for example, when we discuss the relationship between a movie and the novel on which it is based), we turn drama into narrative. An emphasis on the unique features of narration leads to the conclusion that it is *not* "essentially the same" as drama. That is Barthes's view (1966, 121); Chatman, on the other hand, accepts Aristotle's emphasis on their similarity.

Depending on how they view these two issues, narratologists develop four different kinds of theory. (1) Is the essential structure of a narrative to be found in its plot? If the theorist thinks so, the theory will resemble those discussed in the previous chapter. (2) Are the methods of narrative best understood by reconstructing a chronological account of what happened, and then determining how the narrator has altered it? Those who would answer in the affirmative develop accounts of temporal rearrangements of the story line and the ways in which changes in point of view control our perception of the action. This is the approach of Genette and some Russian formalists. (3) Theorists who think that narrative and drama/movies are fundamentally similar, differing only in their methods of representation, usually begin by discussing action, character, and setting; then they treat point of view and narrative discourse as techniques that are used in narration to convey those elements to the reader. Chatman and Shlomith Rimmon-Kenan employ this organization to integrate traditional theories with formalism and structuralism. (4) Some theorists discuss only those elements of fiction that are unique to narration—point of view, the narrator's discourse in relation to the reader, and the like; they are the subject of the next chapter.

With the exception of the first group, these theories are analytic: they treat the parts, elements, or methods of narration. In order to reduce the terminological baggage of this chapter to a minimum, I have summarized it in a series of figures. These terms have the instrumental value of a model, map, or grid: they serve to focus attention and to make visible certain phenomena that would otherwise be unnoticed and unnamed. Rather than showing how they have been applied by Genette, Chatman, and Rimmon-Kenan, I shall illustrate their use in the "synthetic" theories of Tomashevsky (1925) and Barthes (1966). These two critics show how narrative elements fit together in hierarchic groupings, each element serving as part of a larger unit, and those units serving as parts in relation to the whole. Chatman (1969) and Culler (1975) have applied Barthes's method to James Joyce's story "Eveline," and Scholes used the same story to illustrate the methods of Todorov, Genette, and the later Barthes. I shall use Katherine Mansfield's "Bliss" for the same purpose, but my interest is less in developing a detailed analysis (which one can do at leisure, with interesting results) than in showing how terms are applied and what other theorists can contribute to this approach.

Functional and Thematic Synthesis in Tomashevsky and Barthes

As indicated in chapter 4, there are many ways to name and group elements of narrative, depending on the assumptions and purposes of the analyst. If the object is to reveal the total structure of a story, the parts will be named in relation to the hypothesized whole, and that whole will control the identification of the parts. Now this is obviously an example of circular reasoning that will always generate the same "narrative of reading": the analyst knows what the whole is supposed to look like before beginning to read, and the process of fitting one element after another into a pattern is less a voyage of discovery than a repetition of a route planned in advance. Every theorist is in the same position as Oedipus: he sets out to discover a truth that the audience knows is predestined, given his background and assumptions.

We cannot escape the fate of reading, but we can at least try to re-

111

main aware of it and to understand the process and purpose involved. For all but the most formalistic of critics, the object of reading is to experience and understand. Assuming that we don't know the meaning beforehand—that we are not among those who pick up a book thinking, "I wonder how *this* author will disguise the monomyth"—we will continually readjust our construal of parts and wholes as we go along, recognizing that they are interdependent. As Culler says, if an approach to narrative structure "is to achieve even rudimentary adequacy it must take account of the process of reading so that . . . it provides some explanation of the way in which plots are built up from the actions and incidents that the reader encounters. . . . The reader must organize the plot as a passage from one state to another and this passage or movement must be such that it serves as a representation of theme" (219, 222). While not escaping circularity, this approach is one that enters the circle consciously.

In defining the basic unit of narration, the "motif," as "the smallest particle of thematic material," Tomashevsky emphasized the reciprocal relationship between parts and wholes. The identity of an element is determined by its purpose, as in Propp's idea of the "function"; the two conceptions are complementary, as Barthes implies in his "Introduction to the Structural Analysis of Narrative" (see also Doležel). As Figure 5b indicates, Tomashevsky and Barthes construct their theories by fitting the smallest units together in molecular structures and then integrating these at higher levels. Other theories provide fixed definitions of the elements of narrative—actions, characters, description, etc. Tomashevsky's motifs and Barthes's functions cannot be defined until we have decided how they interact with other elements. This difference is easier to illustrate than it is to describe; rather than undertaking a laborious exposition of Figure 5b, I shall assume that you can quickly acquaint yourself with its general structure and the definitions of the terms, knowledge of which is assumed in the next few pages. (If curiosity or boredom has not already led you to read "Bliss," which appears in the Appendix, you might do so now.)

Functions and Motifs

Having returned home and begun preparing for a dinner party by arranging fruit in the dining room, Bertha Young goes upstairs to the nursery, where the nanny is feeding the baby. She decides to feed the baby herself, thus offending the nanny; shortly afterward she is called to the phone. The "functions" involved form what Barthes calls a "se-

Aspect of Narrative structure	Words used to describe it		
	Tomashevsky (1925)	Barthes (1966)	Chatman (1978)
Basic unit of narration	motif—"smallest particle of thematic material"	functional unit (cf. Propp)	narrative statement
Categories of units		functions (actions linking story surface) and indices (static elements integrated at thematic level)	process statements (events) and stasis statements (existents)
Subclasses of units	bound motifs: can't be omitted in retelling; dynamic (change situation) or static	cardinal functions—kernels (nuclei)[a]—related actions that open/close uncertainty indices: character traits, thoughts, atmosphere that require deciphering	actions (brought about by agent) happenings
	free motifs: can be omitted (not essential to plotline)	functional catalyzers (satellites)[a]: optional actions filling narrative space between cardinal functions informants: minor indices that fix setting, time	character (combines traits and existents) setting
Integration at level of action	sequence of situations—conflicts between characters	kernels (nuclei) with associated satellites make up a sequence from opening (choice) to end (consequences)	kernels and satellites
Integration at higher level	character, "the usual device for groupings together motifs"	action—a complex of character roles involved in particular kinds of situation (cf. Greimas)	narrative macro-structures as described by Aristotle, Propp, Frye, others: types of action—pattern, theme
Further integration	syuzhet theme	level of "narration" that reintegrates "functions and actions in the narrative communication"[b]	

[a]"Kernel" and "nucleus" translate Barthes's *noyau*; "catalyzer" and "satellite," his *catalyse*.

[b]Beyond Barthes's "narration" lies the level of "discourse." He says that "narrative analysis stops at discourse—from there it is necessary to shift to another semiotics," one that involves the audience and social conditions.

Figure 5b

113

quence" that opens and closes with "nuclei" or "kernels," which are functions that imply each other (start feeding the baby—stop doing so). Some functions, such as turning to face the fire, are optional within the sequence ("satellites"). Corresponding to these two types of action, there are two kinds of static elements or "indices": "informants" that make the scene concrete (e.g., "the baby had on a white flannel gown"), and "indices proper"—traits and thoughts that require deciphering ("her feeling of bliss").

In this theory, the parts of a narrative are not labeled by recourse to a list of fixed definitions; each one can be named in different ways, depending on the relationships being emphasized. Functions link a story together on the time line from beginning to end. The sequences in which they are grouped may in turn serve as functions in relation to a higher level of sequences. "Bliss" can be represented by the diagram in Figure 5c.

"Feeding the baby" is a sequence for which social practice provides a label, and as such it contains kernels. At the next higher level, "preparation for dinner" is a sequence, and feeding the baby is a satellite— a function that could have been omitted without breaking up the causal continuity. I have indicated how the sequences "receive guests" and "drawing room/coffee" can be broken up into functions, each of which could in turn be dissected as a microsequence, down to the level of sentences and phrases.

The flexibility of the theory, in which a kernel on one level ("of direct consequence for the subsequent development of the story") becomes a catalyzer or satellite at the next higher level, inevitably leads to questions about how we decide what is consequential. Glancing at

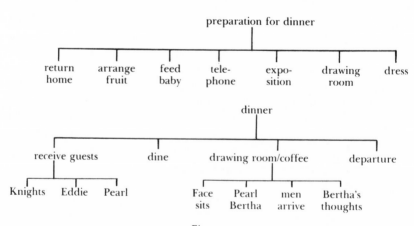

Figure 5c

the sequence of scenes in "Bliss," we might conclude that while they make up a story, few of the functions are crucial to its development. Bertha need not have arranged the fruit, fed the baby, or rearranged pillows in the drawing room (cook, nurse, and maid perform the essential tasks offstage, and she just adds a final touch); admittedly, she must return home and change clothes, but after that events unroll in a conventional social order with little of the "uncertainty" involving choice that Barthes associates with cardinal functions. Short of simply saying that every function is a kernel in one sense and a satellite in another, we must move to a level of integration above action analysis to understand narrative structure. (Barthes applied his theory to Ian Fleming's James Bond novel *Goldfinger*, in which action is paramount; I have deliberately chosen a story of another sort, as a test of the theory's flexibility.)

Here Tomashevsky's approach is particularly useful because it classifies actions or motifs on the basis of not one principle, but two: relevance to the fabula (what happens) and relevance to syuzhet (what the story is "about"; to translate the word as "plot" is misleading). Some motifs are essential in retelling the fabula: we could not eliminate reference to Bertha's return home, her activities before dinner, the arrival and eventual departure of the guests, without making it unintelligible. But these commonplace events take on a different order of significance in relation to the syuzhet in which, as Tomashevsky says, "static motifs"—those not contributing to the development of the action—"may predominate."

The traditional account of a plot describes it as a passage from one state of affairs to another that is different; each change establishes a new situation in a series linked from beginning to end. Without some progression of this sort, there would be no way to distinguish kernels from the less important satellites. And indeed we cannot make this distinction in modern stories that consist entirely of static motifs—conventional action sequences (feeding the baby, dressing) and inconsequential actions (those that do not lead to a change of situation or to understanding, even if intended to do so). John Holloway calls such static motifs "identity elements"—they are like the mathematical operation of multiplying a number by one—or "density elements," in that they build up multiple associations grouped around particular figures and concepts (53–73). In light of what he and Tomashevsky say, we can conclude that while Barthes's satellites may be inessential from the point of view of the action sequence, they may be necessary elements at the next hierarchic level of narrative organization, which is that of character.

The Composition of Character

In their methods of describing the concept of character, the difference between analytic and synthetic theories of narrative becomes clear. Most textbooks and treatises on fiction have for the past century discussed it in a series of sections entitled plot, character, setting, and point of view. Thus they imply that these are the "parts" of a narrative, in the same sense that engine, chassis, and wheels are parts of a car. In "The Art of Fiction" (1888), Henry James inveighed against this method: "People often talk of these things as if they had a kind of internecine distinctness, instead of melting into each other at every breath, and being intimately associated parts of one general effort of expression. I cannot imagine composition existing in a series of blocks. . . . What is character but the determination of incident? What is incident but the illustration of character?" On this point, I find Propp, Tomashevsky, and Barthes in complete agreement with James: functions and characters cannot be separated because they are always in a reciprocal relationship, one determining the other.

In oral tales, as we have seen, a monk can replace a merchant without a drastic change in structure. But in modern narratives such as "Bliss," the balance seems to be reversed: we might imagine changing an action sequence in the story, but in doing so we would want to preserve Bertha's character, as it is constructed from the action. The point, in either case, is that both action and character are "built up" along the time line of reading and narrative development. When Tomashevsky says that "character is a guiding thread which makes it possible to untangle a conglomeration of motifs and permits them to be classified and arranged" (88), and Barthes (1966) says that sequences, as independent blocks, are recuperated "at the higher level of the Action (of the characters)," they acknowledge the dominance of character over action in modern narrative. Their polemics against the traditional conception of character are best understood as objections to the idea that fiction necessarily refers to some person or "story" that existed before the writer started to write; or that as a result of the writing, some ghostly person, having all the attributes of people except bodily existence, has been added to the stock of the world's inhabitants.

Strands of action, information, and personal traits are woven together to form the thread of character. In relation to the sequences that precede and follow it (preparing the dining room, arranging the drawing room), feeding the baby is a satellite that fills a chronological space but disrupts a causal chain. All three incidents, however, are stages in the construction, by the reader, of Bertha, and each is marked by recurrence of the "bliss" that she and the reader are attempting to integrate into her experience and the theme. Her domestic contentment (". . . she had everything. She was young. . . . She had an adorable baby. They didn't have to worry about money") is poised between the unaccountable bliss, the "curious shiver" triggered by seeing the cats at dusk, and her tendency to "fall in love with beautiful women." Thus her character, like the phrase "Harry and she were as much in love as ever," is reinterpreted in retrospect as the story moves onward. Like stars appearing as the sky clears, the motifs lead us to imagine lines that form a recognizable constellation of character, but each new motif can lead to radical redrawings, just as one more fact about someone we think we know well can prompt us to see the person differently.

Once character has been written back into the story line (rather than removed from it, so that the husk of action can be thrown away), the inseparability of plot and character becomes clear—as Aristotle and Tomashevsky point out. For Aristotle, the crucial elements of plot structure are recognition (involving ignorance and knowledge) and reversal (of intention, or of situation). For Tomashevsky, these are "dynamic motifs" that form hinges between one narrative situation and the next. If an event such as recognition is removed from the description of the action and stored away for discussion under the heading "character" or "point of view" (because it involves the interiority of consciousness, not the outer world), the process of narrative movement is misunderstood. Even theorists who formerly reduced characters to "actants," defining them only as byproducts of the functions they performed, have come to recognize that ignorance and knowledge, vested in character as an independent entity, are crucial to an understanding of narrative structure (Greimas and Courtès).

In place of what James called "the old-fashioned distinction between novels of character and novels of incident," the modern theorist offers a variable equation (this one from Genette): $A \times C = k$ (action times character equals a constant). Emphasis on action or plot— for example, in the detective novel—leaves little space or need for complexity of character. Everyday incidents become interesting if complex characters participate in them, or if they are perceived by a consciousness remote from our own (the clown, the madman, the naif, the visitor from another culture). The recognition and reversal in a story may occur in the outer world; they may be inner events (as in Bertha's recognition of a new desire and consequent reversal of intention); and in some fiction it is the reader who is to experience the recognition, as a result of the narrative created by reading (O'Grady; Honeywell; Josipovici).

In the same way, the division of characters into "flat" and "round," depending on whether they are static or capable of change, might give way to a more flexible conception of the interaction of character and fictional world. Because of his simplicity, Huck Finn might justly be called a flat character; his pangs of conscience, in two short passages in the novel, are prized by those who think round, "deep" characters are better, and often they cannot conceal their disappointment with his failure to grow. But the prejudice, violence, credulity, conformity, and even the humanity of the world he inhabits would not even be visible if we did not see them through the transparency of Huck's amoral eyes, which strip away the conventions of "sivilization" to reveal what we civilized readers would not otherwise see. If Huck were round, American literature would gain a slightly more interesting character but lose a world. In the case of flat characters who have no new vision to offer, it is often the very intricacy and inevitability of their connections with the reality they inhabit that makes them interesting.

Tomashevsky emphasizes the interdependence of action and character in his discussion of "motivation" (see "Realism Viewed as a Convention" in chapter 3). The writer must create both at once because a story will not gain our credulity if we think they have been harnessed together like a donkey and cart that the writer can't get moving. An example of their perfect interaction occurs at the end of "Bliss" when Eddie Warren remains with Bertha as the other guests leave (a sign of the poet's obliviousness to the fact that he should go, too). He wants to show Bertha a poem that contains the line "Why Must it Always be Tomato Soup?"—further evidence of his lack of social grace, since Bertha had served tomato soup—and at the same time a revelation of how conventional she is. Bertha crosses the room to get the book, and as a result sees her husband with Pearl, which is the final revelation of the story. Tomashevsky would ask: was it Eddie's character that led him to linger behind the other guests, or was it the writer's need to separate Bertha from her husband and Pearl that led to the creation of Eddie's character? Or as James says, "what is character but the determination of incident? What is incident but the illustration of character?" If the motivation is successful, we will find these questions unanswerable.

In making characters an integral part of the narrative, Tomashevsky and Barthes are almost too successful, for they seem to imply that a character is nothing but verbal scraps (physical appearance, thoughts, statements, feelings) held loosely together by a proper name. Though they did not create this view, they helped spread it. A reaction against detailed, realistic depiction of character is evident in the writings of early twentieth-century novelists. By the 1960s, American fiction was being populated by fantastic, formulaic, and metafictional creatures that bore only a remote resemblance to people as we know them. The theory and practice of the French *nouveau roman* and of German and Italian novelists show that this antirealistic trend was international. Structuralist theories asserting that characters are simply collections of words, on a par with other verbal elements of narrative, were ideally suited to explain the innovative fiction then being written. Such theories can be applied retroactively to earlier narratives, as Barthes and Thomas Docherty have shown. But in their militant opposition to realism, they do not provide an adequate account of either the relationship between fiction and reality or the reader's experience of realistic fiction. Therefore, a brief discussion of more recent theories of character seems in order.

From the fact that narratives are verbal constructs, critical theorists have drawn two polemical conclusions. Since the relationship between words and the world is conventional, and conventions vary, some say that there is no reason to think one representation of character more realistic than another. The observation that all representation (factual or fictional) is conventional brings with it a valuable insight: we must allow each convention its own frame of reference. Comparison of characters in Dostoievsky, Henry James, and William Gass cannot, in itself, lead us to conclude that one is truer to life than another, or that any of them is less true than a biography. In the same manner, one cannot say that a map showing elevations is truer than one that depicts the distribution of population. Yet within its own convention, a map or verbal representation can be true or false. Once they are referred to the reality they map (how many people are there in the New York area? how high is Pike's Peak?), we can indeed call one of them more or less informative or useful than another. This is a point that Martin Price makes in his excellent discussion of character (17–19).

Conceding this point, a second group of theorists grants that factual accounts may be true representations, but points out that fictional characters are purely imaginary constructs, with no relationship to reality. Yet the difference between fact and fiction is reduced when we consider the ways in which we put together our knowledge of people who exist. Fiction is like gossip. I hear verbal reports of the traits and acts of a person who circulates at the edge of my acquaintance. These I piece together with bits of personal observation. From all such fragments, I project a whole: what kind of person is she? A character in fiction or the character of a person in fact is a conjectural configuration. Often I can't quite make them out; they are neither flat nor round but three-dimensional polygons with some points undefined. The ultimate reference of fact and fiction is our experience, and it is entirely consistent with experience to say that I understand Huck Finn more or less well than I understand my next door neighbor. Our sense that fictional characters are uncannily similar to people is therefore not something to be dismissed or ridiculed but a crucial feature of narration that requires explanation.

Formalists and structuralists inherited the category "character" from earlier theorists. Like their predecessors, they treated it as a static element of narrative, opposed to the dynamic, unfolding progress of plot. Chatman and Rimmon-Kenan try to free the concept of character from this limitation, but their method of doing so needs to be supplemented by more radical theories that redefine the very idea of character. If, as structuralists argued, a character or person is not a fixed entity with an essence, that may be because self and world exist for us only as a project, a becoming. From this point of view, no accumulation of point-by-point correspondences between words and realia can ever show what is real. Human reality is a projection from a past toward a future, and it is the enactment of this process in oneself and its replication in narrative that endows both with their sense of truth.

Character can of course be static, moving through changing circumstances of plot without adapting to them, and succeeding or failing in attempts to achieve fixed goals (freedom from want, marriage, the admiration of others, more money, a pleasant life). No matter how animated their action, narratives containing such characters do not convey the "sense of depth, and the movement from the surface of the self to a deeper self" which, as Price says, "is the most characteristic structure of the novel" (xiv). The type of character that Docherty calls "static" is "one whose existence is entirely accounted for in the fiction: this character is simply a function of the plot or design of the whole and cannot step outside the bounds of the fiction." The "kinetic" character, "on the other hand, is one who is able to be absent to the text; this character's motivation extends beyond that which is merely necessary for the accomplishment of the design of the plot, and he or she 'moves' in other spheres than the one we are engaged in reading" (224).

Structuralists paid scant attention to the latter type of character because they suspected that it presupposed a religious or idealistic conception of the self. Three alternative explanations of depth of character have attracted more recent critics. One springs from psychoanalysis, especially from the rereadings of Freud proposed by Jacques Lacan. The impulse to attain defined goals (material, sexual, and egotistical) and to be content once they are attained is what Lacan would call a *need*. Static characters who exist only to satisfy such impulses are common in some kinds of fiction. The character whose demands exceed needs is subject to what Lacan calls *desire*, and "seems to be real only insofar as it desires: that is, real, actual, or present only insofar as it is deferred or projected into a future. . . . Need aspires to the condition of stasis and selfhood, while desire aspires to that of kinesis or subjectivity" (Docherty, 225, 228).

We experience the depth and power of desire in this sense whenever the achievement of definable goals seems somehow less satisfying than we thought it would be; or when we find it hard to define what we want; or when we ask, for whatever reason, "Who am I?" The distance that separates need and desire, in fiction and life, leads Lacan to the exploration of two other gaps: those between unconscious and conscious, and between the self of experience and the verbal "I" (seemingly unified) that we use in referring to ourselves and stating what we are. By facilitating our participation in the psychic life of characters, the novelist allows us to experience and assess the workings of desire, which, as Peter Brooks says, can be seen "as that which is initiatory of narrative, motivates and energizes its reading, and animates the combinatory play of sense-making" (48).

The desires that psychoanalysis explores in depth can be interpreted, from a philosophic perspective, as a necessary product of our situation in time. Character and plot, like self and world, derive their present significance from their position on a path that gathers together all the past and projects it toward a future. The conviction that characters are static entities can come only after reading, when the narrative cuts them off from the possibility of a future and they can therefore be fixed in retrospect. (In this sense every narrative, like every life, ends in a death, as Walter Benjamin suggested in "The Storyteller.") A third explanation of the depth and dynamism of character subsumes the psychoanalytic and philosophic explanations by anchoring them in history. Human desires and plans for the future are actualized in specific historical circumstances. To understand the realistic portrayal of character, we must study the concrete reality it depicts, in relation to the forces that impel society to a new future. This point of view is most fully explored in Fredric Jameson's *The Political Unconscious*.

Characters are not, then, mere collections of attributes, nor is our sense of their wholeness an illusion based on mistaken assumptions about the soul or spirit. They may remain static, change gradually, undergo a transformation (as does Francis Macomber), or never achieve self-definition within the limits of the narrative (as in the case of Bertha Young); though fused with the action, as Barthes and Tomashevsky suggest, they are not dissolved in it.

Indices, Informants, and Static Motifs

The same process of fusion is at work in all the details of the text that are traditionally named setting or description. For Tomashevsky, these are static motifs; Barthes calls them informants or indices. Traditional discussions of description emphasize its importance in establishing a believable time and place for the action and in providing the writer with opportunities to set the mood ("It was a dark and stormy night") and to invest objects with thematic or symbolic significance (Bland; Liddel; Hoffmann). All of these functions are apparent in "Bliss." But this treatment, by separating description from the dynamics of action and character, suggests that it is a fixed element of the text, added to provide emotional coloring or decor, and thus of secondary importance. The conventional distinction between narration and description has reinforced the artificial boundary between the two.

Genette questioned this distinction, and other critics have shown that it is difficult to maintain when they look carefully at narration: "It is easy enough to speak of description of an object, but often one cannot decide between these naive labels when faced with any given passage" (Kittay, 225). When Tolstoy describes a battle, or Huck a thunderstorm, should we call the passages descriptions or actions? "Action" and hence "narration" tend to be applied only to accounts of what human beings do; other kinds of change may be called events or happenings. But this contrast between the living/changing and the inanimate/static is blurred when one realizes that if an event is defined as a transition from one state of affairs to another, it must entail static description of one or both states (Klaus). Furthermore, changes within the mind may be marked by verbs implying dynamism, yet not involve external change. As Bertha and Pearl look at the pear tree— "caught in that circle of unearthly light, understanding each other perfectly, creatures of another world, wondering what they were to do in this one with all the beautiful treasure that burned in their bosoms"—we may find it hard to tuck the passage in the pigeonhole "description," but that is where it would traditionally be placed, since nothing really "happens." In view of the ways that narration and description interpenetrate, they can both be considered "functions of discourse," either of which may be dominant in particular textual zones (Sternberg).

Barthes calls attention to the functional importance of indices: unlike notations of fact, they raise questions that impel us onward in the text. The informants that fix the setting may seem to be the unavoidable lumber of any story, but they are more than that. The society and culture of England in the 1910s are not just the backdrop of "Bliss"; in large part they create the characters. Regardless of whether we consider them informants or indices, some textual details may connect a narrative to the literary tradition, as Tomashevsky points out (such connections are now called "intertextuality"). For example, the pear tree in "Bliss" has been transplanted from a well-known poem by H. D. (Hilda Doolittle), and the "cat, dragging its belly" that "crept across the lawn" in Mansfield's story was to reappear a few years later in T. S. Eliot's *The Waste Land* as "the rat" that "crept . . . dragging its slimy belly on the bank."

The classification of a descriptive detail as free/bound or index/informant may be altered when we move up one level in the hierarchic organization of the text. There is a fire burning in the nursery, and Bertha lights one in the drawing room (informants: it is spring, and the story takes place before houses were centrally heated). But there is a fire burning in Bertha's bosom—"she hardly dared to breathe for fear of fanning it higher" (index), and thus the informants are pulled into the orbit of the theme, where they too become indices. To make such connections is to presuppose a purpose: by accident and design the text was produced by a writer. At times we may wonder if odd textual conjunctions were planned (should we associate "she was so tired she could not drag herself upstairs" with the cat "dragging its belly"?). But before discussing the final integrating levels—theme and narration—I want to review another aspect of narrative design.

Narrative Temporality

Temporal organization, mentioned by Tomashevsky and treated in detail by Harold Weinrich and Genette (1972), is summarized in Figure 5d.

The narrator's hand is clearly at work organizing the time-line of the story everywhere that there is summary rather than scene, as Fielding noted in *Tom Jones*: "When any extraordinary scene presents itself . . . we shall spare no pains nor paper to open it at large to our readers; but if whole years should pass without producing anything worthy his notice, we shall not be afraid of a chasm in our history." Some chapters, he says, will contain only a day, and others, years (II, i). The conventions and techniques of omitting time vary. Chaucer's story covers about two weeks; more than half of it concerns a single morning. His ellipses are explicit and formulaic: "And thus I lete him ete and drynke and pleye, / This marchant and this monk, a day or tweye." In "Bliss," the time line appears to begin in late afternoon and continue without break through the evening. But to study the art of

Elements of Narration

Scene, showing, mimesis: Direct presentation of words and actions of characters; often called "dramatic." Quotation of thoughts—interior monologue—is in this sense *scene.*

Summary, telling, diegesis: Narrator describes what happened in his/her own words (or recounts what characters think and feel, without quotation). The narrowest definition of *narration* equates it with summary or telling.

Point of view: A general term referring to all aspects of the narrator's relation to the story. It includes *distance* (variations in the amount of detail and consciousness presented, in the range between intimacy and remoteness), *perspective* or *focus* (whose eyes we see through—the angle of vision), and what the French call *voice* (identity, position of the narrator).

Narrative Temporality: Chronology, Narrated Time, Reading Time

Duration: In *scene* (see above), the time period described and reading time are about equal; detailed description may make reading time longer than the time of the event (*stretch*). In *summary,* reading time may be much shorter than chronological time (e.g., "year passed"). Some temporal periods may be left out (*ellipsis*); narrated time stops, in a sense, in passages of commentary and description. The narrator's generalizations in the present tense (e.g., "life is hard") are said to be in the *gnomic present*. The length of the temporal period recounted in a segment of narrative is its *extent* or *amplitude.*

Order: Narrator/character can describe the past (*flashback, analepsis*) or future events (characters may guess about them—*premonition, anticipation*; or narrator may know about them—*flashforward, prolepsis*). Events recalled or anticipated may be minutes or years from the narrative "now" (variations in *reach, distance*). They may lie within the time period of the main narrative (*internal* analepsis, prolepsis) or outside it (*external,* as when the narrator recounts something that happened before the beginning of the story). The incidents may or may not be part of the main story line (*homo-* or *heterodiegetic*), and may fill in something that had been left out earlier (*completing analepsis*).

Frequency: A single event may be described once (*singulative narrative*) or several times (*repetitive* narrative). Repeated occurrence of the same event may be described once (*iterative*—e.g., "he saw her every day"). If essentially similar events are described every time they occur, they are *indentity* or *density elements* (see Holloway).

Figure 5d

narrative, one must examine such apparent continuity carefully—for example, by drawing a chronological line and then trying to pinpoint exactly what happens when, and how reading time matches clock time. Mansfield often slides the reader's attention over a temporal gap through the continuity of her sentences, as when she moves Bertha and Pearl from the hallway to the first course of the meal by putting us briefly in Bertha's mind.

Temporal condensations such as summary and ellipsis involve *duration*. Another important category is *order* (flashback and flashforward, the latter occurring when the author leaps ahead to tell what happened later, or when a character imagines the future, as Bertha does at one crucial point). When we enter a character's memory, the ordering can become complex, since reminiscence about an earlier period may evoke thoughts of still earlier ones, and references to the narrative "present" will be flashforwards within memory (Genette). Modern techniques of smoothing over temporal discontinuities are exemplified in an ellipsis and flashback in Hemingway's story. In the afternoon, when Francis refers to his cowardice in face of the lion, the hunter Wilson replies, "Anyone could be upset by his first lion. That's all over." After a paragraph break, the text continues: "But that night after dinner and a whiskey and soda by the fire before going to bed, as Francis Macomber lay on his cot with the mosquito bar over him and listened to the night noises it was not all over." The following lines concern the noise he heard the previous night—the roaring of the lion. "All over . . . not all over" is the verbal hinge of the passage, and night noises provide the associative transition for the twenty-four-hour flashback to the lion hunt. The length of time remembered, its "duration," is about two hours, but the memory occupies nearly a third of the story.

Genette's third category is *frequency*—the number of times an incident is recounted. Of particular interest is the "iterative"—one description of an event that occurs repeatedly—because once named, its frequent use in narrative becomes noticeable, and it calls attention to a weakness in the demarcation between the traditional categories of scene, summary, description, and exposition. In modern stories, exposition often dissolves into reminiscence—leaving us uncertain about its borders—or is entirely remembered by a character. Exposition can also blend into both scene and summary through the use of iteration. In "Bliss," one sentence concerning Bertha's sexual relationship with her husband—"They'd discussed it so often"—is iterative summary (the writer tells what happened repeatedly in the past), exposition (the passage describes a state of affairs), and possibly scene ("*so* often" seems to be Bertha's thought, not the narrator's; the next chapter will treat this sort of ambiguity).

Consider the first two pages of *Huckleberry Finn*. After returning to live with the widow Douglas, Huck says: "Well then, the old thing commenced again. The widow rung a bell for supper, and you had to come. When you got to the table you couldn't go right to eating. . . ." It seems that Huck is describing something that happened repeatedly ("the old thing"), but some of the following details clearly concern a single incident, and at the end of the passage we conclude that this is an account of Huck's first night back with the widow. What we have here is iteration within a "singulative" scene (Genette 118–20).

Exposition? Certainly, since it provides a general account of life with the widow. Summary? Yes, because it selectively recounts what happened repeatedly between dinnertime and bedtime. Scene? Definitely, in that some of the actions and statements occurred only once. For well over a century, writers have been confuting the categories of the critics, as Mark Twain does in this case, and also complaining about them, as Henry James did. But we had no convincing analytic account of the inadequacies of traditional categories until Genette pushed them to an Aristotelian extreme by labeling everything. Criticism is a struggle to name that which has never been noticed.

Syuzhet, Theme, and Narration

Functions are grouped together in sequences, which may themselves form larger units; character is a higher level of organization in that it binds sequences together, as well as being defined by them; and a narrative as a whole can be conceived as a single syuzhet or Action (in Barthes's sense) of which sequences and characters are parts. It is at this level of abstraction that characters exemplify "roles" in typical situations: the contest (protagonist/antagonist), the quest (subject/object, donor/receiver, helper/opponent), adultery (married couple, third party), coming-of-age or metamorphosis (incompetent youth changed to mature, powerful adult).

Action, plot, or fabula is generally held to be the dynamic (Barthes would say the "distributional") aspect of narrative, moving it forward in causal and chronological order. Elements such as character and setting are considered static: they accumulate into wholes (which is why Barthes calls them "integrational") in an additive fashion, since they were there in the first place, so to speak, and it is only the necessary delay caused by language that spreads them out across the time of reading, rather than presenting them in an instant—which would be possible in film. Likewise, "theme" is considered a static feature, since it too is an entity that does not change, though it is discovered gradually.

In keeping with Tomashevsky's conception of motifs, recent critics have proposed an alternative to the foregoing view, one that emphasizes the reader's part in producing meaning—fitting motifs together, evaluating characters, seeking causal connections. Some aspects of this conception were mentioned in the discussion of character and description. As applied to theme, it suggests that the reader integrates story materials in two patterns simultaneously. One is prospective, involving action more than theme: given the trajectory of events up to this point, what is the likely outcome, and how will the enigmas (questions, indices) be resolved? But like Janus, the reader is always looking backward as well as forward, actively restructuring the past in light of each new bit of information. This is the "double reading" identified by Culler (1981). Assumptions about causality lead to conjectures about the future; at the same time, the facts of the present lead to the construction of new retrospective causal chains. This gathering together of the past produces the theme, and we engage in it most fully when the story has no more future. We read events forward (the beginning will cause the end) and meaning backward (the end, once known, causes us to identify its beginning).

Thus theme—the construction of significance backward in time—appears to be as dynamic an element as plot. Culler calls these "the ethical and referential dimensions of narrative." In his review of Hawthorne's *Twice-Told Tales*, Poe says that the writer should begin from theme or effect. "If wise, he has not fashioned his thoughts to accommodate his incidents; but having conceived, with deliberate care, a certain unique or single *effect* to be wrought out, he then invents such incidents . . . as may best aid him in establishing this preconceived effect." The end would then cause everything that preceded it, rather than vice versa.

Greimas illustrates the "double logic" of narrative with an action sequence that Propp called the ordeal: confrontation . . . victory . . . transfer of an object. As a causal series, the three stages are at best probable. If read backward, they form a logical series: transfer of object implies a victory, which implies a confrontation (803–4). Aristotle exemplifies the contradiction of the two points of view when he says that in a good tragedy "the incidents are unexpected and yet one is a consequence of the other." His example: when Mitys was at a festival, a statue fell and killed him (an accident in the referential sphere). It was a statue of a man Mitys had killed (the logic of the ethical dimension, reading backward in time).

In its forward movement, "The Short Happy Life of Francis Macomber" shows that Macomber was a coward; as a result, his wife committed adultery; in his consequent fury, he forgot his fear of death, thus becoming a man and taking authority over his wife, who then accidentally killed him. As in the case of Mitys, we seek meaning in the accident. To make it probable, Francis must be close to a charging animal, and therefore must be made courageous. The reader, like the hunter Wilson, may reason backward in a search for further meaning. Because Margot would not subject herself to an authoritative husband, Francis had to die. Attempting to integrate the accident into the theme, where it will be caused, we impute an unconscious intention to Margot. Thus the ending can satisfy the requirements of Aristotle's double logic—unexpected but, in retrospect, inevitable.

A backward reading of "Bliss," beginning from Bertha's accidental discovery of her husband's infidelity, is too complex to undertake here, but it might involve the possibility that since the awakening of her desire for her husband was in part a product of her experience with Pearl, her husband's adulterous relation with Pearl may have been a precondition of the birth of her desire. Girard's theory of desire, discussed in chapter 2, helps interpret these relationships. At the same time, in view of Bertha's association of the closing scene with "the black cat following the grey cat," we must ask if our reading of the theme, and her own, may not be deluded, insofar as her bliss is seen as leading to sexual desire. I will leave a reconstruction of Chaucer's tale, from the ending as cause to the beginning as effect, to your ingenuity.

The process of glancing backward is at work in both the narrative and the reader, as is evident in temporal rearrangements of story materials. Passages that fill in facts about the past are often named "exposition" and "delayed exposition." Critics suggest that the writer must unload some information on us before getting the story under way, or put off doing so until we need to know more about the characters. Flashbacks in memory, if not expository, may be explained as a device to round out our picture of the character. But the most significant use of exposition, as Culler implies, involves the search for the origins of meaning in the past. In itself, the past consists of an enormous amount of information that we might better do without, as Nietzsche suggested—except that it contains everything we want to know about how the present came to be. It is irrelevant until something happens that suggests the possibility of a new future and, at the same time, a new past, one that leads to this moment. Thus many narratives construct the past, building backward by inserting expository passages about earlier blocks of time, even more audaciously than they move toward the future. In "Bliss" and "The Short Happy Life of Francis Macomber," each step forward in the action unlocks a wider range of the relevant past. The stories stretch out in two directions, not one, from the narrative "now." And this double movement is possible only because the present moment of reading is irrevocably past, in the past tense of narrative, already written.

This conception of theme leads back to the discussion of historical and psychoanalytic narratives in chapter 3, and to the possibility that we identify or imagine causes retrospectively in a search for understanding that is a form of blindness. But it also calls attention to the ways that narrators spin the thread of a tale so that it appears to be one continuous strand, not a series of overlapping motifs. This is the level of "narration." "There can be no narrative without a narrator," Barthes says, and adds, "banal perhaps, but still little developed." Neither he nor Tomashevsky has much to say on this subject, in part because they were not in sympathy with traditional views that identified the narrator with the writer (tracing meaning back to a biography) or treated the narrator as a necessary encumbrance that should whenever possible be concealed from the reader's view. Narrative discourse as defined by Benveniste—direct address from the narrator to the reader—had been identified with technical clumsiness since the beginning of the century. Wayne Booth's spirited defense of authorial commentary in *The Rhetoric of Fiction* (1961) revived discussion of the subject. Since 1966, the date of Barthes's essay, point of view (or "focus" and "voice") has been treated in more detail than any other aspect of narrative technique. Even a superficial review of the subject requires a separate chapter.

6

Points of View on
Point of View

Until now I have continued discussing narration as if it added descriptions, internal views of characters, and temporal rearrangements to a story that might otherwise be presented dramatically. Though this approach may suffice when dealing with traditional tales, which in oral cultures are both narrated and enacted, it proves inadequate when applied to written narratives. The great novels of the twentieth century have not been impressive when turned into movies. The success of some films based on novels results from the fact that since the 1930s, novelists have known that the best way for them to make money is to get a book turned into a film; therefore, many of them write with a scenario in mind, deliberately constructing the action along the lines of a screenplay.

The idea that a story may remain the same despite alterations in the manner of telling it is apparently confirmed by some novelists. Jane Austen changed *Sense and Sensibility* from an epistolary to a third-person novel; early versions of Dostoievsky's *Crime and Punishment* and Franz Kafka's *The Castle* were written in the first person, then changed to the third. On the other hand, they would not have undertaken such laborious rewriting if they thought point of view did not matter (Cohn 1978, 171). In many cases, a story would be altered beyond recognition or simply disappear if the point of view were changed. Mansfield's "Bliss" could not exist as a tale told by her husband, since from his perspective nothing significant happened that evening; if *Huckleberry Finn* were recounted by Mark Twain rather than Huck, it might not be much more interesting than *Tom Sawyer*. Rather than being added as an appendage that will transmit the plot to an audience, narrative point of view creates the interest, the conflicts, the suspense, and the plot itself in most modern narratives.

Novelists have of course long recognized the overriding importance of narrative method. Richardson said that one technical advantage of the epistolary form, in addition to its "novelty," was that in contrast to narration, letters use the present tense, thus inducing in readers a sense of immediate involvement and anticipation. In addition, as Anna Barbauld noted in 1804, "it makes the whole work dramatic, since all the characters speak in their own persons." She conceded that traditional narration had other advantages: by entering the minds of characters, the author can "reveal the secret springs of actions. . . . He can be concise, or diffuse, as the different parts of his story require it." Knowing everything, he can reveal things not known to any of the characters and comment on the action. But narration as such can become tedious; "all good writers therefore have thrown as much as possible of the dramatic"—what we would all call scene, rather than summary—"into their narrative." She identified the memoir, "where the subject of the adventures relates his own story," as a third method of presentation, citing as its advantages that "it has a greater air of truth" and allows for a more intimate revelation of character than the fictitious authorial novel. But "what the hero cannot say, the author cannot tell" in this form, restricting its range of revelation and interest. And the possibility of dramatic presentation is limited in memoirs and autobiographical forms because it is implausible for someone to remember conversations years later. If the events described occurred in the distant past, their presentation may lack immediacy and suspense (Barbauld, 258–60).

Though writers have discovered new methods of narration since Barbauld's time, her conceptual distinctions survive in current criticism. First there is that of *grammatical person* or *voice*: who writes? Apart from experimental fiction, the narrator tells either a story about others (referring to all characters in the third person, as in "The Short Happy Life of Francis Macomber"), or one in which he or she is involved (as in *Huckleberry Finn*). Second, there are different *kinds of discourse*: narration, dramatic presentation (quoted dialogue or monologue), and a catchall category often called "commentary" (exposition, interpretation, judgment, and possibly digressions interpolated by the narrator). *Access to consciousness* is a third basis of classification. The narrator may be able to enter many minds (he or she is omniscient, all-knowing—Hemingway's story is an example) or only one (as in "Bliss"), and of course has the option of keeping the story in the outer world. *Time* and *tense* are also indispensable axes of analysis.

131

Letters, journals, dialogues, and monologues (whether spoken or unspoken) can use the present tense; narration is always in the past tense; and there are narrative sentences that, as we shall see, combine the two systems. Barbauld did not explicitly note one feature of narrative that is often mixed in with the others in the phrase *point of view* and more precisely designated by the words *perspective* and *focus*: who sees, from what position? But even in current criticism, this perceptual category is not clearly distinguished from access to consciousness.

One virtue of Barbauld's approach is that she does not attempt to create an all-encompassing logical taxonomy. Beginning with the novels available to her, she poses two questions: what are the advantages and liabilities of each method for the writer, and what effects do they create for the reader? Her answers, at the beginning of the nineteenth century, reveal that there was a gap between (a) authorial narration, which could create a varied fictional world lacking in authenticity (the "I" who wrote was compelled to admit that the story was a fabrication), and (b) the first-person form that claimed to be true, and thus attained credible representation of psychological detail but did so by confining itself to the form of memoir or autobiography. The great achievement of the nineteenth-century novelists was to close this gap.

As we have seen, there are many ways to characterize "realism" by reference to subject matter and content. Yet if we cannot experience a narrative as an authentic representation of life, the pains that the writer may have taken to ensure its accuracy will have been wasted. From the perspective of narrative theory, the problem confronting the would-be realist involves form as well as content. What is required is a method combining the advantages of third-person narration with the authenticity secured in the first person. Our understanding of others involves communal forms of judgment (the narrator's responsibility); yet our own experience, like that of others, is inevitably partial and subjective. Nineteenth-century novelists developed not only new narrative methods but a new use of language—one that is "ungrammatical" outside literature—that we now experience as the veritable stamp of authenticity in narrative, and they did so through new combinations of the narrative methods listed above. The barriers between narrator and character, between outside and inside views, dissolved—as did that between the past and the present. This example indicates that technique is not simply an auxiliary aspect of narration, a necessary encumbrance that writers must use to convey meaning, but rather that the method creates the possibility of meaning.

And that is why the most spirited debates about narrative theory at present concern point of view.

Point of View in American and English Criticism

Henry James and the German novelist and critic Friedrich Spielhagen (1883) were among the first writers to discuss point of view in detail. In 1932, Joseph Warren Beach complained that the study of technique "has been much neglected by critics, with the result that not merely does great confusion prevail in the criticism of novels . . . but we do not even have available for the description of novelistic technique terms approximately precise and generally understood" (3–4). Three decades later, point of view was the most frequently discussed aspect of narrative method (cf. "Theories of the Novel, 1945–1960" in chapter 1).

Of particular interest to critics were the ways in which novelists had overcome the limitations of authorial and first-person narration. James identified what many consider the best means of doing so. An authorial narrator (one who plays no part in the action) tells the story but does not indulge in commentary or use of the pronoun "I"; the reader is never reminded that a writer has created what is in fact a fictitious tale. Further, the narrator presumes access to the mind of only one character, thus reproducing an aspect of authenticity found in the first-person novel, in which, as in life, we do not know what goes on in other minds. This "limited point of view" often involves a visual as well as a psychological constraint: the narrator represents only what the character sees, as if looking through the character's eyes or, as "invisible witness," standing next to him. As Percy Lubbock pointed out, James and other novelists who use this method often step to one side of their protagonists so that they can describe conversations dramatically.

Advocates of this method agree with Barbauld in preferring dramatic presentation (scene) to narration (summary), since the latter always serves as a reminder of the narrator's presence. Dialogue, in the present tense, has the immediacy that Richardson gained by having the characters write letters. To summarize: third-person limited point of view evades the category of grammatical person by suppressing the narratorial use of "I"; with respect to kinds of discourse, it eliminates commentary and substitutes dramatic presentation for narration when possible; it assumes access to only one mind and often uses the

133

visual perspective of that character. (English and American critics failed to notice the importance of "time" and "tense" in this form, as we shall see.) Since "third-person limited point of view without self-reference by the author" is an unwieldy phrase, we might accept Stanzel's suggestion that it be called "figural narration," as opposed to "authorial narration" (see Figure 6a). Mansfield's "Bliss" is a technically perfect example of the method.

An emphasis on dramatic immediacy reveals that figural narration has certain limitations. When representing actions, the narrator can substitute present-tense dialogue for past-tense summary easily enough; but how can the same shift be effected when conveying thoughts and feelings? Since they are unspoken, they must be narrated and will therefore be in the past tense. One alternative—which eighteenth-century novelists borrowed from drama—is to use present-tense soliloquy, in which, by convention, characters put their thoughts in well-formed sentences. But "convention" betokens artifice and breaks the spell of authenticity that realists try to create. There appears to be only one alternative solution to the problem: dramatic presentation of consciousness requires a shift to first-person narration. This technical conclusion is confirmed by the history of the novel. Figural narration, characteristic of the late nineteenth and early twentieth centuries, is poised between the dominance of the less dramatic authorial narration that preceded it and an increasing use of first-person forms (either in long sections of novels, as in James Joyce and William Faulkner, or in entire works). The interior monologues and stream-of-consciousness techniques of this "inward turn" of the novel are not a creation of the twentieth century. For example: "N.B.—Southern gentlemen.—Churchyard—apostrophe to grim death—saw a cow feeding on a grave—metempsychosis—who knows but the cow may have been eating up the soul of one of my ancestors—made me melancholy and pensive for fifteen minutes; —man planting cabbages—wondered how he could plant them so straight—method of mole-catching . . ." (from Washington Irving's *Salmagundi*, 1807). Popular romances explored the extremes of subjective experience before they became a central concern of highbrow novelists. The history of these techniques remains to be written, but their use in recent fiction has been discussed in detail (Melvin Friedman; Humphrey; Cohn, 1978).

The theoretical framework used by most English and American critics in discussing point of view was fully developed by 1960 and survives in introductory literature textbooks (see Norman Friedman for a survey of this tradition). Every aspect of this theory has been chal-

134

An Inventory of Narrators

Term	Meaning and synonyms
Author/writer Implied author	An author who uses the word "I" in a narrative often seems different from the writer—the person who may be described on the dust jacket. Even in fiction lacking reference to an authorial "I," we may form a conception of the author based on the style and manner of telling. Most critics accept Wayne Booth's suggestion that whether overt or covert, we should refer to this persona as the "implied author."
Authorial narration	An implied author who refers to himself as "I" tells a fictional story in which he does not appear, though personal knowledge of the characters may be implied. Using the Greek for "same" and "different" (homo-, hetero-), "outside" (extra-, intra-), Genette refers to the authorial novel as extradiegetic and heterodiegetic—outside narrator, different from characters.
Third-person narration	The writer refers to all characters in the third person. This category can include authorial narration, but usually refers to a fiction in which there is no reference to the "I" who writes. In the latter sense, it is also called "figural narration" (Stanzel), "Er-Erzählung" (German).
First-person narration	The narrator-writer is also a character in the story, who may tell his own story ("'I'-as-protagonist," Genette's "extradiegetic-homodiegetic") or someone else's ("'I'-as-witness", or "Ich-Erzählung" in German).
Implied author vs. narrator	If an authorial narrator recounts a story, there is no apparent difference between the implied author and the narrator. In third-person/figural narration, since there is no reference to an "I" who writes, there is no linguistic way to distinguish the implied author from the narrator. In first-person fiction, the narrator is usually different in obvious ways from the person who did the writing. Some critics claim they can discern an implied author behind the first-person narrator, despite the lack of linguistic signs differentiating the two.
Embedded narration	A story told by a character in a story is "embedded." Some critics refer to it as "metanarration" or "hyponarration."
Voice	Following Genette, some critics use "voice" with reference to the act of narrating—the situation involving a teller and an audience. More narrowly defined, "voice" answers the question "who speaks?" In American criticism, "voice" often refers to the unique qualities in an author's works.

Figure 6a

lenged in the past twenty years. The points at issue range from the interpretation of grammatical conventions to the ways in which stories communicate meaning, the features that should be used in defining point of view, and the relationship of narratives to reality. Six books on the subject, representing four national traditions, have been published since 1978. Rather than glossing over these disputes in the

135

hope of discovering the truth about point of view, I shall emphasize them, for this is one area in which each uncompromising theory reveals something that the others fail to notice.

In order to give my account of these issues a semblance of order, I have divided my discussion of them into three parts: (1) linguistic features of narration—grammatical person, tense, and kinds of discourse; (2) recent theories concerning the structures of representation in narrative—the spatial and perceptual relations of narrators to characters and characters to each other; (3) critics who approach point of view from the perspective of language as a cultural phenomenon. Analysis of narrative as a particular use of language yields one form of classification; other issues become important when it is viewed from the middle distance, as representation; and when seen from the outside, which is the position we all occupy as readers and members of society, point of view requires a different treatment. These three categories correspond roughly to the phraseological, spatial-temporal, and ideological planes discussed by Boris Uspensky.

The Grammar of Narration

Given the division between scene (dramatic, present tense) and summary (narrative, past tense), it would appear that the narrator must shuttle back and forth between the two; and that the contents of consciousness, if not rendered in monologues, must be conveyed by the narrator, summarizing what characters thought and felt in the past tense. But this is not the case, as can be demonstrated by looking carefully at the language of narration.

Consider the opening words of Hemingway's story: "It was now lunch time and they were all sitting. . . ." Something is awry here. The sentence is ungrammatical. One can say "was then" but not "was now," because "now" refers to the present, the moment at which I speak or write. Fiction is rife with this aberrant use of adverbs and other strange combinations of time and tense. Here is an example from the second page of "Bliss": "This, of course, in her present mood, was so incredibly beautiful." One can say "this . . . present . . . is" or "that . . . past . . . was," but not mix the two in ordinary discourse. Considering the oddity of such sentences, it is remarkable that their use has been so little noticed. An old-fashioned grammarian will tell us that there is a similar mixture of time reference in what is called the "historical present tense," used in classical languages to bring past actions into the "now" of telling. But we need more than a name for such linguistic aberrations. In what contexts do they appear, and what do they imply?

Words such as "here," "now," "this," "there," and "today" are known as *deictics*. Their meaning is determined in relation to the location of the speaker in space and time. By eliminating all self-reference, a narrator cuts deictics loose from their normal connection to an identifiable speaker; thus they are free to gravitate toward the here-and-now of the characters. Hemingway's "now" applies to Wilson and the Macombers, not to himself. The narrative remains in the past tense, of course, and this might appear to be an insuperable barrier to any further step in bringing the story into the present time of reading. But writers have discovered a way to modify, if not efface, this bifurcation of past and present. The second half of Hemingway's opening sentence shows how they do so: "It was now lunch time and they were all sitting under the double green fly of the tent pretending that nothing had happened." The past perfect tense, "had happened," represents an action that took place before a specific time in the past. By consistently using the past tense or past progressive with deictics, and the past perfect for anything earlier in time (e.g., "today she was feeling the same thing she had felt yesterday"), the writer may create the impression that the past tense indicates the present, and the past perfect serves the function normally performed by the past tense. The whole tense-system is shifted forward in time.

These features of fictional narration, first analyzed by Käte Hamburger in 1957, help close the gap between past and present, narrator and characters. But in the representation of mental states, the gap seems to remain. They can be described ("For the first time in her life Bertha Young desired her husband"), paraphrased in indirect discourse ("Bertha thought that she desired her husband"), or quoted in direct discourse ("Bertha thought, 'I desire my husband'"). The distance between the narrator's past-tense summary and the character's present-tense interior monologue is not bridged by indirect discourse, which simply preserves the antithesis by including its two poles. Scene *or* summary, past *or* present—as recently as 1970, well-known critics assumed that these were the only choices available to narrators in rendering consciousness. Yet in 1897 a philologist named Adolf Tobler wrote an article about a peculiar mixture of direct and indirect discourse he had found in novels. And at that time, as Roy Pascal shows in *The Dual Voice*, novelists had been using it for nearly a century.

Instances of this "ungrammatical" mixture abound in "Bliss." After Harry has said on the phone that he'll be late, Bertha apparently wants to tell him something: "'Oh, Harry!' 'Yes?' What had she to say?

137

She'd nothing to say." Who is the speaker, or thinker, of the last two sentences? They cannot be thoughts in Bertha's mind because she would use "I" and the present tense. They are not indirect discourse ("she wondered what she had to say") because that form requires a subordinate clause and excludes questions. But surely it is not the narrator asking "What had she to say?" This would imply either that the reader is being asked to supply the answer, or that the narrator has momentarily paused to ask, self-reflectively, "Now let me see, what was it that Bertha had in mind to say?" and then replied "Oh yes, now I've figured it out, she really really had nothing to say." Therefore the sentences are neither the narrator's discourse (summary) nor the character's discourse (scene). But more surprising than any of these linguistic and logical puzzles is the fact that they do not bother us in the least. We know the thoughts are Bertha's and are not disturbed by the first/third person ambiguity; we assume that the words used are close in verbal form to what she was thinking. Because of our competence as readers of literature, we understand the passage without any consciousness of the conventions on which it is based, just as many critics did until recently.

The narrative method I have been discussing has accumulated a variety of names. It is called *style indirect libre* by the French, who first studied it in detail, and writers in English often follow them in naming it free indirect style or discourse. Charles Bally called it "indirect" because he thought it was derived from indirect discourse, "free" because it was free of conjunctions; he considered it a "style," not a grammatical form, because it entails an astonishing range of departures from normal usage and, in his opinion, occurs only in writing. The Germans term it *erlebte Rede*, experienced speech, because the critics in their tradition who first studied it thought that its use implied that narrators had actually experienced what the characters did, leaving no trace of their own presence in the form (Pascal). For the Russian critic Bakhtin, however, this form is a "dual-voiced discourse," always a mixture or merging of narrator and character. Other names are "represented discourse" (Doležel 1973), "represented speech and thought" (Banfield), "substitutionary narration" (Hernadi) and, as applied only to thought, "narrated monologue" (Cohn 1966). It does not always take the same form in different languages, in part because of differences in their structure. In eastern European languages, for example, it is commonly a substitute for speech, whereas in Germanic and Romance languages it is used almost exclusively to convey unspoken thoughts (Vološinov, 126–27).

Despite these differences, it appears to be a universal phenomenon—appearing, for example, in Japanese and Chinese—especially, if not exclusively, associated with literature.

In English, represented speech and thought make use of the tense shift characteristic of third-person narration—past tense for the present, past perfect for the past. It also uses a systematic shift of modal tenses. In Hemingway's story, when the hunter Wilson decides that his friendly relationship with the Macombers has ended, he thinks about the consequences: "He would see them through the safari on a very formal basis. . . . Then he could read a book with his meals." We know that he is thinking something like "I will see them through. . . . Then I can read a book." In addition to "would" for "will" and "could" for "can," we find "should" for "shall" and "might" for "may"; the third person is of course substituted for the first; and words like "here" and "now" refer to the space and time of the character. Exclamations and questions are acceptable in represented speech and thought, as are incomplete sentences. The words used often seem appropriate to the character but in other cases may preserve the style of the narrator.

For the theorist, my list of formal features characterizing represented speech and thought is not sufficiently precise. But this is one area of criticism in which theory outruns practice: of the thousands of pages written on the subject, only a few hundred in English concern its application to narrative texts. (See McHale for a survey of over fifty discussions of the subject that appeared between 1957 and 1977). Having read an essay on its main features and uses (those by Cohn 1966, Hernadi, and Bickerton are excellent), any reader can return to fiction and discover aspects of structure that may not yet have been noticed by critics. Theorists isolate the phenomenon so that it can be scrutinized; readers find it in its natural habitat, a novel or short story, where sentences and paragraphs flow across the zones of narration, represented speech and thought, and monologue (with or without quotation marks) in such a way that it is often impossible to tell where one ends and another begins. For convenience of reference, I have listed the main grammatical forms through which narrators give us access to consciousness (Figure 6b), but these are not the only ones available. "Bliss" begins as narration. In the fourth paragraph, a sentence of quoted monologue enables us to conclude that we have previously been following the words in Bertha's mind. How, and where, did we get from authorial narration into her mind? The question can be answered quickly and arbitrarily, but since theorists have not iden-

Methods of Representing Consciousness
(based on Cohn 1978, 104–5)

	Mode of Representing Thought	Example
FIRST PERSON	Past recounted (first person, past tense), usually as journal, diary, autobiography; speaking to someone (*skaz*, dramatic monologue); writing to someone (epistolary novel); or addressing a reader. Direct discourse.	As I approached the house, I wondered if I was late.
	[a]Present consciousness represented: "interior monologue" (first person, present tense), either talking to oneself, or transcript of mind. Direct discourse.	That's the house. I wonder if I'm late.
THIRD PERSON	[b]Psycho-narration: narrator describes contents of character's mind (Third person, past tense). Indirect discourse.	Mary approached the house. She wondered if she was late.
	[a]Quoted monologue: "interior monologue" quoted by narrator (narrative—third person, past tense, character's thought—first person, present tense). Direct discourse.[c]	Mary approached the house. "Am I late?" she thought. "Should I tell them why I was delayed?"
	[a]Represented speech and thought, or narrated monologue: character's thoughts, in her own language, third person (both narration and thoughts in third person, past tense).	Mary approached the house. Was she late? Should she tell them why she was delayed?

[a]These three types are sometimes called "stream of consciousness."

[b]Unconscious thoughts and feelings can be represented only in psycho-narration, since by definition a character cannot be aware of of that which is unconscious. Narrative summary of a character's thoughts is generally considered an old-fashioned technique, but some twentieth-century authors have used it because it allows them to explore the terrain that psychoanalysis makes available for narration. A narrative description of mental processes can also make use of metaphors ("psycho-analogies") and (as a means of creating an impression of dramatic immediacy) the present tense. See Cohn 1978, 41–57.

[c]Joyce and some other writers suppress pronouns, quotation marks, and sometimes verbs, to blur the boundary between the narrator's and the character's discourse. ("The cab pulled away. House etched against opalescent sky. Darkening toward dissolution. May be late. Deferential gestures suffice for apology. Manner ingests matter. Into the pool of porchlight. 'Stephanie, we thought you might have forgotten!'")

Figure 6b

tified the grammatical methods that make this particular transition possible, it would take patience to answer the question convincingly (Vološinov, 137–78, provides some clues).

The test of a literary theory is its usefulness, and books by Pascal and Cohn have shown that we can learn a great deal about the art of narrative by studying represented speech and thought. Considering the preference for dramatic presentation that has prevailed since the time of Richardson and Barbauld (for that matter, even Aristotle held that the epic poet should narrate as little as possible), we can now see that critics who intuitively appreciated dramatic immediacy were not only hampered but misled when they tried to explain it by reference to the scene/summary dichotomy. At a more general level, it is possible to argue that the grammatical features of fictional narration are not simply techniques that it happens to use but its defining characteristics (Hamburger). In the first three words of Hemingway's story ("it was now") we are moved outside the time and space of the real world, where these words always take on meaning in relation to someone who exists, into the here-and-now of what we call, appropriately, "fiction." While journalists and historians sometimes use this shift (W. J. M. Bronzwaer), they may well have borrowed it from literature, which remains the only domain in which it is common.

To these arguments claiming that there is a radical difference between fictional and factual language, Banfield adds another. Unlike the sentences of ordinary language or discourse, she says, those in fiction are not used for communication, which always presupposes a speaker/writer and hearer/reader. Her argument (based on careful grammatical analysis) leads to the conclusion that, strictly speaking, in fiction there is no person who narrates, telling us something. Sentences such as "What had she to say?" separate pronouns from their usual association with one or another speaker. Consciousness and the self are thus cut loose from "I," and we as readers are allowed to experience something we cannot otherwise experience in this world: subjectivity freed from its connection with our own bodies and voices. The emergence of fiction in the seventeenth century, Banfield implies, may be connected to new ways of conceiving the self.

The position of Hamburger and Banfield, which gains support from Benveniste (cf. Figure 5a), has important consequences for other aspects of narration. Some critics try to classify the "reliability" of third-person narratives on the assumption that a diary or letter contains exactly what a character wrote; quoted dialogue is a less precise index of what was said; an implied author's summary of a conversation or description of a character's thoughts may not be entirely accurate. If Hamburger is right, the fictional world created in third-person narration is simply posited, beyond any questions concerning reliability. Quotations are neither more nor less reliable than narratorial summary, since there is no reality about which these "unspeakable sentences" could be right or wrong.

Carried to its logical extreme, this theory leads to a controversial conclusion. First-person narrators who witness or participate in the action they describe do not employ the tense shift, the transposed deictics, and the access to the minds of others characteristic of third-person forms. If these are the signals by which we recognize fiction, and if first-person narrators—unlike their third-person counterparts—may misperceive or lie (we can determine this by comparing the facts they present with the interpretations they offer), in what sense can first-person narration be called "fiction"? Hamburger's answer is categorical: it is not fiction. Since the "I" who writes in this form uses the conventions of ordinary language and addresses someone, the discourse implicitly claims that it is about the real world; indeed, this is one basis of its authenticity, as noted by Barbauld. Therefore, Hamburger says, first-person fictional narratives are "feigned reality statements."

Here the logic of linguistics seems to lead to conclusions not confirmed by experience. Banfield shows that some first-person narratives use the timeless "now" of third-person narration in recounting past experiences, marking a separation of the "I" who narrates from a different "I" in the past. First-person narratives sometimes employ free indirect style (narrated monologue), as Cohn has demonstrated. In these respects, at least, first-person forms use the conventions of Hamburger's "fiction." Stories that involve a tale-teller speaking to an audience (in Russian known as *skaz*; O. Henry's "The Haircut" and Twain's "The Celebrated Jumping Frog of Calaveras County" employ this form) can be considered "dramatic" fiction, similar to plays.

There is something counterintuitive about the absolute separation of first- and third-person narratives. It does, however, have one virtue: it calls attention to the fact that there is a categorical difference between the two, disregard of which (mainly by French theorists) has led to unnecessary confusions. We cannot question the reliability of third-person narrators, who posit beyond doubt or credulity the characters and situations they create (Martínez-Bonati, 21–42; Głowiński). Any first-person narrative, on the other hand, may prove unreliable because it issues from a speaking or writing self addressing someone. This is the condition of discourse, in which, as we know, the possibility of speaking the truth creates the possibility of misunderstanding, misperceiving, and lying.

Structures of Narrative Representation: Focus

Hamburger and Banfield correct a weakness in earlier accounts of point of view by providing a rigorous analysis of time and tense. They also lend support to the formalist contention that fictional narration is categorically different from nonliterary uses of language in that it is not created to communicate messages to an audience. By bringing analysis of represented speech and thought into American criticism, Hernadi, Pascal, and above all Cohn have shown that modern narration consists not of two types of discourse (mimetic and diegetic, showing and telling) but of three, and the third is crucial for an understanding of narrative technique.

Though these critics might object to being grouped together, in view of their differences, they share an emphasis on the importance of the language of narrative to which many are opposed. The most congenial of their opponents would accept much of what they say but attempt to go beyond it by examining aspects of narration that they do not discuss. Granting the importance of linguistic signs that tell us we are reading fiction and of the subtle techniques used to convey consciousness, we know that these are not the only uses of language involved in telling a story. Most novels lead us in and out of the minds of characters as part of a more encompassing design. Until we see how the interiority of thought is related to action and interaction, the purpose of point-of-view techniques, which are too often considered in isolation, will be misunderstood.

Narrators may set their writings apart from reality through the time and tense of certain sentences, but there are other sentences lacking these signs of fictionality that use, in a straightforward way, the language of discourse and communication. Every narrator that cannot be located in time and space creates a fictional world containing characters for whom that world is a reality. In order to understand the functional importance of point of view, we must extend its range of meaning to include the relationships between characters, as well as their relationship to the narrator. Each one can provide a perspective on the action just as the narrator does.

In treating grammatical person and access to consciousness as the defining features of point of view, traditional accounts of the subject overlooked a crucial distinction. "Access to consciousness" has two meanings: a third-person narrator can look *into* a character's mind or look *through* it. In the first case, the narrator is the perceiver and the character's mind is perceived. In the second, the character is the perceiver and the world is perceived; the narrator seems to have delegated the function of seeing to the character, as if a first-person story containing phrases such as "I noticed . . . then I realized" had been rewritten in the third person ("she noticed . . . then she realized").

This distinction between "focus of narration" (who writes?) and "focus of character" (who perceives?), first proposed by Cleanth Brooks and Robert Penn Warren in 1943, was more fully developed by Genette in 1972. It is crucial for an adequate account of omniscient narration, which earlier critics tended to disregard and even discount. James and his successors found it diffuse and undisciplined, since it lacked the obvious (and simpler) unity of figural narration. They would be able to explain the virtues of a story such as "Bliss," but not those of "The Short Happy Life of Francis Macomber," which jumps from one focus or perspective to another without apparent logic.

At the beginning of Hemingway's story we see the scene through the eyes of the narrator who, after the opening dialogue, dips back in time and gives us visual access to the inside of the Macombers' tent. We are then brought back to the scene with which the story opened, and after a remark by Wilson, we find the following sentence: "Mrs. Macomber looked at Wilson quickly." Then, a few lines later: "She looked at both of these men as if she had never seen them before. One, Wilson, the white hunter, she knew she had never truly seen before." He is then described, as seen through her eyes. The narrative "voice" remains unchanged, but "focalization" of the scene shifts from narrator to character. This passage might seem technically clumsy to some critics, based on the following line of reasoning: Hemingway wanted to describe Wilson but knew that narratorial description is old-fashioned and undramatic. Therefore he contrived to have Margaret see Wilson. But this is an improbable ruse, since she already knows what Wilson looks like. Realizing this, Hemingway tried to justify the improbability by saying that she looked at him *as if* she had never seen him. Omniscient narration is full of such contrivance, which is indicative of its shortcomings.

This sort of criticism results from a failure to understand the system of representation based on focus. Hemingway's story is a dazzling display of its resources. It includes panoramic views, close-ups, track shots (Wilson's view of Margaret as he and Francis leave the campsite in a car), and zoom-ins ("the buffalo got bigger and bigger until he could see the gray, hairless, scabby look of one huge bull and how his neck was part of his shoulders"). Such variety, which is also found in Tolstoy, leads me to suspect that narratives may be the source of the varied visual resources of the movies, rather than vice versa. Hemingway even uses the lion as a focalizer: "The lion still stood looking majestically and coolly toward this object that his eyes showed only in silhouette, bulking like some super-rhino." Macomber's single, fatal step, detaching himself from the silhouette of the car (a consequence of having forgotten to release the safety catch on his rifle) is the first turning point of the story; it causes the lion to see him and to move before he shoots, and this incident is dependent on precise visual realization of the scene.

In view of Hemingway's care in presenting visual perspectives, the description of Wilson by Mrs. Macomber deserves reconsideration. Wilson looks like a candidate for the role of Santa Claus at a grade school party; Francis, on the other hand, has the physical attributes of a TV hero. Margaret had never "truly" seen Wilson before his display of courage in facing the lion because, like most of us, she judges people on the basis of their physical appearance. When she is led to compare the two men from what to her is a new point of view, she must rework her idea of the relationship between visual signs and inner meaning.

After Genette (1972) made focus a topic of critical interest, Mieke Bal improved on his theoretical scheme (1977), and Pierre Vitoux suggested further refinements of the concept (1982). It has been accepted by many other critics whose theoretical orientation is structuralist or semiotic. The Russian critic Boris Uspensky discussed the same topic in a less formal but equally revealing way in *A Poetics of Composition* (1970). Though the words used may vary, the two basic concepts involved in the study of focalization are those of a focalizer (a perceiver) and that which is focalized (the perceived). If a story contains more than one focalizer, the shifts from one to another become an aspect of narrative structure. In addition to registering the outer world, a focalizer is capable of self-perception (e.g., Macomber "pulled the trigger . . . until he thought his finger would break"). Further, s/he is capable of reflection—thinking about what is seen or deciding on a course of action. In all three capacities, as perceiver, self-perceiver, and self-reflecter, a focalizer has the option of concealing or revealing the contents of consciousness. A decision about the matter is often crucial, in literature as in life, but this does not alter the fact that someone who talks about another character in a story is as much a focalizer as someone who thinks the same thing but remains silent. Thus the concept of focalization provides a means of reintegrating consciousness and dialogue in the description of narrative structure.

With respect to Hemingway's story, it is hardly necessary to point out that the focalizer in many passages is the narrator. Beyond that, there are obvious differences in the use of variable focalization. We know Wilson as a perceiver and self-reflecter, Francis less extensively as a perceiver and self-perceiver (with a few brief passages of self-reflection), and Margaret only as a perceiver. We know that Wilson does not say much of what he thinks, and Francis does so too often;

almost all we know of Margaret's thoughts is what she says. In general, our sympathies are enlisted by those whose thoughts we know. Most readers tend to qualify the narrator's characterization of Francis as a "coward" after learning what he thought and felt during the lion hunt. But no such possibility of sympathy exists for Margaret, whose thoughts must remain unrecorded in order to preserve the enigmatic ending. One telltale sign of omniscience, beyond the third-person narrator's unnatural access to the minds of others, appears in the story: comments on what a character did *not* think.

When focalization is not treated as an independent category in the definition of point of view, "omniscient narration" becomes a kind of dumping-ground filled with a wide range of distinct narrative techniques. A narrator may "see with" one or more characters, presenting what they see, as if looking over their shoulders. A shift from one position to another does not imply omniscience in the usual sense (access to consciousness), but we have no other word to name the technique. Even if the narrator seems to have crossed the line between inner and outer worlds, using such phrases as "she noticed" or "he was surprised to see," we have no firm evidence that this has happened, because we all draw such conclusions about what others think, having noted their reactions, without claiming access to their minds.

The categorical distinction between first-person narrators, confined to conditions of knowledge in the real world, and third-person forms in which narrators can theoretically know everything (but may restrict themselves to partial knowledge) breaks down in practice. Uspensky characterizes the third-person narrator of *War and Peace* as " a penetrating and intelligent human being, with his own likes and dislikes, with his own human experiences, and with the limited knowledge that is inherent to all human beings" (109–10). In many scenes he is simply a shrewd observer, one whose perception and wisdom we trust. He may use such phrases as "the people in the room appeared to recognize him" or "she seemed startled by what he said," in keeping with the restrictions placed upon a first-person narrator who claims to have been present. At other times, he has access to what characters think. What are we to do with such violations of our categories? At the very least, we must admit that the structures of representation in narrative cannot be reduced to a linguistic ontology, and that "focus" must be treated as an independent constituent of point of view, alongside grammatical person of the narrator and access to consciousness.

The Languages and Ideologies of Narration

Theorists use clear-cut distinctions to identify phenomena that would otherwise pass unnoticed. But clarity is always achieved at a price. When we focus on particular aspects of narrative method, the scene of narration as a whole becomes blurred. Having tried to show why traditional, grammatical, and structuralist-semiotic theories are indispensable for an understanding of point of view, I want to identify their limitations from the perspective of the Russian critics Vološinov and Bakhtin.

Despite their differences, the theories I have discussed are all analytic: they begin with dichotomies (narrator or character, first- or third-person narration, inside or outside the mind, focalizer-subject or focalized-object) and end with classification. In reading, we are less conscious of these divisions than of the effects that result from their interaction. Uspensky discusses this subject (101–29), but even after he has added "ideology" to the list of features that characterize point of view, something seems to be lacking. We experience narrative not as a compendium of categories but as a total movement, the parts of which are perhaps best characterized by the phrase "point of view" in its most common meaning—a set of attitudes, opinions, and personal concerns that constitute someone's stance in relation to the world. And this totality, which contains but exceeds categories, is embodied not in language (as an abstract unity that can be studied theoretically) but in the "languages" through which different points of view are expressed.

We are all expert in discriminating the varied languages that make up our social world. "In real life," Bakhtin remarks, "we very sensitively catch the smallest shift in intonation, the slightest interruption of voices, in anything of importance to us in another person's practical everyday discourse" (1929, 201). On the editorial pages of a newspaper, we find the distinct languages of contending political columnists and of letters to the editor. A single situation or event is described in very different words and styles. "The prose writer confronts a multitude of routes, roads, and paths that have been laid down in the object by social consciousness" (Bakhtin 1934–35, 278). Words, along with the values and attitudes they imply, are not simply detachable from objects that we know apart from them; the word is *in* the object, which we always experience from one point of view or another. The process of becoming an individual is in large part one of learning a language of our own, freeing ourselves from automatic

147

repetition of the words and phrases that we grew up with, choosing ways of naming from available kinds of discourse (for only by using conventions can we communicate), but combining them with our own intentions so that we speak with our own voice.

The contending languages of the everyday world are used for the transmission of ideas and attitudes. They address each other across lines like those separating the columns in a newspaper, not allowing the opposing discourses to penetrate the boundary within which they declare their truth. The purpose of the novel, in Bakhtin's view, is to represent these differences so that they will become visible and to allow them to interact. The features of language that concern him are not stylistic or grammatical; they are "those aspects in the life of the word . . . that exceed . . . the boundaries of linguistics" (1929, 181).

When critics discuss Hemingway's style, for example, they usually call attention to its uniform simplicity and clarity, and from a purely linguistic point of view, they are right. But seen through Bakhtin's eyes, "The Short Happy Life of Francis Macomber" is a battleground or carnival of competing languages. We find the mincing tones of the society column, replete with cliché: "They were adding more than a spice of *adventure* to their much envied and ever-enduring *Romance* by a *Safari* in what was known as *Darkest Africa.* . . ." There is a description of Francis as a representative of the upper class that might have been spoken at his club, except that the narrator's voice replays one phrase, like a cut-over groove on a record, to deflate him: "He knew . . . about duck-shooting, about fishing, trout, salmon, and big sea, about sex in books, many books, too many books, about all court games. . . ."

Because of the vital connection between language and the different codes that we live by, some ideas can be expressed only in foreign tongues. To convey his sense of the hunter's duty, Wilson resorts to the Swahili word *shauri*; to name his social relationship to the Macombers, he is forced to translate a French phrase ("What was it the French called it? Distinguished consideration"). And at the heart of the story, we find that Wilson's whole being, the "thing he had lived by," is a piece of language—a quotation from Shakespeare. That he introduces and follows it with gruff profanity ("Damned good. See if I can remember. Oh, damned good") betrays both his embarrassment in relation to heroic rhetoric and his identification with the social class that "authenticates" its discourse by swearing with every other word. In *Huckleberry Finn*, which can be read as a systematic attack on all attempts to smooth over linguistic differences (which are in fact ideological differences), quotation from Shakespeare serves another purpose.

This jostling of disparate languages is what Bakhtin calls *heteroglossia*. Hemingway's narrator has a style, but it highlights rather than smoothing over linguistic differences. "The words of the author that represent and frame another's speech create a perspective for it; they separate light from shadow, create the situation and conditions necessary for it to sound; finally, they penetrate into the interior of the other's speech, carrying into it their own accents and their own expressions, creating for it a dialogizing background" (Bakhtin 1934–35, 358). Dialogue for Bakhtin is no mere alternation of speakers. In life as in literature, its essential quality emerges most clearly in disagreements, when the way in which things are said becomes as visible an object of contention as the subject of dispute. The words of the other cut deep, penetrate our own language, and we return them as taunt or retort. In Hemingway's story, Margaret reprimands Francis: "'You'll behave yourself.' 'Behave myself? That's a way to talk. Behave myself.' 'Yes. Behave yourself.' 'Why don't *you* try behaving?'" Margaret is patronizing (we say "behave yourself" to children), and Francis cuts through her assumption of authority by using her childish word to name the source of his fury—her infidelity. "Behave," which has a reasonably stable meaning in the eyes of the linguist, comes to life in unexpected ways in the contexts of fiction, which itself is the life of language made visible.

Another kind of dialogue appears in passages of narration. Parody is one of its obvious forms, the author setting another language next to the narrator's and thus highlighting its characteristics, as in Hemingway's use of the society column. Bakhtin holds that a rigid separation of styles is characteristic of authoritarian cultures, which mark the boundary between a sanctioned language and any discourse that differs from it. For at least two centuries, Western societies have seldom produced a dominant language of this sort, and that is one reason authoritative authors have been replaced by deputized narrators who do not exercise verbal and evaluative control over the characters, allowing them instead to speak their own languages. Represented speech and thought, in which it is often difficult to know where the character's words end and the narrator's begin, is a good example for Bakhtin of how different kinds of discourse interact (see also Vološinov 1930, 20–21). The narrator's style may penetrate to the heart of the character's thoughts, tinging them with irony; on the other hand, it often seems that the narrator, through a kind of stylistic contagion, has picked up words from the character (Cohn 1978, 32–33). In Mansfield's story, the narrator's discourse seems infected with Bertha's, reducing the distance between them. Categorical distinctions, such as that between first- and third-person narrators, are often less important than the distance between types of discourse, since the latter can obliterate the borderlines created by grammar.

Bakhtin insists that linguistics alone cannot identify such borders. Often a phrase, or simply a tone or inflection, alerts us to shifts or mixtures of points of view. "There was no man smell carried toward him"—the sentence is third-person narration, but the perception seems to come from the lion. Interactions of distinct languages and perspectives create "dual-voiced discourse," making us aware of the salient aspects of each.

The implications of Bakhtin's theory emerge clearly in his definition of the novel as a "hybrid" form: it is "an artistically organized system for bringing different languages in contact with one another" (1934–35, 361). When conceived as an imitation or representation of life that happens to be written (the traditional view), the novel is first of all stripped of its language, which is set aside for discussion under the heading "style"; then characters and narrator are separated from one another (each one a unique, personal subjectivity) for categorical treatment as focalizer-subject *or* focalized-object, narrator's discourse *or* character's discourse, inside *or* outside the mind. Bakhtin sees characters and narration as "language zones," which may share social attitudes and commitments; on the other hand, he discovers within one character or narrative voice the division of allegiances that results from genuine interaction with the languages of others. This teeming mass of disparate languages is no accidental byproduct of "subjects" encountering "objects"; it is the pulse of social life, from which we draw the ways of naming that make us individuals and constitute our view of the world. "The ideological becoming of a human being, in this view, is the process of selectively assimilating the words of others," just as Wilson assimilated the passage from Shakespeare (1934–35, 341).

The word "ideology" has long seemed to be a foreign interloper in our everyday and disciplinary languages. Its natural habitat is political theory, where it sometimes refers to hidden motives or to factors of which we are unaware that lead to false consciousness. Bakhtin uses it to refer to "a particular way of viewing the world, one that strives for social significance," and in this sense it is close to the ordinary meaning of "point of view." What he adds to more technical analyses is an awareness of how content not only penetrates the form of fiction but constitutes it, and of the centrality of language in any discussion of narrative.

There remains one other perspective on the scene of narration that I have until now avoided. It is that of the person who never appears within the scene yet is as crucial to its existence as the writer: the reader—or rather readers—who, like critics, see it in very different ways.

7

From Writer to Reader:
Communication and Interpretation

If we listen carefully, according to Bakhtin, we may hear two kinds of dialogue in narratives other than those included in quotation marks. Through the tone set in narration, the writer can engage in an implicit conversation with the characters, sympathizing with them or adding ironic overtones to what they say, and through parody and stylistic imitation may also comment indirectly on other authors and conventional uses of language. We recognize such effects because we know a great deal about how language is used in literature and in life. The interaction of our linguistic knowledge with the words on a page produces still other dialogues. Though we do not reply to the writer, we usually feel s/he is addressing us, and we bring a story into being by posing and answering questions (even if unconsciously) about what we read. Those who talk or write about narratives contribute to the total dialogic context of literature, where the production of words entails the creation of value, through the work and pleasure of understanding.

Once the reader enters the scene of narration, we cannot help seeing it from a new perspective. We need not recognize the grammatical features of represented speech and thought to experience its effects, any more than we need study phonemes to use language. Narrative techniques are, after all, not ends in themselves but a means of achieving certain effects. We cannot know what a narrative is except in relation to what it does, and while the purposes of readers and writers vary, they are inseparable from questions of value and meaning.

This is a point that Wayne Booth insisted on in *The Rhetoric of Fiction* (1961). In opposition to prevailing critical views, which emphasized formal features of literature and held as an article of faith that the best novels were ambiguous, Booth argued that fiction is a form of communication. By this he did not mean that writers should try to prove a thesis; nor did he conceive communication as limited to the transmission of propositional meaning. Emotional response, as important in the classics as in popular literature, is part of what writers evoke, and it cannot be separated from values and attitudes. One of the targets of his attack was a highbrow aestheticism that looked down on emotional involvement as a contamination of the purity of art. Having purged it of values, emotions, determinate meanings, and even the human element introduced by an identifiable narrator or author, critics had in his view misunderstood the purposes of fiction. In his emphasis on the importance of values and ideologies, Booth has something in common with Bakhtin, some of whose ideas he would now accept as a modification of his earlier position (Booth, 1984.)

The Communication Model

As a substitute for the taxonomies produced by point-of-view theorists, Booth and others use a linear communication model to explain fiction: an implied author, who may differ from the narrator, presents information about characters and events to a reader. Linguists use a similar diagram to discuss nonnarrative communication: a speaker conveys a message to a listener. Admittedly, the situation in fiction can be more complicated than in everyday conversation, since a number of figures may be introduced to the left and right of the message (as indicated in Figure 7a). But by including the reader as an essential feature of the narrative situation, and by fixing the concept of literary meaning *between* narrator and reader, this model suggests new ways of understanding what happens when we read.

Within the world of realistic fiction, dialogues exemplify the functions of language in everyday life. What the words mean depends on how they are used, not simply how they are defined; the speaker's intention and relation to the hearer are among the many factors we automatically take into account. To understand the passage from Hemingway's story that begins with Margaret saying, "I won't leave you and you'll behave yourself," we must rely on our tacit knowledge of what people are trying to do when they use words this way. Her statement can be interpreted as a prediction (I know you will in the future behave), a promise (if you behave, I won't leave you), a threat (if you don't behave, I will leave you), and an imperative (you *will* behave yourself!). Francis interprets it as a command, and she then repeats it

153

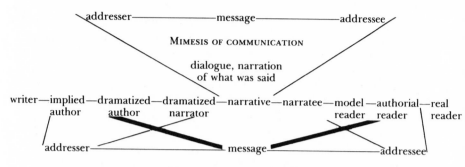

COMMUNICATION

NARRATIVE COMMUNICATION

A narrative may have only one addresser (as in "Bliss"), an implied author and dramatized narrator (*Huckleberry Finn*), or, as in *Canterbury Tales*, an implied author, dramatized author ("Chaucer" as an incompetent tale-teller), and dramatized narrators. In the same manner, there may be one or more addressees. Whenever another addresser and addressee are added to the model, everything between them becomes part of the "message."

Writer: Wayne Booth (1979) argues that two additional figures can occupy the space between the flesh-and-blood writer and the implied author. The sequence of implied authors created during an author's life make up a "career author" (see Lawrence Lipking, *The Life of the Poet*). Writers may also develop a "public character" that is presented to the press and audiences—a role half forced on them by their public image and acclaim (cf. "Borges and I," in Jorge Luis Borges, *A Personal Anthology*).

Implied/dramatized author: The implied author, by definition, never uses "I" or refers to the audience; a dramatized author does so. Lanser shows that the distinction between the former (which she calls the "extrafictional voice") and the dramatized author (her "public narrator") is one of degree, with intermediate stages between the two.

Dramatized narrator: A character in the story (Lanser's "private narrator").

Narratee: Prince's term for the person to whom a narrative is addressed. If not a character, the narratee is the same as the implied reader.

Implied reader: An abstraction used to discuss the kinds of competence real readers possess (see Ong; Iser, 34–38). To emphasize different kinds of competence, critics may call this figure the ideal, super-, or informed reader. If there are addressers other than the implied author, this figure can be divided into:

Model reader: Eco's term for the reader whose characteristics are delineated by, or inferred from, the text (Prince's "virtual reader"; Rabinowitz's "narrative audience"; Lanser's "public narratee"). This is a quasi-fictional role that the reader is expected to play (see Ong).

Authorial reader: Rabinowitz's "authorial audience"; Gibson's "mock reader"; Lanser's "extrafictional reader." Usually this figure is similar to the actual audience addressed by the implied author. Unlike the model reader, this one remains aware that the fiction is a fiction (the implied author may allude to the fact) and reads in light of that knowledge.

Figure 7a

as such. But the issuance of a command presupposes that the speaker has the authority to make it, and when the story was written, wives did not conventionally exercise that kind of authority over husbands (though the "henpecked husband" was a comic stereotype). Francis is especially offended because, as noted earlier, this is the kind of command a mother gives to a child.

Speech-act theorists study these dimensions of language use—what we do *in* saying something, and do *by* saying it. Richard Ohmann and Mary Louise Pratt have shown that literary texts have much in common with ordinary speech acts; and Susan Lanser, in *The Narrative Act*, integrates speech-act theory with point-of-view criticism to produce a comprehensive account of the communication between writers and readers.

Linguists and semioticians add other features to the analysis of communication (in their terminology, "pragmatics"). Above and below the addresser/message/addressee axis, Jakobson lists three factors that are important in any speech event. Successful transmission of the message requires some knowledge of the "context," or what the speaker refers to; some means of opening, closing, and checking the communication channel ("contact"); and a way to determine how the words are intended to function (a matter of the "code" being used). When Francis says "Behave myself? That's a way to talk," he is commenting on the code; when he says "*shut up,*" he is obviously attempting to end the contact. The meaning of some lovers' quarrels and short stories (Hemingway's "Hills like White Elephants," for example) resides in the code or "metalingual" function: it is not the message but the comments *about* the message that reveal what is happening.

As a spectator or voyeur looking into a realistic fictional world, the reader interprets what happens much as we do in ordinary life, fitting together the events, characters, and motives. But what is the purpose of the story as a whole? In everyday discourse, the point a speaker makes in using a story as a message may be clarified by the context. A lawyer, trying to test Jesus, asks, "Who is my neighbor?" Jesus answers with the story of the good Samaritan. But stories are at best ambiguous. Therefore, after telling it, he checks to see whether the lawyer understood the "code" by asking which of the three characters is the neighbor. The lawyer's reply shows that he received the intended message. Writers and readers, however, do not exchange information about contact and code to ensure the accuracy of transmission, and in fiction the context does not involve reference to reality (if it did, we might be able to answer some of our questions by checking other sources of information).

Printed narratives may contain an implied author who addresses the readers, indicating what the story is about and why it is told. If the implied author tells the truth in saying the story is fictional or factual, the normal communication model holds, though readers may need to draw on their knowledge of literary conventions to understand the meaning. As the authorial voice falls silent, however, the reader becomes less certain about the purpose and meaning of the story-as-message. In many modern narratives, the problem is not just one of inferring an interpretation from a sequence of events that we understand, but of understanding exactly what happened—fitting actions, characters, and motives together in an intelligible plot or story. Is Bertha's interpretation of what happens in "Bliss" reliable, or is it distorted by her unusual emotional state and her sexual preoccupations?

In *The Rhetoric of Fiction*, Booth showed that narrative theorists have two choices when faced with such questions. They can maintain that fiction is similar to nonliterary discourse and try to preserve the communication model by showing how literary conventions serve as a substitute for those that are used in ordinary discourse to ensure the accurate transmission of meaning. Or they can forsake the communication model, in view of the fact that there is little agreement about what fictional narratives mean. Given these alternatives, it is understandable that most theorists should try to find a position somewhere between the two.

Some critics accept and even celebrate the fact that interpretations vary. Writers, in their view, cut fiction free from determinate meanings to open a space for the reader's personal involvement in the story. Others argue that the position allotted to the reader as a creator of meaning is more circumscribed by the writer and literary conventions than it may at first sight appear to be. Perhaps the creation of meaning is a cooperative enterprise, reader and writer both contributing a share; possibly the real determinants of interpretation are the literary and cultural assumptions of particular communities in history, since these shape what writers and readers perceive and create. A third group of critics (one I have constituted for my own purposes) holds that the meaning of fictional narratives is inherently unstable. In this last category I place critics who discuss not writers, readers, and conventions, but reading.

Kinds of Readers

Differences of opinion about narrative meaning seems to increase in direct proportion to the importance attached to the story and the care with which it is interpreted, as commentaries on Homer, the Bible, and the Bhagavad-Gita show. So long as popular fiction was regarded as a form of entertainment, it did not seem to require interpretation, though it might be considered frivolous or harmful. Stories intended or pretending to teach might be accepted at face value, on the basis of the moral lessons they obviously offered. But once novels entered the college curriculum, taking their place as an important literary form alongside poetry, drama, and nonfictional prose, disagreements about their interpretation multiplied. Legal systems and some religions have developed methods of settling such disputes by adjudication or authoritative decision; teachers may use discussion, explanation, or their authority to control interpretation in the classroom; but in books and articles, conflicting opinions are the norm.

In this case as in others, an understanding of literary history helps explain current critical theories. The disappearance of the author who addressed readers in the eighteenth and nineteenth centuries, as well as the appearance of problematic and fragmentary narratives in the twentieth century, has forced readers to participate in the production as well as the interpretation of texts. Once we have acquired the skills necessary to construct meanings where none are specified, we can return to the novels of earlier periods and discover interpretations that our former reading habits had led us to overlook (Culler 1982, 38–39; Docherty, x–xiii).

Readers themselves are the most obvious source of interpretive diversity, since each one brings to narratives a different set of experiences and expectations. For Norman Holland, individual differences are a function of one's psychic "identity"—a configuration of defenses and desires that characterize one's way of approaching life and literature. According to his psychoanalytic theory, we each "find in the literary work the kind of thing we characteristically wish or fear the most" (124). Once the reader has carefully set defense mechanisms in place, in order to ward off any potential threat that a narrative poses to psychic equilibrium, s/he can fantasize freely, satisfying individual drives for gratification.

There are, of course, many interpretations of Freud, and psychoanalysts differ from psychologists in their explanations of subjective identity; human beings are "texts" as subject to interpretive disagreements as narratives are. But most analysts accept the premise that each of us has a "script"—a general conception of how the narrative of life tends to develop—which serves as the basis of our interpretations and actions. Whereas earlier psychoanalytic critics held that such scripts can be discovered in novels (see chapter 2), Holland and others transfer them from the text to the reader: a narrative structure remains undefined until someone construes it in relation to a personal identity theme.

The impulse to reject this theory because it implies that we simply impose our own meanings on narratives is itself a defense mechanism, since we don't like to admit how often we repeat our characteristic acts of interpretation. Critics justify their explanations by referring to the text and using accepted interpretive procedures so that they will not be accused of subjectivity in a profession that prizes scientific, objective methods (we are all charter members of the Society for the Suppression of Subjectivity). Individual differences need not be interpreted psychoanalytically, however. David Bleich suggests that personal interpretations can be accepted as such and used as a basis of discussion and negotiation, from which shared knowledge will emerge.

For Bleich and Holland, interpretation is the final stage in the process of reading. They both allude to the earlier stages during which readers turn words into symbols or allay defense mechanisms, but they say little about the processes involved (cf. Mailloux, 27–32). Having read a story, the reader is of course free to interpret it in relation to a personal identity theme or anything else, but the freedom exercised while reading is of a different kind. Readers can choose not to open a book, or to close it whenever they please. Knowing this, the writer must continually solicit their attention, in acknowledgment of their freedom to stop reading. But so long as they continue to read, they voluntarily enter into a nonbinding pact with the writer, who does not impose personal views or purposes on them and asks in return that they set aside their own practical aims in order to bring an imaginary world into existence. As Sartre says, "On the one hand, the literary object has no substance but the reader's subjectivity. . . . But on the other hand, the words are there like traps to arouse our feelings and to reflect them toward us. . . . Thus, the writer appeals to the reader's freedom to collaborate in the production of his work" (39–40).

Though the writer may wish to make a narrative accessible to any potential reader, some conception of the audience is necessary to lead individuals to feel that they are the ones to whom it is addressed. As Saul Bellow says, "The writer cannot be sure that his million [readers] will view the matter as he does. He therefore tries to define an audience. By assuming what it is that all men ought to be able to understand and agree upon, he creates a kind of humanity" (118). By the same token, the writer must consider "whether the *image he creates of himself*, his implied author, is one that his most intelligent and perceptive readers can admire" (Booth 1961, 395). There is nothing hypocritical about this process of constructing an authorial voice that will address a hypothetical audience, any more than it is artificial or insincere to use one form of address in a business letter, another in a note to a friend. Conventions are not a constraint on genuine communication; they make it possible.

When we identify ourselves as readers addressed by the implied author, we become members of what Peter Rabinowitz calls the "authorial audience," on the basis of an implicit understanding with the author that the story being told is a fiction. (Holland might interpret this agreement as a means of setting our defense mechanisms at rest: we know that in reading fiction, we are playing "let's pretend"). As members of the "narrative audience," however, we read as if the story were true, in the sense that we grant existence to the characters and events. Within this world we distinguish facts from lies, and credible from unreliable points of view. If the implied author appears to look down on people of our own background, or seems patronizing or ironic when speaking of those who happen to be women, do not know Latin, or own a small business, then we may simply refuse to consider ourselves members of the authorial audience and not read the book. Yet we may accept that role without liking the implied author, who may appear to be a sentimentalist or a witty snob but still someone who tells an interesting story. Having joined the narrative audience, we can identify with characters or regard them as repellent, just as the narrator can. These variations of psychic "distance" between author, narrator, narratee, and authorial reader are, as Booth argues, crucial to the experience of narrative (155–59).

The importance of distance, empathy, identification, and desire in the reading of fiction has recently been reemphasized by Hans Robert Jauss and Fredric Jameson. These factors help account for the differences between individual responses, but they also operate powerfully in determining our reactions as members of a particular group or culture. Our ideas of courage and cowardice, honesty and hypocrisy, justice, goodness, and fairness are all part of our social being. Narratives have traditionally provided an affirmation of social values, and as Jauss shows, the modalities of response to the traditional hero—ranging from associative or admiring identification to irony—serve as an index of historical and social change (1977, 152–88). At the unconscious level, where Freudian critics locate familial and personal determinants of desire, Jameson sees social patterns of response inscribed, and these change from one socioeconomic epoch to the next.

Rabinowitz's distinctions between the actual, authorial, and narrative audiences are particularly useful in discussing the ways in which we "believe in" a story and identify with the characters. They also help sort out problems created by unreliable narrators and ambiguous stories, which can often be clarified by asking which audience encounters difficulties of interpretation. Other theorists use a variety of terms to designate the role of the reader, depending on what aspect of response they are interested in analyzing. Some hold that a narrative is most fully appreciated by the best of all possible readers, a "superreader" or "informed reader." On the other hand, authors may indicate—through commentary or the manner of presentation—what attitudes and abilities they assume the reader to possess. They may take it for granted that the audience has a wide range of learning, or helpfully supply information it may not happen to know. They can draw us into their confidence, as Huck Finn does; their rhetorical questions, denials, overjustifications, and even their silences serve to characterize not only themselves but their conception of the auditor (Prince). The image of the reader created within the text is variously referred to as the model, virtual, or postulated reader, and some critics argue that we can best understand a narrative by identifying ourselves with that figure. "The author creates, in short, an image of himself and another image of his reader; he makes his reader, as he makes his second self, and the most successful reading is one in which the created selves, author and reader, can find complete agreement" (Booth 1961, 138).

While an attempt to identify with an audience that is historically or socially distant from us can expand our imaginative horizons, it may not result in the best possible reading of a book. Some novels do not please the audience of their own time; a writer may try to change contemporary reading habits, rather than satisfy them. It is of course possible to argue that great writers speak to us of what is eternally human, quite apart from social and cultural change. But if we look at the interpretations of their works through the centuries, we find less agreement than we might expect. Such similarities of opinion as do exist result in part from a process of cultural accretion, through which ideas about literature are woven into a tradition that in large part determines what we see. Revolutionary novels of the past that proved morally offensive or unintelligible to the contemporaneous audience, disrupting what Jauss calls its "horizon of expectations," may be for us the masterpieces of a continuous evolution.

The ways in which literary traditions propagate similar interpretations deserve as much attention as the differences between individual responses. Reader-response theorists emphasize an important point:

narratives do not contain a definite meaning that sits in the words waiting for someone to find it. Meaning comes into existence only in the act of reading. But it is equally wrong to conclude that interpretation must therefore be "in" the reader, regardless of the words on the page. In order to read them, we must know the language—the "code," in Jakobson's communication model—though we need not be conscious of its complex rules. Similarly, we have been trained since childhood in the conventions of storytelling. And just as we learn our own regional dialects, so those who acquire their interpretive skills from a particular critical school tend to talk and interpret the same way. Social, cultural, and literary change combine to produce new kinds of narrative and new methods of interpretation. Interpretations differ because readers differ; differences between readers are a function not just of their personalities but of the conventions they employ in reading. When asked why I find a particular meaning in a story, I usually point to certain passages, but they support my interpretation only on the basis of assumptions about conventions: certain words and actions imply certain meanings.

Of the theorists who attempt to account for the process of reading narratives, none has been more successful than Wolfgang Iser. He holds that the writer does exercise control over the way readers perceive the text, through the use of mutually understood conventions, and to this extent he accepts the assumptions of the communication model. But fictional narration alters the conditions of communication in fundamental ways, he points out. The "implied reader" (his term for the reader implied by the text) is part of the fictional structure, and as such this role is not one to which we can commit ourselves without qualification. The meaning we infer from the text emerges from a productive tension between "the role offered by the text and the real reader's own disposition" (1976, 37). Furthermore, he suggests, the implied reader is not the "addressee" of a fictional narrative, as the communication model suggests, but simply one of several standpoints that provide perspectives on its meaning. The implied author, the characters, and the plot offer different points of view on the action as it unfolds. The reader's role is to bring about the convergence of these perspectives; their meeting place is the meaning of the text, which is perceived from an imagined standpoint that combines them.

Narrative texts, then, unlike speakers in ordinary discourse, provide several channels of communication, governed by different intentions. (This conception has something in common with Bakhtin's "heteroglossia," discussed in the last section of chapter 6). Each viewpoint is derived from a repertoire of conventions and attitudes that we use in understanding life. But in fiction, we must construct the schematic "reality" to which the words refer by imagining it, rather than filling in missing details by taking another look at the world or at other sources of information. Here the individuality of the reader comes into play, and the writer has provided for it in the gaps and blanks that exist in the text.

To these aspects of reading that are specific to fiction, Iser adds others characteristic of narrative. In their successive presentation, each character and viewpoint become the "theme" of the reader's attention, viewed against the "horizon" of what has gone before. In Hemingway's story, for example, after experiencing Wilson's view of Francis as a coward and something less than a man, we enter the perspective of Francis and learn how fear can paralyze the will. Later, if capable of sympathizing with an attitude that the narrator does not seem to endorse, the reader may see that from Margaret's point of view, the thrill men get from killing large animals is, if not repugnant, at least inhumane. Each perspective tends to be negated by those that follow, leading the reader to readjust his understanding of the past action and form new expectations concerning the future.

When a perspective on life proves inadequate, the reader tends to question the entire repertoire of conventional assumptions on which it is based. In Iser's view, narration progresses as a negation of partial and inadequate ways of understanding the world, leaving in its wake not a constructed meaning but a variety of hypothetical viewpoints, depending on how the reader has filled in meanings, questioned social practices, and tried to find positive alternatives to the inadequate views represented in the text. If open to the experience the text provides, we are likely to find negations of some of our own views; as a result, the self that begins reading a book may not be quite the same as the one that finishes it. That is why, for Iser, "the reader" is not the fictitious figure addressed by the implied author, the real person reading, or some combination of the two; rather, the reader is a transcendental possibility, not yet realized, that exists and changes only in the process of reading.

Reading

Iser's theory occupies the middle ground between conceptual analysis of literary communication and a process-oriented account of reading. The communication model (Figure 7a) is a synthetic representation of all the possibilities that can be actualized as we pass through texts. At one moment, a dramatized author may address us as the intended audience; at another, we may overhear a conversation between characters or be addressed by a narrator who obviously misperceives the events described. A comprehensive reader-response theory must consider all these alternatives; but when they are listed on an atemporal chart, they do not tell us much about reading itself. That is why, after discussing abstractions such as implied readers, Iser tries to show how they are mobilized and altered in their journey through a story. His theory leads to a persuasive account of what happens when we read, though he does not attempt to describe the process in detail.

Rather than proposing a theory and then showing how it might work in practice, one can use an inductive approach—simply begin reading a text and develop conclusions about the process along the way. The most brilliant example of this method is Roland Barthes's *S/Z*, an analysis of Balzac's story "Sarrasine." After a few introductory pages, Barthes begins quoting the story, a few words or sentences at a time, and commenting on each segment. In the title and first sentence he finds the five "codes" that will create multiple possibilities of meaning as the reader follows them through the text. No two readers are likely to obtain the same results when they use this method. Chatman and Scholes have used it to analyze Joyce's story "Eveline"; I will try to exemplify it by discussing a few sentences of Mansfield's story.

Though titles may prove to be apt summaries of stories after we have read them, they usually appear enigmatic when we begin. "Bliss"—who feels it, in what circumstances, and with what results? Such questions belong to the *hermeneutic code*, which leads the reader through a series of partial disclosures, delays, and ambiguities as the story moves toward its final revelations. We know from the beginning that "bliss" is an emotional state, one of transport beyond the ordinary; when it is connected to other bits of information about thoughts and traits, the totality will be the locus of a person (the *code of semes*). The first few words of the story—"Although Bertha Young was thirty"—give us a proper name around which many semes will gather, though they may never crystallize as a fixed "character." Her age, thirty, is a fact we construe as part of the *referential* or *cultural code*, that enormous storehouse of knowledge we automatically use in interpreting everyday experience. With the phrase "she still had moments like this," the *code of actions* or *proairetic code* begins. We will collect these actions in groups (returning home, feeding the baby) that move the story from beginning to end; the hermeneutic code also works in this sequential fashion. The phrase "waiting for something

. . . divine to happen," which appears on the second page of the story, brings these two codes together and, like a signpost pointing toward a city we have never visited, draws us toward new revelations.

Barthes later reshuffled these first four codes (in an essay published in 1973, which provides a conveniently brief example of the method); their names are less important than their general character. A glance back at Figure 5b will show that the codes can be derived from his earlier analysis of narrative structure. The sequence of "functions" in the 1966 essay has been split into two codes—one of actions, the other of enigmas. Some of the static elements that he formerly called "indices" have entered the code of enigmas, or hermeneutic code, and others create the code of semes. The "informants" of the earlier theory have become the referential code. Instead of arranging elements in a hierarchic, atemporal structure, his new method simply treats them sequentially as they occur in reading.

The fifth and final code in *S/Z* is the *code of symbols*, based on antithesis. In "Bliss," the sentence "Why be given a body if you have to keep it shut up in a case like a rare, rare fiddle?"—a simile Bertha denies as soon as she has created it—is the first in a complex chain that opposes inside to outside, closed to open, hot (the burning in her bosom) to cold (the rooms), and warm to cool colors. Hovering between these extremes is a series of objects—a mirror, Miss Fulton "all in silver," the silver flowers of the flame-shaped pear tree—that reflect, by turns, each side of the antithesis. According to Barthes, the site on which symbolic opposites meet is the body—in this case, Bertha's body. But in leaping ahead in the story, departing from line-by-line comment to discuss the symbolic code, I have violated Barthes's method. "If we want to remain attentive to the plural of a text," we must avoid such atemporal "*construction* of the text: everything signifies ceaselessly and several times, but without being delegated to a great final ensemble, an ultimate structure" (1970, 11–12).

Reading, thus described, is like listening to music. Actions and enigmas are the lines of melody, leading forward, interweaving as in a fugue; semes, symbols, and cultural references add harmonies and rhythms in recurring patterns (29–30). At times these levels of the text may seem to coalesce in a single thematic meaning, "even while the discourse is leading us toward other possibilities"; the meaning skids, "each synonym adding to its neighbor some new trait, some new departure" (92). Like Iser, Barthes holds that narratives employ several channels of communication—between one character and another, narrator and narratee, writer and reader. Sometimes the reader has information the character is struggling to discover, and a message received by the character has an entirely different meaning for the reader. "Thus, like a telephone network gone haywire, the lines are simultaneously twisted and routed according to a whole new system of splicings" (132). In modern texts, there is often no identifiable narrator; "the more indeterminate the origin of the statement, the more plural the text. . . . Whereby we see that writing is not the communication of a message which starts from the author and proceeds to the reader; it is specifically the voice of reading itself; *in the text, only the reader speaks*" (41, 51).

But who is the reader? By identifying different roles that the reader may need to fill, reader-response theorists imply that there is no simple answer to this question. To be absorbed in reading is to be forgetful of the daily self, drifting toward imaginary identification with characters, or veering away toward a wry view of their fate. To a second reading of the text I may bring a different mood, and certainly bring awareness of what will happen next, with the result that a different "I" reads, seeing new patterns. What remains constant, within and between readers, is a collection of habits and conventions mobilized in the act of reading, and these are the cumulative product of our experience with literature. "This 'I' which approaches the text is already itself a plurality of other texts, of codes which are infinite or, more precisely, lost (whose origin is lost). . . . The meanings I find are established not by 'me' or by others, but by their *systematic* mark: there is no other *proof* of a reading than the quality and endurance of its systematics; in other words: than its functioning" (10−11).

If construed as an assertion that there is no such thing as a self, unique to each of us, this passage may have a slight shock value. Barthes probably intended that effect, but his denial of the reader's individuality is carefully qualified. The "'I' which approaches the text" is not the one who talks to friends; it is the one willing to lose itself in reading. When I read, the text may trigger all sorts of ideas and associations that others would not experience. These thoughts *occur*, but they are not "*established*." To establish meaning—which involves explaining it to myself or someone else—I relate one part of the text to others, and in doing so I assume (as others do) that meaning arises from connections between things. The meaningful system I find may appear plausible (if it is based on codes everyone knows) or eccentric. In any case, it will be one or the other not because I said it but because of the system I explain.

Forsaking the communication model, Barthes makes the codes the real heroes of his story of reading. There is no longer an author-as-addresser, an authoritative source of the meaning that readers try to recover; there is only writing. The five codes that he claims we use in reading are already written into the "readerly" or "classical" narrative, just as they are written in us, and because of their conventional nature, they limit the meanings we can impute to the text. Any systematic interpretation is ultimately arbitrary, since there is no message "in" the text to which it might correspond. However, in solving the problem of how and why interpretations differ, Barthes creates another. His theory is based on the assumption that the codes remain fixed, creating both the freedom and the constraints of the narrative system. Does the evidence support this conclusion?

As Frank Kermode points out, the history of interpretation does not bear out Barthes's view; cultural and interpretive conventions change. "In fact, the only works we value enough to call classic are those which, as they demonstrate by surviving, are complex and indeterminate enough to allow us our necessary pluralities" (1975, 121). Such is the power of cultural and institutional traditions that the classics are perpetually renewed through reinterpretation so that they can help us preserve our connection with the past, while accommodating themselves to current concerns. Two factors contribute to our success in finding new meanings. One is the disappearance of the facts and interpretive conventions that tied earlier literature to its cultural context. "We can say that it is the very *alien-ness* of texts that makes interpretation possible [and] that this estrangement is caused by the action of history" (Kermode 1983, 29). The interpretive convention that allows us to take an active part in the production of meaning, which has a long history and has become a necessity in dealing with modern texts, is a second factor that helps us discover the current relevance of the classic.

In explaining why literature is perpetually open to reinterpretation, Kermode does not imply that historical change and individual caprice justify any interpretation whatsoever. Like Barthes and Iser, he holds that a narrative marks out a definite range of interpretive possibilities, but he differs from them in his explanation of the constraints and liberties involved. To interpret, in his view, is not simply to discover systematic relations, as Barthes asserts, but to integrate them in a system. Since writers and readers create meanings by connecting parts of the text to form a totality, Barthes's argument that there is no system *in* the text is beside the point; the text doesn't exist apart from its readings and interpretations.

Given the sheer mass of information contained in any narrative, we inevitably attach more importance to some elements than to others. In detective novels, we attend to the plot and the clues (the proairetic and hermeneutic codes), setting aside other details. Barthes sees the latter, which belong to the referential, semic, and symbolic codes, as the accessories of narrative, furnishing realistic detail and ideological props to the story's readability. Kermode holds that such details always have the potential to coalesce in meaningful patterns that supplement or contradict the interpretation implied by the main sequential elements. In his readings of classic, modern, and popular fiction, he spots seemingly random elements that point to "secrets" in the text. The subtlety and persuasiveness of his own interpretations provide convincing support for his theory and show that details we consider irrelevant, pushed aside in our search for larger structures, may yield their meanings to patient analysis. One such detail in "Bliss" is a sentence before the arrival of Pearl Fulton that has no apparent relation to the rest of the story: "Came another tiny moment, while they waited, laughing and talking, just a trifle too much at their ease, a trifle too unaware." I suspect that this odd intervention of the narrator, marking a brief interruption in temporal continuity and in consciousness, has a meaning that might transform everything else the story says. To determine whether it is a clue carefully planted or a seed of my own imagining, it would be necessary to read Mansfield's short stories as fragments of a larger design, looking for similar details.

Recent theories of reading are products of a critical dialogue, each participant staking out his position in relation to the others. Before discussing the nature and significance of their disagreements, I want to describe the position of a critic who adds another twist to the thread that binds current theories of narrative together: J. Hillis Miller. In common with Barthes and Kermode, he holds that a text establishes the range within which plausible interpretations are possible and that "more is to be gained by talking about the words of the work than by talking about the reader as such and his responses" (40, 20). Like Kermode, he distinguishes the singular events that move a narrative forward from the other details that, because of their similarities, enter into systematic patterns of meaning (1). But he disagrees with Kermode on one crucial point. He does not think that readers can discover one secret after another in a text, each involving details that were overlooked in earlier interpretations; there are no secrets, because any detail can enter into antithetically systematic explanations (25, 51). A simplified explanation of Miller's position cannot do it justice, but its importance leads me to provide one.

As we progress through a story, we discover repetitions—of words, events, images, actions—that can be grouped in meaningful patterns. The traditional themes identified in literary study (archetypes, sym-

167

bols, patterns of conflict) offer a rich variety of templates in terms of which we tend to perceive narratives. Assuming changeless patterns of meaning—an assumption sanctioned by our culture—we are equipped to recognize the similarities on which systematic interpretation is based, and we do so by disregarding incidental differences between one event and another. But there is another way to view narrative and meaning. It begins from the most basic, observable fact about the world; objects and events are separate, distinct from one another, and subject to change. From this point of view, *only differences exist*. No matter how exactly an event repeats one that occurred earlier, they are separated by time, context, and probably by their consequences. Similarities thus appear to be accidental and phantasmal— in the sense that it is my mind, removing them from time and circumstance, that sees two things as the same (1–17). Since narrative is based on the estranging distance that time puts between events that appear similar, it can always undercut the meaning we find in "repetition of the same" by showing that it is really repetition with a difference. Both patterns seem necessary, but they are contradictory.

The contrary patterns created in narrative by these two kinds of repetition can be found in a detail from "Bliss"—the color of Pearl Fulton's dress. Early in the story, Bertha sees "the lovely pear tree with its wide open blossoms as a symbol of her own life," symbolic identity being an exemplary instance of the first type of meaning, based on archetypal similarity. Later Pearl arrives, "all in silver"; and after dinner, when she and Pearl stand looking at the pear tree with its "silver flowers," she feels they are joined in a more inclusive unity, "understanding each other perfectly." A true union with her husband, across the gap of sexual difference, now seems possible. But time proves this is a delusion. Her bliss is shattered by the sight of Pearl with her husband. Difference has destroyed the unity based on silver (an ideal symbol of similarity, since it reflects like a mirror, rather than asserting its own color and presence). Therefore Bertha does what any perceptive interpreter of narrative does: she recalls a repugnant difference that she had excluded from her identification with the pear tree—the two cats on the lawn—and develops a new interpretation of the original experience. When Pearl leaves, with Eddie following, she sees them as "the black cat following the grey cat." Having previously seen Pearl's dress as silver, like the pear tree, she now perceives it as gray, like the cat. The actual hue of a silver dress makes both interpretations plausible, but they are contradictory. Miller would find this example representative of interpretation in general. Neither narratives nor the characters they represent provide a fixed locus of meaning. Pearl (like the gem after which she is named) is both gray and silver.

If interpretations can be "related to one another in a system of mutual implication and mutual contradiction," as Miller says (40), he has proved that interpretive diversity is not simply a product of subjective differences, historical change, or a failure to interpret with systematic rigor. It may result from an inescapable difference between logical (atemporal) and narrative meaning. However, even apart from the philosophical arguments that might be mounted against this conclusion, it seems to contradict the most obvious fact about fictional narration: stories are after all written by authors who presumably intend them to be meaningful; the communication model (from author to work to audience) remains basic to our thinking about literature.

In reply to this objection, Miller and others would point out that there is a difference between a meaningful story and a story that has only one interpretation. The latter would be meaning-impoverished and, as authors know, probably not very interesting. Furthermore, the communication model, by simplifying the representation of what happens when we read, creates a misleading picture of the process. The author is not the only source of meaning, nor is the reader the only interpreter. As indicated in the analysis of "Bliss," the characters usually "read" and interpret the events in which they are involved. The fact that critics often argue about whether a character has interpreted his or her world correctly serves as evidence that interpretations exist *within* a story as well as in what readers say about it. Narrators are also readers and interpreters. And finally, the writer is a reader and interpreter, just as the real reader, by posing and answering questions, becomes a writer or rewriter of the story. In other words, the entire communication model exists within each of its discrete parts.

In order to show that these paradoxes are not just sophistries, it is helpful to return to the criticism of Frank Kermode and the situation of narrative before the modern period. In writing "The Shipman's Tale," Chaucer followed the typical practice of his time: he took a well-known story and turned it into a work of art. From a literary point of view, the shortcomings of the earlier versions are obvious: they do not explain the motives of the characters, who are stock figures; the incidents, which seem contrived for the creation of a joke, are not accompanied by authenticating details that would make them believable. Having heard or read the tale, Chaucer interpreted it by rewriting it. Rather than complaining about its faults (the activity of the reader as critic), he repaired them. And this procedure was, for at least 2,000 years, the most common method of creating a narrative: expanding on inherited materials. In the Christian tradition, it led to the creation of the Lives of the Saints and the apocrypha concerning the life of Jesus. In the multitude of stories that grew up around the "matter" of Troy, Thebes, and Rome, writers answered questions raised by lacunae in classical literature: What happened after Odysseus returned home? What became of the other heroes after the sack of Troy? The same process led to the integration and elaboration of romance narratives concerning Carolingian France and Arthurian Britain.

In *The Genesis of Secrecy*, Kermode provides a brilliant analysis of this process at work in the creation of the four gospels. Mark is the shortest; it contains enigmatic and even unintelligible incidents that are explained more satisfactorily in Matthew, Luke, and John. The method they used to clarify the story, one common in their time, is a particular form of the method of exegesis known as "midrash": "instead of interpreting by commentary, one does so by a process of augmenting the narrative" (81). As a result, a figure whose presence is unexplained in Mark acquires characteristics and motives in the other gospels; as an intelligible character, he may engage in new actions, and these in turn may require further interpretation. Once the canon had been fixed and many gospels declared apocryphal, Biblical interpretation took the form of commentary, not rewriting. Interpretation remains necessary because so many questions about the Bible remain unanswered. But it is doubtful that they could all be answered by a more complete, circumstantial narrative. Every increase in length adds to the complexity of the whole, and details that resolve one interpretive puzzle often create others.

This conception of the writer as an interpreter and rewriter may not seem to apply to modern narratives, prized because they are original. But the notebooks of novelists indicate that in generating a story from the germ of an idea, they too use the techniques of midrash. Action leads to the creation of a character, and the character gives birth to new actions. Tolstoy, whose description of this process was cited in the second chapter, once said that "in a writer there must always be two people—the writer and the critic." The latter is a reader who has the special privilege of rewriting the story. Before stories became personal property (through copyright laws), anyone could retell them and put an interpretation right in the text by altering the characters and actions or by introducing commentary. Since that kind of participation is now forbidden, our rewriting must take the form of external commentary (a paper or essay), which a story tends to slough off in its passage through time. But such commentaries, in their totality, make up interpretive traditions, which in their diversity enable us to perceive and understand narratives in different ways.

This chapter began with the obvious premise that if we want to understand narrative structure and meaning, we should see how they function in the process of reading, rather than analyzing them in the abstract. The communication model provides a starting point for this endeavor, but the differences between literary and pragmatic communication, resulting in part from those between writing and speech, allow readers more latitude than conversationalists in the construction of meaning. The hypothesis that the lack of agreement about interpretation results from differences between readers can account for interpretive diversity, but it cannot account for the equally obvious continuities of interpretive traditions. These continuities result from shared conventions of interpretation and the ways in which writers mark out, within a text, the position from which the intended reader will view the narrative. However, the reader occupies only one of several interpretive positions, those of characters and narrators being equally important. Barthes does not think that the information conveyed by these separate lines of communication can be integrated in an inclusive interpretation. Kermode and Miller hold that readers can legitimately integrate textual elements in total systems of meaning and that any significant narrative will give rise to varied interpretations, though they have different reasons for arriving at this conclusion.

How do we in fact read narratives? In one sense, the question is unanswerable. George Dillon has described the strategies readers use to understand literary sentences, but the conceptual operations required to make sense of a fictional world do not lend themselves to linguistic analysis. When a reader recounts the thought processes involved, the result is not a transcript of experience but a "story of reading," as Culler says—one composed after the fact, in the form of a narrative that is at best plausible: "It proves no easier to say what is in *the* reader's or *a* reader's experience than what is in the text" (82).

The theories of reading produced during the past fifteen years have, nevertheless, made significant contributions to the understanding of narrative. First, they have reinstalled the writer and reader alongside the text as elements that must be taken into account in any adequate theory. Second, by revealing the complexity of literary communication, they have encouraged more careful readings of narrative texts. Patience reveals that they are quite as worthy of close analysis as poetry. And finally, something of importance may be revealed by the

171

very failure of the attempt to determine the extent to which reader and text, as separate entities, contribute to interpretive diversity. Any such effort presupposes that the theorist can step outside the field of analysis, escaping the conditions of narrativity and reading, in order to identify them. But any essay or book that treats this subject is itself another reading, another interpretation, another narrative. If the failure of this theoretical effort leads to a realization that we cannot separate ourselves from those activities when we analyze them, then reading, interpretation, and narration would appear to be necessary aspects of understanding, not just concepts that are useful in discussing fiction.

8

Frames of Reference:
Metafiction, Fiction, and Narrative

In developing a theory of narrative or of anything else, the
first step is to define the field of study. In chapter 4 I discussed
critics who define plot, or the structure of action, as their subject, and
much of what they say applies to plays as well as to narratives. Chapter
5 concerned critics who analyze plot but also take account of specific
features of narration lacking in drama, such as descriptions and the
verbal presentation of characters. The field of study expands further
when theorists consider the role of the narrator. As chapter 6 showed,
a narrator frames and shapes the action presented; he or she can be
inside the story as one of the characters or outside it as an anonymous
observer, and beyond those borders we are confronted with questions
of the narrator's relationship to the writer. Chapter 7 extended the
discussion to what might appear to be the final feature of the narrative situation—the reader, who can also be inside the story (as one of
the characters to whom it is told or as someone addressed by the author) but is ultimately outside it.

The last expansion of the field of reference leads the theorist to
step outside our experience of narrative—to speak not as a reader
but as someone talking about what readers do and how they differ
from one historical epoch to the next. Kermode and Jauss show that
cultural change leads inevitably to reinterpretation of the literary
canon. Shklovsky compares a text to an iceberg that drifts southward
into warmer currents, which melt away the bottom until "the upper
portion that looms above the water becomes heavier and the iceberg
capsizes. Now it has acquired a completely different aspect—no
longer pointed, but flat-topped, more massive, smooth. . . . Such are
the fortunes of a work of literature. There are periodic upheavals in

the way they are understood. What was once funny becomes tragic; what was beautiful is perceived as banal. A work of art is, as it were, continually being rewritten."

The conceptual progression from analysis of plot to consideration of more encompassing contexts can be taken as evidence of progress toward a comprehensive understanding of narrative. Just as one might verify a scientific theory that applies to a limited range of phenomena and then expand it by identifying variables that would account for other classes of events, so by considering more and more features in the narrative situation, we should be able to produce theories of increasing generality and precision. Unfortunately, however, the analogy does not seem to hold. Theories of narrative do not fit together in a neat, hierarchic relationship; taking more features into account can overturn the conclusions derived from a simpler model rather than subsuming them.

Another difference between scientific and narrative theories results from the instability of the frameworks used in the latter. To construct an explanation, one must fix the elements to be analyzed within a frame of reference, establishing what scientists call the "boundary conditions" of the theory. Some facts are excluded from its purview, and the language of the theory is distinct from the "object-language" that it uses to name facts. But as previous chapters show, many features of the narrative situation have a disturbing tendency to move back and forth across the border that should separate what is inside a narrative from what is outside it. The narrator/writer and implied/real reader are two obvious instances of such shifting elements. The first section of this chapter treats critics who show how demarcations between text and context, story and interpretation, and writing and reading can become blurred or reversed, overturning a theory intended to fix meaning in place. An obvious disruption of the line between a narrative and its readings occurs when the story includes reference to theories, other narratives, or itself. In the second section, I will discuss some types of fiction (such as parody and metafiction) that exemplify these dilemmas.

For many critics, the theories and narrative techniques of recent years are oversophisticated departures from the basic facts that determine the difference between fiction and reality, or falsity and truth. The third section of the chapter returns to these facts to see whether recent theories can add anything to the traditional conception of how literature is related to life. Section four concerns the larger issue of whether narrative, fictional or factual, is a distinctive and legitimate mode of explanation, comparable in importance to theories in the natural sciences that call its explanatory usefulness into question.

Crossing Theoretical Borders: Models of Misreading

Unlike plants and planets, stories and their writers know that readers are observing them. The knowledge that an observer is present can affect behavioral patterns; that is why social scientists often conceal their purposes from people who are used in experiments. The writer, knowing how readers respond and critics theorize, can take their propensities into account and try to control the way a text will be experienced. Thus the text may neutralize or co-opt the theories that would explain it.

In *Story and Situation*, Ross Chambers shows that many texts are *"situationally* self-referential," not only creating a role for the implied reader but "specifying the conditions—the necessary understandings between reader and text—for them to be successful as acts of literary communication" (25–26). Once we recognize how a narrator attempts to control our perception of a story, we may choose to read it differently: "By reading this self-situation as *part of the text*, one should free oneself to recontextualize it (that is, interpret it) along with the rest of the text. . . . The text needs to be thought of in terms other than those available to it in the historical and ideological circumstances of its own production" (27). The passage of time may effect this change (as Kermode and Shklovsky say), quite apart from our intentions ot those of the writer.

Realistic writers encourage us to lend credence to their stories by suppressing all evidence that they use narrative conventions, and they must be particularly careful to keep us from noticing their attempts to control our responses, if that is their intention. Should we come to suspect that our credulous absorption results from technical manipulation, we are doubly shocked—not just by the deception but by the reversal of roles whereby the writer reads and interprets us, rather than we the story. Some modern theorists oppose realism for the same reason that Plato opposed mimesis: it is the falsest form of fiction precisely because it appears true, hiding the fact that it is illusion.

Rather than neutralizing or co-opting theoretical scrutiny, a writer may deliberately reveal that a story is an illusion, baring the devices that make it seem real. Gabriel Josipovici looks on the realistic novel as a deviation from traditional and modern narratives which, by includ-

175

ing an authorial narrator and referring to literary conventions, acknowledge their fictional status. In his view the best modern novelists use realistic techniques only to set the stage for an awakening of consciousness that will jolt us out of our solipsistic dreams:

> First, they lull us into taking the "picture" for "reality," strengthening our habitual tendencies, and then suddenly our attention is focused on the spectacles through which we are looking, and we are made to see that what we had taken for "reality" was only the imposition of the frame. But for this to work we must first be taken in, and what better way of taking in the reader than through the medium of the novel, which is almost not a medium at all, almost like life itself. . . . We become aware . . . with a shock of recognition, suddenly realizing what we had dimly sensed all along, that what we had taken to be infinitely open and "out there" was in reality a bounded world bearing the shape of our imagination. . . . The playful inversions of the novel form and the parody of language and conventions in modern fiction have the opposite effect, making us realize with a shock that we are dealing not with the world but with one more object in the world, one made by a human being. [Josipovici, 297, 299]

Josipovici's account of how modern novels can affect readers is not a theory in the usual sense, and the same could be said of other critics I shall be discussing. By calling attention to the spectacles and frame (the techniques and structures) that create the effects of reality, the novelist shows that they are entrancing and dangerously false, often doing so at the very moment when a satisfying theme seems to be emerging. The exposure of illusion raises awareness to a new level. Many champions of realism think that allegory, metafiction, and parody (in general, any overt signs that a narrative is conventional) are a form of game-playing, indicating that a writer or critic is not really serious. That is not true; advocates of self-conscious fiction may, like others, be frivolous, or sensible, or (as in the case of Josipovici) much more serious than most of us.

Like Josipovici, Paul de Man views nineteenth-century realism as a deviation from narrative methods that "prevent the all too readily mystified reader from confusing fact and fiction and from forgetting the essential negativity of the fiction" (1969, 219). But he is less optimistic about the possibility of escaping from fiction and theory to attain some reliable higher knowledge about reality. Instead of attempting to summarize his position, I shall simply introduce it, trusting that interested readers will consult other sources (Culler 1982; Johnson 1984) and de Man's writings for a fuller account.

Constructing a narrative involves two activities: *naming* objects and

176

events accurately (so that the words represent all important aspects of the reality depicted), and *ordering* the names (putting words and sentences in a sequence corresponding to their temporal occurrence). The resultant narrative should have a meaning, which is not something that the words have "added to" the story (this would imply that the meaning wasn't really in the events but had been imposed on them by the words); ideally, the words make visible and highlight a meaning that was there all the time, so that we can "read" it.

But what if the story told is one that leads to a realization that the process of naming and ordering was false? This would be the sort of narrative that Josipovici discusses: the protagonist or reader finally sees that the events and words don't match, either because the protagonist imagined something that was not really present, or because the conventional words and perceptions did not represent the reality of the situation. The consequent shock of recognition frees us from illusion, returning us to the real world. De Man acknowledges that in dealing with narratives of this type, "such a reading is a necessary part of the novel's interpretation. . . . This does not mean however that it can stop there" (1979, 200). In other words, we cannot call a halt to the interpretation by concluding that the narrator or protagonist misperceived the events. We must go on to consider how they might be re-presented truthfully, for the very conclusion "it was an illusion" (what de Man calls "the negativity of fiction") implies that there is another, more reliable way to present them.

What we or the narrator must do, then, is return to the beginning of the story and reread it in light of our new knowledge. Where before we had seen love, true understanding, external difficulties, and disappointment, we may now recognize not a literal reference to the "facts" but an imaginary (figurative, metaphorical) representation of a desire or need that shifts from one person to another and can never be satisfied, a false conjunction of opinions, a projection of our own inadequacies onto the outer world, and a refusal to accept the difference between what we want and how things are. The words are no longer a record of what really happened; they are now seen as an *allegory*, a text in which every word stands for some idea that is different from what it names. The text now "narrates the unreadability of the prior narration"; it tells an entirely new story, "a story of the failure to read," to make proper connections between words or ideas and things (de Man 1979, 205).

But knowledge that the first story was false and the second one less delusory does nothing to solve the real problem posed by literature and life—how to live. To accept the new understanding of life (my love is a psychological desire based on a physical need) is intolerable; to revert to the belief that "I" am a conscious self that can "know" and "act" rationally is impossible. Therefore, I must make an arbitrary ethical choice: since truth and falsehood cannot produce any prescription concerning how to live, I must decide what might be the right way to live (as opposed to some way that, whether true or false, is wrong). At the same time, the very decision to make this choice is based on the conclusion that I have some knowledge about reality and literal meaning; therefore, it plunges me back into a repetition of precisely those false assumptions that I had tried to escape. If narrated, the consequences of this ethical choice will probably appear arbitrary, naive, or incoherent. Indeed, many readers may not even recognize that the story I tell is an allegory (my "reading" of the falsity of the literal story), and as a result they may accuse me of making the very mistakes that I have tried to expose.

Different as they are, I find in these three critics a shared concern with the ways in which writers and readers can change the borders that in theory should separate the story from its interpretation. The subtlety of these analyses serves as a reminder that writers are not inspired transcribers but readers and interpreters of experience. Our conflicting attempts to say what a narrative means may result from the fact that our interpretations have already been inscribed in the story, and the writer has refused to choose between them, as Barbara Johnson (1980) suggests in her reading of *Billy Budd*. If a theory is the simplest explanation of a variety of phenomena, and we want to explain how critics can come to such varied conclusions about the meaning of a narrative, we might be forced to say that the narrative itself is the only "theory" that could explain the phenomena (why critics say such different things about it).

Irony, Parody, and Metafiction

Often writers make it clear that we should not take their stories at face value. Literary tradition and ordinary language have a number of names for a disparity between statement and meaning—irony, sarcasm, overstatement, allegory, mockery, parody—and their very abundance testifies to the pervasiveness of the phenomenon. It is pertinent to the discussion of narrative theory not just because the fiction of the past two decades has made increasing use of such devices, but because they pose problems for any theory of narrative.

In "ordinary language," we mean what we say (speech-act theorists tell us that we are serious, sincere, and committed to the truth of our statements). Writers of narratives often say one thing and mean another—this is why "literary interpretation" is necessary—but with an adequate theory, we would be able to show that they really *do* mean what they say, though they have a special way of saying it. But within literature itself, the "imp of the perverse" (Poe's name for it is as good as any other) reinstalls itself, without apparent reason, to wreak theoretical havoc, to ridicule or dismantle systematic explanations. We find in literary history a continuous tradition of narratives that satirize or mix generic conventions, breaking the one-to-one relationship between convention and meaning. Since they are not subsumable in a third-level theory, all we can say of them is that they violate the others (the ordinary and the literary).

For my purposes, it is useful to sort the techniques of perverse narratives into two groups on the basis of the ways in which they deviate from the generally accepted conventions of the period in which they were written. In the first group I place those that challenge literary and social conventions through satire, parody, irony, and the like. The second group contains those techniques associated with the word "metafiction." If a character in a novel discovers that she is a character in a novel, or feels unfairly treated and decides to murder the novelist—in general, whenever the "fictional narrative/reality" relation becomes an explicit topic of discussion—readers are removed from the framework normally used in interpretation. This thematization of the narrative situation may be implicit rather than explicit, as when the story can be understood as an allegory about storytelling. To characterize these two techniques schematically: writers can look at prevailing literary and social conventions from another *position*, thereby questioning the validity or authenticity of the norm; or they can step outside the conventional framework of telling a story to another *level*, where the story being told, its audience, reality, and even narrative theory may be subjects of discussion.

Though the distinctions between irony, satire, and parody are easy to explain and illustrate, they tend to break down when examined in detail. Dictionaries of literary terminology say that parody is essentially a stylistic phenomenon—exaggerated imitation of the formal characteristics of a writer or genre, signaled by verbal, structural, or thematic disparities. It exaggerates traits to make them visible; juxtaposes disparate styles; uses the techniques of one genre to present subject matter usually associated with another. Margaret Rose neatly encapsules these possibilities in a formula: two codes, one message. Irony, on the other hand, conveys two messages through one code

(52–53, 61). Yet we traditionally distinguish two kinds of irony—verbal and dramatic (the latter being irony of situation). And one of my literary reference works argues that parody belongs to the genus satire. In short, the more carefully we discriminate among irony, satire, and parody, the more they appear to have in common, both conceptually and empirically. When we find one of them in a narrative, the other two are often lurking in the vicinity, and all three are common in novels that mix generic conventions. They can appear as a localized tone or technique, yet can also be modes encompassing an entire text.

What they have in common, except in their most exaggerated uses, is that no rule can tell us how to recognize them. We must catch the tone, feel the hitch that tells us something is awry—that words and meaning don't match. No wonder, then, that we tend to characterize them in emotional rather than theoretical terms. Irony can be dispassionately distant, an Olympian calm that notes and may sympathize with human weakness; or it can be savage, destructive, consuming even the ironist in its wake. Parody is funny (unless we happen to be friends of the parodied text, in which case it may be in bad taste). Yet even here, as Rose points out, our categories break down: some classical critics allied parody to "imitation" of an author, since the parodist may admire and elsewhere use the very techniques he pokes fun at (28–35; see also Tynjanov). So long as two codes are present, those of the source text and the parodist, there are two meanings. The parodist cannot completely efface, and may even sympathize with, the "serious" meaning of the original.

When viewed as instances of a general class of narrative methods, parody, irony, satire—and even allusion, quotation, puns, and verbal comedy—might be called "dual-voiced discourse" or "defamiliarization." I suspect that Bakhtin and Shklovsky used these words not only to emphasize the generic similarities involved, but also to free these techniques and the narratives that use them from their subordinate position in most histories of literature. In characterizing a narrative as funny, parodic, or ironic, we distinguish it from serious, normal, and "great" literature. However, if instead we say that such narratives call attention to the formal and ideological frameworks that govern literature and society, by showing that from another perspective the conventions involved may not depict the world or human conduct as it is or should be, we are likely to assess them in a different way. Reality, then, would be something that can be revealed when two codes intersect, since their simultaneous presence helps us see how conventional frames condition our understanding (Lotman, 72). Cervantes and Mark Twain are great realists not despite their use of parody but because of it.

Metafiction suspends normal meaning in another way. Like irony and parody, the prefix "meta-" designates phenomena found in non-literary uses of language. Normal statements—serious, informative, and truthful—exist *within* a framework that they do not name. They have an addresser and addressee, make use of a code (a language), and presuppose a certain context, as described in the last chapter. If I talk *about* the statement or the framework, I move up one level in the language game, suspending the statement's normal meaning (usually by putting it in quotation marks). Likewise, when a writer talks about a narrative within that narrative, s/he has put it in quotation marks, so to speak, stepping beyond its boundaries. Immediately the writer has become a theorist, everything normally outside the narrative being reproduced within it.

Probably most readers are familiar with metafictional techniques, which are not only as old as narrative itself but often turn up in the minor writings of well-known authors. In addition to producing major (symbolic, realistic) works, Hawthorne, Melville, and Twain wrote metafictions such as "Main Street," *The Confidence Man*, and "The Great Dark" (in which dreams and reality become indistinguishable). *Huckleberry Finn* begins as metafiction in reverse: a fictional character created by Mark Twain begins to speak about him.

The difficulties that theorists and critics encounter in dealing with complex metafictions are conceptual or ethical. "Fiction" is a pretense. But if its writers insistently call attention to the pretense, they are not pretending. Thus they elevate their discourse to the level of our own (serious, truthful) discourse. For the ethical critic, the writer's acknowledgment that he is just pretending is taken as evidence not of seriousness and sincerity but of frivolity, game-playing, literary high jinks. The writer's duty is to pretend seriously—not to say, seriously or playfully, that it's a pretense. What is at stake here is the whole system of traditional distinctions between reality and fiction on the one hand and truth and falsity on the other. To escape from the confusions that writers can create when they play with these terms, it is best to return to more solid ground—philosophy—in order to see whether it can tell us anything new about them.

What Is Fiction?

Modern answers to this question, like those in the past, are governed by the purposes of the writer. Philosophers no longer seem worried, as Plato was, about the threat that fiction can pose to reliable knowledge and good citizenship. But if they propose theories of truth, meaning, and reference, they must—like Plato—show why fiction, or reference to what does not exist, lacks all three. Once that is done, they have little need to say more about it. Critical theorists, on the other hand, usually set out to show why fiction can be of value, how it is structured, and how it functions in relation to other social institutions. L. B. Cebik classifies the main approaches to the analysis of fiction as epistemic, aesthetic, and heuristic; G. C. Prado divides them into the logical, aesthetic, and ethical. Recognizing that we must shift gears in moving from one kind of talk to another, we might best, like Socrates, go to the philosophers and ask not what is truth (a subject about which they disagree) but—what is fiction?

In the first half of the century, English and American philosophers tried to develop theories of knowledge that would serve as a bedrock foundation for the truths discovered in the natural sciences. For this endeavor, they needed a well-developed logic and an explanation of how, relying on sense data, words can be accurately linked to the world. "Fiction," in this context, meant a false connection between words and things, or reference to something that doesn't exist. Because of technical difficulties that arose in the development of this theory, more recent philosophers have conceived of truth not as a relationship between statements and reality but as an offshoot of the conventions involved in language use. Stating a true proposition is, after all, only one use of words. Most of our talk involves informing, persuading, asking, expressing attitudes, reminding or warning people, and the like. In *How to Do Things with Words*, the British philosopher J. L. Austin proposed what is now known as a "speech-act" theory of language, the purpose of which was to identify the conventions that make words meaningful in various situations. Aristotle had anticipated the development of such a theory in the *Poetics*, when he remarked that the art of rhetoric included study of "what is a command, a prayer, a statement, a threat, a question, an answer, and so forth" (19.4).

For the questions "what exists?" and "what is true?" Austin substituted "how are utterances meaningful? what do we achieve by using them? what conventions govern their uses?" From this point of view, fiction is not exactly false, nonexistent, or imaginary; it is just oddly empty. An utterance is *"in a peculiar way* hollow or void if said by an actor on stage, or if introduced into a poem, or spoken in soliloquy. . . . Language in such circumstances is in special ways—intelligibly— used not seriously, but in ways *parasitic* upon its normal use—ways which fall under the doctrine of etiolations of language" (Austin, 22; see also 104, 121). Though lovers of literature may be hurt by Austin's attitude toward fiction (which indicates how little has changed in philosophy since Plato), creative theorists found that his ideas suggest a new way of defining literature. It can be conceived as an imitation not of reality—in which case, questions of its truth or falsity loom large—but as an imitation of speech acts, ordinary uses of language.

Among the earliest critics to use Austin's theory for a new definition of fiction and literature were Richard Ohmann, Barbara Herrnstein Smith, and Mary Louise Pratt. In Ohmann's view, "Literary works are discourses with the usual illocutionary rules suspended, acts without consequences of the usual sort. . . . The writer puts out imitation speech acts *as if* they were being performed by someone" (97–98). This view works well for plays, which Ohmann used to illustrate it; what about novels? Smith (whose ideas are not simply derived from Austin's) points out that novels are usually imitations of nonfictive writing acts, such as the production of histories and biographies. Pratt goes one step further: since the stories people tell in everyday life are similar in structure and purpose to those in "great literature," she sees no reason to claim that the latter are "imitations." We are left with one category, narrative speech acts. This is a logical result of the theory. For if, as Smith argues, "the essential fictiveness of novels . . . is not to be discovered in the unreality of the characters, objects, and events alluded to, but in the unreality of the alludings themselves" (29), then fiction can be defined as *pretended* speech acts. The nonexistence or falsity of the things represented is irrelevant. By mutual agreement of writer and reader, the language means just what it usually means, except that in a peculiar sense it is empty, hollow, void (see Culler; Hutchison). But it is no more peculiar than a narrative told in conversation.

Some may think that this parasitic use of philosophy by literary theorists leaves us just where we started. What is the difference between saying that a writer really depicts a pretended world (the traditional view), or pretends to depict a world the reality of which doesn't matter? For those whose purpose is to show how literature is or can be used, the difference is this: the speech-act theory underwrites the claim that literary study can show us something significant—how language and society work (most social action involving the use of words). The shortcoming of this view, for those who are interested in other uses of literature, is that it makes no provision for the possibility that literature can do anything *other* than mimic reality. By sweeping questions about fiction (representation of what doesn't exist) under the carpet, this theory denies literature any unique function. It is what Prado calls a "cognitive pretender" theory, one suggesting that literature really shows or can teach something about life but has an odd way of doing it. Though this view may be true, it must establish and defend its truth in the arena where other disciplines claim that they can teach the same things better (rhetoric, philosophy, linguistics, and perhaps sociology and political science would be among the challengers).

Prado and Richard Rorty imply that this defense of literature is a mistake from the beginning. It springs from tacit acceptance of the entire philosophical tradition that has tried to guarantee the reliability of distinctions between truth and falsity, reality and imagination/fiction—a tradition that is itself doggedly committed to a mimetic picture view of the relation between concepts and the world. Rather than subjecting ourselves to this view or fighting it head on, Rorty suggests we simply forget it. We use language in all sorts of ways; so long as we understand each other and accomplish our purposes when talking about electrons, social practices, novels, or history, it is pointless and in fact peculiar to puzzle over the fact that Sherlock Holmes exists in some sense but doesn't really exist in another. If we accept fully the idea that the meaning of words depends on how they are used, the only questions remaining, should we care to study them, will concern the conventions involved in the varied language games that make up our discourse.

Rorty's view has proved increasingly popular with theorists who discuss literature from a philosophic perspective. Some of those who think that fictional narratives can best be understood through empirical study, rather than conceptual analysis, reject both his view and that of speech-act theorists. For Austin and his follower John Searle, there are no significant differences between ordinary and fictional language use, aside from the parasitic emptiness of the latter. What we do *in* saying something, or do *by* saying it can be determined by inspecting the mood of the sentence (declarative, imperative, interrogatory), the kinds of verbs used, the context, intentions, and results. When critics use speech-act theory to define literature, they naturally gravitate toward literary examples that use language exactly the same way it is used in conversation and non-fictional writing. This is "discourse," as Benveniste defined it (see chapter 5). But as we know from the theorists discussed in chapter 6, third-person fictive narration is *not* discourse; it has specific grammatical and referential features not found in plays, histories, poems, and autobiographies.

Lubomír and Doležel and Thomas Pavel (1981) maintain that the hollowness of fictional uses of language, as defined by philosophers, is full of things that the philosophers weren't looking for. When pre-

184

sented with the opening sentence of Hemingway's story—"It was now lunch time and they were all sitting . . ."—speech-act theorists see someone pretending to assert, or asserting a pretense. The systematic backward-shift of tenses ("was now") and the illegitimate use of the word "they" (which violates the rule that we must identify the reference of a pronoun before using it) are of no interest to them. Here a philosopher, P. F. Strawson, is of some help: the sentence does not *assert* the existence of "they"; it *presupposes* their existence. Reading on in the story, we find the narrator not just giving us fictional information but assuming the impossible ability to know what others are thinking, and conveying their thoughts in sentence forms never found in discourse. The full force of what Cebik and Prado say about the different standpoints from which theorists view fiction here strikes home: though speech-act theorists may explain meaning in discourse, they do not explain what one needs to know in order to understand the meaning of any third-person fictional narrative (Cebik, 119–26).

Doležel shows that the statements of a third-person narrator carry "*authentication authority*," and thus represent *narrative facts*; the speech acts of characters, who are subject to the rules proposed by Austin and Searle, do not have this reliability. Doležel, Pavel, and Félix Martínez-Bonati do not have the same view of fictional language, but they agree on this point. Regardless of how we decide to classify what the narrator writes, we rely on the narrator's assertions to decide whether the *characters* are telling the truth or lying, perceiving accurately or delusively, and the like. From this fact, several kinds of speculations emerge. What about first-person narratives and plays? Since they use only discourse, one must develop a different account of their fictionality (or accede to that provided by speech-act theory). Another line of thought is suggested by the ontological status of the facts posited in third-person narration. It leads toward discussion of "possible worlds" on the basis of the assumption that reality might, in other circumstances, be something different from what it is. Rather than discussing this possibility, I encourage readers to pursue it in the fascinating essays of Pavel.

Although possible-worlds theories have a disquieting tendency to populate the universe with imaginary objects, they can also provide insights into the ways in which realistic fiction recreates a world to all appearances like our own. When philosophers inspect fictional sentences, their training leads them to look for material objects (referents) and in particular for proper nouns: Andrew Chase-White never existed (fiction); Dublin exists (fact). Any attempt to understand what goes on in novels by making such discriminations is singularly unproductive. The effects.of realism depend not on the relative number of actual and imaginary objects named but on the "referential entailments" that link both together in accordance with what we know about the world. A sentence as simple as "All John's children are asleep" presupposes not only the existence of children of John, but of children as such, of men with proper names, patrilineal relationships, and sleep (Cebik, 137–38). A few sentences of a realistic novel are sufficient to evoke a dense network of such relationships without naming them. Given so many verifiable presuppositions (though the writer has not *asserted* them), it is no wonder that readers are less puzzled by proper names without reference (we expect them in fiction) than engrossed in reconstruction of a reality so like our own.

Having discussed empirical objections that critics have lodged against philosophic conceptions of fiction, I want to mention one current argument among philosophers about this subject before leaving it—as they have left it—unresolved. As Searle reveals, our philosophic tradition defines fiction beginning logically from the rule of truth. Since "any regulative rule at all contains within it the notion of a violation," and "lying consists in violating one of the regulative rules on the performance of speech acts," telling the truth and lying are logically born at the same moment (67). One might have thought that truth and falsity came into existence together but that serious sincerity and conscious deception involved a separate moment, since there is no necessary connection between the two pairs; but regardless of these logico-temporal connections, Searle makes it clear that they precede the birth of fiction. "Fiction is much more sophisticated than lying. To someone who did not understand the separate conventions of fiction it would seem that fiction is merely lying" (67). Fiction (pretending without intent to deceive) is, then, the child of lying, not the father of lies, as Plato said.

But what this system leaves unexplained is how to establish its first antithesis—the distinction between rules and no rules. Before one follows or violates them, one may decide not to play a language game; prior to that, one must be able to distinguish such games from other behavior. Creation of the rule-governed system entails a paradox. To state a rule, one must be able to suspend the rule. The sun shines; but to say "'the sun shines' is true" or "'the sun does not shine' is false," I must in some way suspend the truth, sincerity, and speech act of just *saying* the two phrases in order to "cite" them. To explain truth and falsity, I must give examples—pretend to assert, without actually asserting. That is fiction. My motive in establishing this system is to exclude falsity, lying, fiction; but I can't institute the system without reproducing, within it, the very errors I want to exclude.

The point at issue is a logical one, but as Searle's account shows, it is often presented in the form of a narrative that implies a particular history of man and truth. In taking issue with Searle, I rely on Gregory Bateson, who discovered playful pretending in the behavior of animals. What fascinated him was the necessary premise of the play: "'These actions, in which we now engage, do not denote what would be denoted by those actions which these actions denote.' The playful nip denotes the bite, but it does not denote what would be denoted by the bite" (180). Thus the animals enacted Russell's paradox (the nip is and is not a member of the set "bites") and *had* to enact it, if they wanted to play. Their behavior was metacommunicative, and it suggests the possibility that metafiction, in some form, is logically entailed in the distinction between fiction and fact.

Bateson and Jacques Derrida discuss the problem with more philosophic precision than I can claim or pretend. Both use a picture frame to illustrate the issues involved. The frame tells us to interpret everything inside it differently from the way we interpret what is outside it. But to establish this distinction, the frame must be part of the picture yet not part of the picture. To state the rule that separates picture from wall, or reality from fiction, one must violate the rule, just as Russell had to violate his rule for avoiding paradoxes in stating it (Bateson, 189; Waugh, 28–36).

What Is Narrative?

In light of the philosophic quest for truth, the connection between fiction and narrative becomes clearer. Just as fiction can be opposed to fact and truth, narrative is opposed to atemporal laws that depict what is, whether past or future. Any explanation that unfolds in time, with surprises during its progress and knowledge only through hindsight, is just a story, no matter how factual. What histories and biographies share with novels and romances is temporal organization. Treatises, essays, and nonnarrative poems at least organize their materials around thematic assertions; they accept the burden of saying what they mean, even if they fail to state the truth. But narratives, no matter how peppered with generalizations, always provide more information or food for thought than they have digested. Either they aren't worth interpreting (mere entertainment) or they engender too many interpretations. Their multiplicity of meaning is not a product of excessive critical ingenuity; from a hardheaded philosophic viewpoint, it is one of the necessary features of narrative as such (Cebik, 123–25). Peter Jones is surely correct when he argues, in *Philosophy and the*

Novel, that these meanings can come only from the reader. That is why reader-response criticism is particularly relevant to fictional narration.

In these circumstances, as Prado says, our need for a *theory* of narrative/fictional meaning is "a consequence of trying to square fiction, conceived of as 'nonreferential' but communicative, with discourse deemed communicative by virtue of being referential. . . . If fiction does enrich us, it must somehow operate as does descriptive, assertive discourse. That is, it must operate by presenting or 'intimating' content to which we can assent. The content must be propositional, if only indirectly or implicitly" (92, 88). To say fiction gives us insights, themes, or an enrichment of experience is not to deny what Prado says, because such meanings are ultimately propositional, no matter how attenuated.

How then do we extract or create meaning from narratives? The previous chapter treated a few of the many ways of doing so; most are variants of a process aptly described by Cebik (111–22). Narrative sentences presuppose many generalizations about human behavior. In order to understand what is happening in a story, we must connect the events, and do so by assuming the existence of general laws that interrelate them. Afterward, we may want to check some of these generalizations by comparing them with what we know of the world. Most of the presuppositions (hunger leads people to eat, there are hot days in the summer) go without saying; some generalizations may seem dubious to us; and still others may be difficult to construct because the events can be interpreted as examples of different lawlike connections.

I hope this explanation of the process seems so obvious as to be self-evident. To show that it can generate paradoxes or to discover fallacies in its assumptions, as many critics do, can be considered a worthwhile activity in that it prevents us from being held captive by a theory of narrative meaning that we know is, in some sense, inadequate. What is more important, I think, is to recognize that since the 1950s, theorists in other disciplines have been attempting to construct an *alternative* to this "covering-law model" that not only scientists but most literary critics accept as the only legitimate mode of explanation. Instead of imitating or jeering at the philosophic tradition which assumes that there is only one way to know truth, we might better participate in the formulation of a theory of narrative better able to account for human action.

The roots of this alternative tradition go back to the 1950s, when W. H. Dray and others showed that historical explanation was not an inadequate attempt to state timeless scientific generalizations but something altogether different. This movement, which I discussed briefly in chapter 3, is admirably summarized in Paul Ricoeur's *Time and Narrative*. But history was not the only discipline in which it was important. In philosophy, there was G. E. M. Anscombe's analysis of intention and a renewed interest in the philosophy of action; in sociology, Erving Goffman's "dramatistic" theory of behavior; in anthropology, Victor Turner's concept of "social dramas"; in experimental psychology, countless figures who have shifted the discipline from a concentration on rat conditioning to an emphasis on cognitive and linguistic processes; in psychoanalytic thought, Schafer, Spence, and others mentioned in the third chapter; and in the philosophy of science, where our claims to knowledge may always (for better or worse) be grounded, there is G. H. von Wright, whose discussions of explanation, understanding, and human action are too little known among humanists.

To this movement toward an understanding of narrative as a fundamental mode of explanation, one not reducible to the covering-law model, some literary theorists have contributed. Best known are the structuralists and semioticians; less known are those who toil away at complex theoretical projects in discourse analysis, or analyze the narrative conventions of remote tribes. Of recent attempts to see what other disciplines can contribute to an understanding of literature, Charles Altieri's *Act and Quality* is probably the best. The fear that many humanists have, on considering all this theoretical activity, is that if it were introduced into literary study, it would destroy what little we have left of humanism by turning it into a debased form of scientism. Such fears are understandable. But for those who are genuinely interested in fiction and narrative—which are *not* confined to novels and short stories written since the Renaissance but are fundamental to mass culture, social behavior, and our conceptions of our own lives—it is undesirable to shut the rest of life off from its connection with literature, or to sever any ties literary study might have with other disciplines.

So long as narrative theorists are willing to confine their interests and enthusiasms within the arena that traditional philosophy and scientific theory have staked out for them, they are assured a fairly secure place in the university and society. Provision is made for the study of narrative fiction. When they start to talk about fiction outside literature, or narrative in philosophy and science, even their colleagues may be disturbed. After all, the claim that we do somehow learn something important from literature, a claim we make and others grant, is based on our willingness to admit that we know the (accepted) differences between fact and fiction, between narrative and the truth that can, with care and imagination, perhaps be extrapolated from it.

To explore, even hypothetically, the possibility that narrative is something other than a defective version of the covering-law model might require us to suspend our claim that fictional narratives give us knowledge—in the traditional sense. Perhaps—probably, in view of their pervasiveness—they give us something else, or some other kind of knowledge; but the premise (we don't know what narrative is) precludes the presupposition that we know what knowledge narratives give us. What then is narrative?

Having reached the point at which a genuinely interesting book on narrative would begin, I can only say that I would never have undertaken a discussion of recent theories if I had known how to answer the question. An understanding of narrative is a project for the future—and not only the future of literary study. In *Time and Narrative*, Ricoeur has made a beginning, one many will find useful even as they dismantle and reconstruct it. Historians and philosophers have yet to realize how much they can learn from the literary theories of narrative I have discussed, and we have as much or more to learn from them. While waiting for the essays and books that give us the theory we are waiting for, we might best read narratives, for they will be the source of anything of value we might contribute to the subject.

Appendix

The Lover's Gift Regained

An oral version of this traditional folk motif was recorded in 1968 in South Carolina. The transcript of the tape recording reads as follows:

> This man was a bachelor and he lived in this big residential area, and this man and woman moved in beside him, you know, and the woman was real beautiful—she had long blonde hair and she was built real good, and every day she'd get out and cut the grass and all, in short shorts and tight pants and everything. Now the man, he said, "I just got to have a little bit of that." So finally one day he got up nerve to go over there and ask her. And he said, "Can I have a little bit of that?" And she said, "Well, tomorrow when there ain't nobody around, you come over here and bring fifty dollars and I'll let you have it." So the next day he went over there and took the money and he got it, you know, and it was real good, and he goes back home. And that night her husband come home and he says, "That man next door come over today?" (And she says, "Oh, I'll bet he knows.") She says, "Yeah, he come." He says, "He bring that fifty dollars?" (She says, "I know he knows now.") She says, "Yeah, he brought it." He says, "Well, I's just wondering, 'cause he come by my office this morning wanting to borrow fifty dollars and he said he'd bring it back to you today." [Moreland H. Hogan, Jr., "A New Analogue of the 'Shipman's Tale,'" *Chaucer Review* 5 (1970–71): 245–46]

Variants of the story were recorded in New York and California in the 1940s. Both involve a wife whose admirer gives her an expensive fur that she wants to keep. She pawns it or puts it in a railway station locker, then tells her husband that she has found a pawn ticket or key and asks him to go collect the item. In each case the husband returns with something that is worthless (see Ernest W. Baughman, *Type and Motif Index of the Folktales of England and North America* [The Hague: Mouton, 1966], 357).

Behind these jokes lie centuries of tale-telling in Europe and the Near and Far East. As J. W. Spargo shows in *The Lover's Gift Regained: Chaucer's "Shipman's Tale"* (Helsinki: Folklore Fellows Communications, 1930), the earliest versions appear in the *Shukasaptati* (Seventy Tales of a Parrot), a tenth-century "frame-tale" (a story that contains other stories, like the *Canterbury Tales*) written in Sanskrit. It tells of a man who takes a sixty-nine-day trip, leaving his wife in the care of his pet parrot. When the wife is tempted by prospective lovers, the parrot asks her to delay until he finishes telling a story. One story follows another, and several of them involve the "lover's gift regained" motif. In the thirty-fifth, a merchant visits the house of a grain merchant and finds that he is not at home. He induces the wife to yield her favors by giving her a ring. Regretting the bargain afterward, he finds her husband at the market and demands delivery of the grain that the wife said her husband would provide in exchange for the ring. Enraged, the husband has his son return to the house and obtain the ring in order to annul the business transaction.

By the fourteenth century, there were Persian and Arabic translations of the *Shukasaptati*, greatly altered; most of them did not contain the tales that employ this motif. But it does appear in twelfth-century Arabic stories which, as Spargo shows, continued to generate Middle Eastern variants into the nineteenth century. In Europe, the motif spread from fourteenth-century Italian versions to Germany, France, and England. Those that appeared in Boccaccio's *Decameron*, Chaucer's *Canterbury Tales*, and La Fontaine's *Fables* ("A femme avare galant escroc," taken directly from Boccaccio) are the best known. The synopsis of Boccaccio's version (the eighth day, first story) reads as follows: "Gulfardo borroweth of Guasparruolo certain monies, for which he hath agreed with his wife that he shall lie with her, and accordingly giveth them to her; then, in her presence, he telleth Guasparruolo that he gave them to her, and she confesseth it to be true."

In other variants, the lover accidentally damages something in the house, and then tells the husband that the wife has demanded money or a valuable article to pay for it, whereupon the husband makes the wife return the gift; or the lover, not knowing the husband, happens to tell him about the incident, and the husband confronts the wife with the facts; or the lover pays the wife with worthless goods or counterfeit money (Stith Thompson, *Motif-Index of Folk-Literature*, rev. ed. [Bloomington: Indiana University Press, 1955–58], 4:410–11).

There is some question in my mind as to whether these should be called variants of "the same tale," in that there are significant *structural* differences between them. If we decide to call them the same, we should be able to describe precisely what they have in common. Chaucer's extension of the anecdote—having the wife say that she will repay the husband in bed—seems to involve a significant statement about cultural practices, in the following sense: marriage, as a social and legal institution, defines husband and wife as one entity (credits and debts incurred by either party are their joint responsibility). But on the other hand, Western societies define marriage as a contract between two persons, and the wife is legally obliged (on pain of divorce) to grant only her husband's sexual desires. What Chaucer's version suggests is that marriage is based on an exchange of money for sexual favors, and if that is the case, the wife of the merchant in his tale is one of the first women to have stated the fact in literature. This tale, then, would make sense only in societies that define husband and wife as one legal entity, but also define marriage as a contract of exchange (money for sex) between two legal entities.

But these speculations do not capture the subtlety and vitality of Chaucer's story, retold in modern English by Sharon Robinson as follows.

Geoffrey Chaucer, "The Shipman's Tale"

There once lived in St. Denis a merchant whose wealth had earned him a reputation for wisdom. He had a wife of great beauty who was companionable and who loved revelry—a thing that costs more than all the good cheer and respect that men do such women at feasts and dances are worth. Such greetings and approving looks pass away as does a shadow on the wall. But woe to him who must pay for it all!— the foolish husband, who must deck us out richly for the sake of his own honor's sake, while we do a jolly dance. And if perchance he can't afford it, or won't put up with the expense because he thinks it a waste of money, then another man must pay, or lend us gold; and that is dangerous.

This worthy merchant kept a noble house, and owing to his generosity and his wife's fairness, he had a great many visitors there. But listen to my tale! Among all his guests, the great and the lowly, there was a monk both fair and bold—about thirty years old, I think—who was always visiting that place. This handsome young monk had become so well acquainted with the merchant since their first meeting that he was as much at home there as it was possible for a friend to be. And since both the monk and the merchant had been born in the same town, the monk claimed kinship with him; and as for the merchant, he had no objection to that, but was as happy as a bird at dawn, for it brought great joy to his heart. Thus were they knit in an everlasting alliance, and each of them promised the other lifelong brotherhood.

Dan John was generous, especially with money, and he was full of diligence to give pleasure and to spend his money. He never forgot to tip the lowliest page in the house, and when he visited, he gave some appropriate gift to the lord and then to all his household, according to their station. Because of this they were as glad at his arrival as a bird is when the sun comes up. But no more of such now, for this suffices. But it befell thus, that the merchant one day made ready to travel to the city of Bruges, to buy some goods. Therefore he sent a messenger to Paris, asking Dan John to come to St. Denis to divert himself with him and his wife for a day or two, before he went to Bruges.

This worthy monk of whom I tell you had permission of his abbot to go as he wished, because he was a man of great discretion, and also an outrider, whose job it was to oversee their granges and barns throughout a wide region; and so he came anon to St. Denis. Who was as welcome as my lord Dan John, our dear cousin, full of courtesy? With him he brought a jug of malmsey and another full of fine vernage, and game fowl for eating, as was his custom. And thus I leave them to eat and drink and disport for a day or two, this merchant and this monk.

On the third day this merchant rose up and soberly considered his needs, and went up into his counting-house to make a reckoning of how things stood with him that year, and how he had spent his holdings, and whether he had gained or not. He laid his ledgers and his many money-bags before him on the counting board; full rich was his treasure and his hoard, and thus he shut tight his counting-room door, for he wished not to be bothered in his accounting for a time. And thus he sat till it was past nine in the morning.

Dan John had also risen in the morning, and walked to and fro in the garden, and said his devotions reverently.

This good wife then came walking privily into the garden where he softly trod, and greeted him as she had often done before. A maid-child accompanied her, whom she ruled and guided as she would, for the maid was under her rod.

"Oh my dear cousin, Dan John," she said, "what ails you that you rise so early?"

"Niece," he said, "five hours of sleep a night ought to suffice, unless one is a tired old soul, like these married men who lie and cower, as a weary hare sits in her burrow, all distraught by hounds. But dear niece, why are you so pale? I think, certainly, that our good man has worked you since nightfall, so that you need to rest soon." And with that, he laughed full merrily, and blushed at his own thoughts.

This fair woman began to shake her head, and spoke thus: "Aye, God knows," she said, "no, no, my cousin, that's not the way it is with me; for by the God who gave me soul and life, there is no woman in the realm of France who has less desire for that sorry game. For I may sing 'Alas' and 'welaway that I was ever born,' but to no one," said she, "dare I reveal my problem—wherefore I think I may leave this land, or else make an end of myself, so full am I of dread and care."

This monk began to stare at the woman, and said, "Alas, my niece, God forbid that for any sorrow or any dread you should destroy yourself! But tell me of your sorrow—perhaps I may give council or help for your troubles; therefore tell me all your problem, for it shall be secret. For on my breviary I swear that never in my life, for neither love nor loathing, shall I betray any confidence of yours."

"The same again I vow to you," she said. "By God and by this breviary I swear to you, though men tear me to pieces, I will never—even if I go to Hell—betray a word of anything you tell me. I say this not out of kinship, but truly for the love and trust there is between us." Thus were they sworn, whereupon they kissed, and each of them spoke freely to the other. "Cousin," said she, "if I had time, as I don't have now—especially in this place—then I would tell a tale of my life, what I have suffered since I became my husband's wife, albeit he is your cousin."

"Nay," said this monk, "by God and St. Martin, he is no more my kin than is the leaf hanging from this tree. I call him thus, by St. Denis of France, to have more reason to know you, whom I have loved especially of all women, truly, This I swear to you upon my vows. Tell me your grief, and make haste, and then go on your way, lest he come down."

"My dear love," said she, "oh my Dan John, much rather would I hide this secret, but out it must; I can bear it no longer. To me my husband is the worst man there ever was since the world began. But since I am a wife, it becomes me not to tell anyone of our private matters, neither in bed nor out. God of His grace forbid that I should tell it! A wife should say nothing but good of her husband, that I know, but to you I shall tell just this: So help me God, he isn't worth in any way the value of a fly. But what grieves me most of all is his stinginess. You know as well as I that all women naturally desire six things: They want their husbands to be bold, and wise, and rich, and generous with those riches, and obedient to their wives, and lusty in bed. But by the very Lord that bled for us, to array myself for his honor, I must pay one hundred francs by next Sunday, else I am lost. I'd rather I had never ever been born than that I be caught in a scandal or disgrace. And if my husband should discover it, I am lost. Therefore I pray you, lend me this sum, or else I must die. Dan John, I say, lend me these hundred francs. By God, I will not fail in gratitude if you do as I ask. For on a certain day I will repay you, and do you whatever pleasure and service I may do, just as you please. And if I don't, may God take on me vengeance as foul as Ganelon of France received."

This good monk answered thus: "Now, truly, my own dear lady," he said, "I have such great pity for you that I swear to you and plight you my troth, that when your husband has gone to Flanders, I will deliver you from this care, for I will bring you a hundred francs." And with that, he caught her by the flanks and hugged her hard, and kissed her again and again. "Go quietly on your way now," he said, "and let us dine as soon as we can, for by my dial it's nine o'clock. Go now, and be as true as I shall be."

"God forbid it should be otherwise," she said, and she went forth as jolly as a magpie, and bade the cooks to hurry so that the men might dine. Then up to her husband went this woman, and knocked boldly at his counting-house door.

"Who's there?" he asked.

"By St. Peter, it is I," said she. "What, sir, how long would you fast? How long will you reckon and figure your sums, and your books? The devil take a share of all such reckonings! You have enough, by God, of His gift. Come down today, and let your money bags be; are you not ashamed that Dan John shall keep a dreary fast this whole day long? What, let us hear a mass, and then go dine."

"Wife," said this man, "you can hardly understand what complicated business we merchants have. For, God save me, and by that lord named St. Ive, out of twelve of us businessmen, scarcely two shall thrive continually into old age. We must make good cheer and put up a good front, and go forth thus into the world, and keep our business affairs secret till we are dead, or pretend to go on a pilgrimage, or disappear elsewhere. And therefore I must carefully consider this strange world, for always we must stand in dread of accident and fortune in our trading.

"Tomorrow I will go to Flanders at daybreak, and will return as quickly as I can—for which, my dear wife, I beseech you, be courteous and meek toward every person, and be careful to protect our property, and govern our house well and honestly. You have enough, in every manner and kind, to provide for a thrifty household. You want for neither clothing nor food, and you shall not lack silver in your purse."

And with that he shut the door to his counting room, and down he went; no longer would be delay. But hastily a mass was said, and speedily the tables were laid, and quickly they hurried to dinner, and the merchant fed the monk richly.

After dinner, Dan John soberly took the merchant aside, and spoke privately to him, thus: "Cousin, I see it stands so that you will go to Bruges. God and St. Augustine speed and guide you! I pray you, cousin, be careful as you go. Be moderate in your diet, especially in this heat. Neither of us needs exotic fare. Farewell cousin; may God keep you from care. And, day or night, if there is anything in my power that you would have me do in any way, it shall be done exactly as you say. One thing, before you go, if it may be: I pray you to lend me a hundred francs for a week or two, for I must buy certain beasts to stock a farm of ours; God help me, I wish it were yours! I shall not fail my day, you may be sure, not for a thousand francs, a mile away. But let this thing be a secret, I pray you, for I must buy these beasts tonight. And farewell now, my own dear cousin; many thanks for your generosity and friendliness."

This good merchant answered courteously, at once, and said, "Oh my cousin, Dan John, certainly this is a small request. My gold is yours whenever you wish it, and not only my gold, but my goods as well. Take what you will; God forbid that you should spare.

"But there's one thing about merchants—you know it well enough: their money is their plow; our credit is good when our reputation prospers, but it is no jest to be without gold. Pay it back at your ease; I will full gladly please you as best I can."

He fetched these hundred francs anon, and took them privately to Dan John. No one in all the world knew of this loan, save this merchant and Dan John themselves. They drink, and talk, and ramble about for a while, and so divert themselves until Dan John rides off to his abbey. The morrow came, and this merchant rides forth toward Flanders; his apprentice guides him well until he came merrily into Bruges. Now this merchant goes quickly and diligently about his business, buying and borrowing. He neither gambles nor dances, but, shortly to tell, carries out a merchant's business—and there I let him be.

The Sunday after the merchant had left, Dan John is come again to St. Denis, with head and beard all freshly shaved. In all the house there was not a knave so small, nor anyone else, who wasn't delighted that Dan John had returned. And, to get right to the point, this fair wife agreed that, in return for these hundred francs, Dan John should have her, flat on her back, in his arms all night; and this agreement was carried out in deed. In mirth all night they led a busy life till it was day, when Dan John went his way and bade the household, "Farewell, have a good day"; for none of them, nor anyone in the town, suspects Dan John at all. And he rides forth, home to his abbey, or wherever he pleased; I'll say no more of him.

When the fair had ended, this merchant returned to St. Denis, and makes great cheer with his wife, and tells her that merchandise is so expensive that he must borrow some money, for he was bound by a contract to pay twenty thousand shields right away. And so he went to Paris, to borrow some francs from friends he had there, and some francs he took with him. And when he arrived in Paris, out of great friendship and affection he went first to meet Dan John—to amuse himself, not to ask or borrow money of him, but to find out about his welfare, and to tell him of his trading—as friends do when they meet. Dan John greeted him merrily, and the merchant told him in great detail what good purchases he had made on all his goods, and how well his business had gone—except that he had to borrow money as best he could, and then he could have some time for joy and rest.

Dan John answered, "To be sure, I am happy that you have returned home in good health. And if I were rich, as I hope for eternal bliss, you should not want for twenty thousand shields; for you so generously lent me gold. And in so far as I am able, I thank you, by God and by St. James. But nonetheless, I took unto our lady, your wife, at home, the self-same gold upon your bench; she knows it well, surely, by certain tokens that I can tell you of. Now, by your leave, I may stay no longer. Our abbot wishes to leave this town anon, and I must go with him. Greet our lady, my own sweet niece, for me, and farewell, dear cousin, tell we meet."

This merchant, who was very prudent and wise, has borrowed some money on credit and paid that sum of gold into the hands of some Lombards in Paris, and got his bond from them; and home he goes as merry as a poppinjay, for he knew well that, as things stood, he would earn a profit on that trip a thousand francs above his expenses.

His wife met him eagerly at the gate, as she was long accustomed to do, and all that night they spent in mirth, for he was rich and cleanly out of debt. When it was day, this merchant began to embrace his wife anew, and kissed her on her face, and up he goes and makes it fairly rough.

"No more," she said, "by God, you've had enough!" And wantonly she played with him again, till at last the merchant spoke thus: "By God," he said, "I am a little angry with you, my wife, although it grieves me to be so. And do you know why? By God, I think you've made a bit of coolness between me and my cousin, Dan John. You should have warned me, before I went, that he had paid you a hundred francs, and had a token of it. He felt badly treated because I spoke to him of borrowing money—I could tell it by his face. But nonetheless, by God our heavenly King, I never thought of asking anything of him. I pray you, wife, do so no more; always tell me before I leave you if any debtor has paid you in my absence, lest through your negligence I might ask him for something that he's already paid."

This wife was not frightened, but boldly and quickly said: "By the Blessed Virgin, I defy the false monk, Dan John! I care nothing about his tokens. He brought me some money, that I know well. What! Evil luck on his monk's snout, for, God knows, I believed absolutely that he had given it to me because of you, to use for my own honor and advantage, out of kinship and the good cheer that he has oftimes enjoyed here. But since I see I am in trouble, I will answer you to the point: you have slacker debtors than I! For I will pay you well, and speedily, from day to day; and if I should fail, I am your wife—mark it on my tally and I shall pay as soon as I can. For, by my troth, I've spent every bit on my clothing, and haven't wasted a bit. And because I have spent it so well, for your honor, for God's sake, I say, be not angry—but let us laugh and play. You shall have my jolly body for a pledge. By God, I will not pay you except in bed! Forgive me for it, my own dear spouse. Turn to me, and make better cheer."

This merchant saw that there was no help, and that it was foolhardy to chide because the thing could not be changed. "Now, wife," he said, "I forgive you, but by your life, stop being such a spendthrift. Take better care of my property, I charge you."

Thus ends my tale now, and may God send us fair tales enough until our lives shall end!

Katherine Mansfield, "Bliss"

Although Bertha Young was thirty she still had moments like this when she wanted to run instead of walk, to take dancing steps on and off the pavement, to bowl a hoop, to throw something up in the air and catch it again, or to stand still and laugh at—nothing—at nothing, simply.

What can you do if you are thirty and, turning the corner of your own street, you are overcome, suddenly, by a feeling of bliss—absolute bliss!—as though you'd suddenly swallowed a bright piece of that late afternoon sun and it burned in your bosom, sending out a little shower of sparks into every particle, into every finger and toe? . . .

Oh, is there no way you can express it without being "drunk and disorderly"? How idiotic civilization is! Why be given a body if you have to keep it shut up in a case like a rare, rare fiddle?

"No, that about the fiddle is not quite what I mean," she thought, running up the steps and feeling in her bag for the key—she'd forgotten it, as usual—and rattling the letter-box. "It's not what I mean, because—Thank you, Mary"—she went into the hall. "Is nurse back?"

"Yes, M'm."

"And has the fruit come?"

"Yes, M'm. Everything's come."

"Bring the fruit up to the dining-room, will you? I'll arrange it before I go upstairs."

It was dusky in the dining-room, and quite chilly. But all the same Bertha threw off her coat; she could not bear the tight clasp of it another moment, and the cold air fell on her arms.

But in her bosom there was still that bright glowing place—that shower of little sparks coming from it. It was almost unbearable. She hardly dared to breathe for fear of fanning it higher, and yet she breathed deeply, deeply. She hardly dared to look into the cold mirror—but she did look, and it gave her back a woman, radiant, with smiling, trembling lips, with big, dark eyes and an air of listening, waiting for something . . . divine to happen . . . that she knew must happen . . . infallibly.

Mary brought in the fruit on a tray and with it a glass bowl, and a blue dish, very lovely, with a strange sheen on it as though it had been dipped in milk.

"Shall I turn on the light, M'm?"

"No, thank you, I can see quite well."

There were tangerines and apples stained with strawberry pink.

Some yellow pears, smooth as silk, some white grapes covered with a silver bloom and a big cluster of purple ones. These last she had bought to tone in with the new dining-room carpet. Yes, that did sound rather far-fetched and absurd, but it was really why she had bought them. She had thought in the shop: "I must have some purple ones to bring the carpet up to the table." And it had seemed quite sense at the time.

When she had finished with them and had made two pyramids of these bright round shapes, she stood away from the table to get the effect—and it really was most curious. For the dark table seemed to melt into the dusky light and the glass dish and the blue bowl to float in the air. This, of course in her present mood, was so incredibly beautiful. . . . She began to laugh.

"No, no. I'm getting hysterical." And she seized her bag and coat and ran upstairs to the nursery.

Nurse sat at a low table giving Little B her supper after her bath. The baby had on a white flannel gown and a blue woollen jacket, and her dark, fine hair was brushed up into a funny little peak. She looked up when she saw her mother and began to jump.

"Now, my lovely, eat it up like a good girl," said Nurse, setting her lips in a way that Bertha knew, and that meant she had come into the nursery at another wrong moment.

"Has she been good, Nanny?"

"She's been a little sweet all the afternoon," whispered Nanny. "We went to the park and I sat down on a chair and took her out of the pram and a big dog came along and put its head on my knee and she clutched its ear, tugged it. Oh, you should have seen her."

Bertha wanted to ask if it wasn't rather dangerous to let her clutch at a strange dog's ear. But she did not dare to. She stood watching them, her hands by her side, like the poor little girl in front of the rich little girl with the doll.

The baby looked up at her again, stared, and then smiled so charmingly that Bertha couldn't help crying:

"Oh, Nanny, do let me finish giving her her supper while you put the bath things away."

"Well, M'm, she oughtn't to be changed hands while she's eating," said Nanny, still whispering. "It unsettles her; it's very likely to upset her."

How absurd it was. Why have a baby if it has to be kept—not in a case like a rare, rare fiddle—but in another woman's arms?

"Oh, I must!" said she.

Very offended, Nanny handed her over.

"Now, don't excite her after her supper. You know you do, M'm. And I have such a time with her after!"

Thank heaven! Nanny went out of the room with the bath towels.

"Now I've got you to myself, my little precious," said Bertha, as the baby leaned against her.

She ate delightfully, holding up her lips for the spoon and then waving her hands. Sometimes she wouldn't let the spoon go; and sometimes, just as Bertha had filled it, she waved it away to the four winds.

When the soup was finished Bertha turned round to the fire.

"You're nice—you're very nice!" said she, kissing her warm baby. "I'm fond of you. I like you."

And, indeed, she loved Little B so much—her neck as she bent forward, her exquisite toes as they shone transparent in the firelight—that all her feeling of bliss came back again, and again she didn't know how to express it—what to do with it.

"You're wanted on the telephone," said Nanny, coming back in triumph and seizing *her* Little B.

Down she flew. It was Harry.

"Oh, is that you, Ber? Look here. I'll be late. I'll take a taxi and come along as quickly as I can, but get dinner put back ten minutes—will you? All right?"

"Yes, perfectly. Oh, Harry!"

"Yes?"

What had she to say? She'd nothing to say. She only wanted to get in touch with him for a moment. She couldn't absurdly cry: "Hasn't it been a divine day!"

"What is it?" rapped out the little voice.

"Nothing, *Entendu*," said Bertha, and hung up the receiver, thinking how more than idiotic civilization was.

They had people coming to dinner. The Norman Knights—a very sound couple—he was about to start a theatre, and she was awfully keen on interior decoration, a young man, Eddie Warren, who had just published a little book of poems and whom everybody was asking to dine, and a "find" of Bertha's called Pearl Fulton. What Miss Fulton did, Bertha didn't know. They had met at the club and Bertha had fallen in love with her, as she always did fall in love with beautiful women who had something strange about them.

The provoking thing was that, though they had been about together and met a number of times and really talked, Bertha couldn't yet make her out. Up to a certain point Miss Fulton was rarely, wonderfully frank, but the certain point was there, and beyond that she would not go.

Was there anything beyond it? Harry said "No." Voted her dullish, and "cold like all blond women, with a touch, perhaps, of anæmia of the brain." But Bertha wouldn't agree with him; not yet, at any rate.

"No, the way she has of sitting with her head a little on one side, and smiling, has something behind it, Harry, and I must find out what that something is."

"Most likely it's a good stomach," answered Harry.

He made a point of catching Bertha's heels with replies of that kind . . . "liver frozen, my dear girl," or "pure flatulence," or "kidney disease," . . . and so on. For some strange reason Bertha liked this, and almost admired it in him very much.

She went into the drawing-room and lighted the fire; then, picking up the cushions, one by one, that Mary had disposed so carefully, she threw them back on to the chairs and the couches. That made all the difference; the room came alive at once. As she was about to throw the last one she surprised herself by suddenly hugging it to her, passionately, passionately. But it did not put out the fire in her bosom. Oh, on the contrary!

The windows of the drawing-room opened on to a balcony overlooking the garden. At the far end, against the wall, there was a tall, slender pear tree in fullest, richest bloom; it stood perfect, as though becalmed against the jade-green sky. Bertha couldn't help feeling, even from this distance, that it had not a single bud or a faded petal. Down below, in the garden beds, the red and yellow tulips, heavy with flowers, seemed to lean upon the dusk. A grey cat, dragging its belly, crept across the lawn, and a black one, its shadow, trailed after. The sight of them, so intent and so quick, gave Bertha a curious shiver.

"What creepy things cats are!" she stammered, and she turned away from the window and began walking up and down. . . .

How strong the jonquils smelled in the warm room. Too strong? Oh, no. And yet, as though overcome, she flung down on a couch and pressed her hands to her eyes.

"I'm too happy—too happy!" she murmured.

And she seemed to see on her eyelids the lovely pear tree with its wide open blossoms as a symbol of her own life.

Really—really—she had everything. She was young. Harry and she were as much in love as ever, and they got on together splendidly and were really good pals. She had an adorable baby. They didn't have to worry about money. They had this absolutely satisfactory house and garden. And friends—modern, thrilling friends, writers and painters and poets or people keen on social questions—just the kind of friends they wanted. And then there were books, and there was music, and she had found a wonderful little dressmaker, and they were going abroad in the summer, and their new cook made the most superb omelettes. . . .

"I'm absurd. Absurd!" She sat up; but she felt quite dizzy, quite drunk. It must have been the spring.

Yes, it was the spring. Now she was so tired she could not drag herself upstairs to dress.

A white dress, a string of jade beads, green shoes and stockings. It wasn't intentional. She had thought of this scheme hours before she stood at the drawing-room window.

Her petals rustled softly into the hall, and she kissed Mrs. Norman Knight, who was taking off the most amusing orange coat with a procession of black monkeys round the hem and up the fronts.

". . . Why! Why! Why is the middle-class so stodgy—so utterly without a sense of humour! My dear, it's only by a fluke that I am here at all—Norman being the protective fluke. For my darling monkeys so upset the train that it rose to a man and simply ate me with its eyes. Didn't laugh—wasn't amused—that I should have loved. No, just stared—and bored me through and through."

"But the cream of it was," said Norman, pressing a large tortoise-shell-rimmed monocle into his eye, "you don't mind me telling this, Face, do you?" (In their home and among their friends they called each other Face and Mug.) "The cream of it was when she, being full fed, turned to the woman beside her and said: 'Haven't you ever seen a monkey before?'"

"Oh, yes!" Mrs. Norman Knight joined in the laughter. "Wasn't that too absolutely creamy?"

And a funnier thing still was that now her coat was off she did look like a very intelligent monkey—who had even made that yellow silk dress out of scraped banana skins. And her amber ear-rings; they were like little dangling nuts.

"This is a sad, sad fall!" said Mug, pausing in front of Little B's perambulator. "When the perambulator comes into the hall—" and he waved the rest of the quotation away.

The bell rang. It was lean, pale Eddie Warren (as usual) in a state of acute distress.

"It *is* the right house, *isn't* it?" he pleaded.

"Oh, I think so—I hope so," said Bertha brightly.

"I have had such a *dreadful* experience with a taxi-man; he was *most* sinister. I couldn't get him to *stop*. The *more* I knocked and called the *faster* he went. And *in* the moonlight this *bizarre* figure with the *flattened* head *crouching* over the *lit-tle* wheel. . . ."

He shuddered, taking off an immense white, silk scarf. Bertha noticed that his socks were white too—most charming.

"But how dreadful!" she cried.

"Yes, it really was," said Eddie, following her into the drawing-room. "I saw myself *driving* through Eternity in a *timeless* taxi."

He knew the Norman Knights. In fact, he was going to write a play for N. K. when the theatre scheme came off.

"Well, Warren, how's the play?" said Norman Knight, dropping his monocle and giving his eye a moment in which to rise to the surface before it was screwed down again.

And Mrs. Norman Knight: "Oh, Mr. Warren, what happy socks!"

"I *am* so glad you like them," said he, staring at his feet. "They seem to have got so *much* whiter since the moon rose." And he turned his lean sorrowful young face to Bertha. "There *is* a moon, you know."

She wanted to cry: "I am sure there is—often—often!"

He really was a most attractive person. But so was Face, crouched before the fire in her banana skins, and so was Mug, smoking a cigarette and saying as he flicked the ash: "Why doth the bridegroom tarry?"

"There he is, now."

Bang went the front door open and shut. Harry shouted: "Hullo, you people. Down in five minutes." And they heard him swarm up the stairs. Bertha couldn't help smiling; she knew how he loved doing things at high pressure. What, after all, did an extra five minutes matter? But he would pretend to himself that they mattered beyond measure. And then he would make a great point of coming into the drawing-room, extravagantly cool and collected.

Harry had such a zest for life. Oh, how she appreciated it in him. And his passion for fighting—for seeking in everything that came up against him another test of his power and of his courage—that, too, she understood. Even when it made him just occasionally, to other people, who didn't know him well, a little ridiculous perhaps. . . . For there were moments when he rushed into battle where no battle was. . . . She talked and laughed and positively forgot until he had come in (just as she had imagined) that Pearl Fulton had not turned up.

"I wonder if Miss Fulton has forgotten?"

"I expect so," said Harry. "Is she on the 'phone?"

"Ah! There's a taxi now." And Bertha smiled with that little air of proprietorship that she always assumed while her women finds were new and mysterious. "She lives in taxis."

"She'll run to fat if she does," said Harry coolly, ringing the bell for dinner. "Frightful danger for blond women."

"Harry—don't," warned Bertha, laughing up at him.

Came another tiny moment, while they waited, laughing and talking, just a trifle too much at their ease, a trifle too unaware. And then Miss Fulton, all in silver, with a silver fillet binding her pale blond hair, came in smiling, her head a little on one side.

"Am I late?"

"No, not at all," said Bertha. "Come along." And she took her arm and they moved into the dining-room.

What was there in the touch of that cool arm that could fan— fan—start blazing—blazing—the fire of bliss that Bertha did not know what to do with?

Miss Fulton did not look at her; but then she seldom did look at people directly. Her heavy eyelids lay upon her eyes and the strange half smile came and went upon her lips as though she lived by listening rather than seeing. But Bertha knew, suddenly, as if the longest, most intimate look had passed between them—as if they had said to each other: "You, too?"—that Pearl Fulton, stirring the beautiful red soup in the grey plate, was feeling just what she was feeling.

And the others? Face and Mug, Eddie and Harry, their spoons rising and falling—dabbing their lips with their napkins, crumbling bread, fiddling with the forks and glasses and talking.

"I met her at the Alpha show—the weirdest little person. She'd not only cut off her hair, but she seemed to have taken a dreadfully good snip off her legs and arms and her neck and her poor little nose as well."

"Isn't she very *liée* with Michael Oat?"

"The man who wrote *Love in False Teeth*?"

"He wants to write a play for me. One act. One man. Decides to commit suicide. Gives all the reasons why he should and why he shouldn't. And just as he has made up his mind either to do it or not to do it—curtain. Not half a bad idea."

"What's he going to call it—'Stomach Trouble'?"

"I *think* I've come across the *same* idea in a lit-tle French review, *quite* unknown in England."

No, they didn't share it. They were dears—dears—and she loved having them there, at her table, and giving them delicious food and wine. In fact, she longed to tell them how delightful they were, and what a decorative group they made, how they seemed to set one another off and how they reminded her of a play by Tchekof!

Harry was enjoying his dinner. It was part of his—well, not his nature, exactly, and certainly not his pose—his—something or other—to talk about food and to glory in his "shameless passion for the white flesh of the lobster" and "the green of pistachio ices—green and cold like the eyelids of Egyptian dancers."

When he looked up at her and said: "Bertha, this is a very admirable *soufflée!*" she almost could have wept with child-like pleasure.

Oh, why did she feel so tender towards the whole world tonight? Everything was good—was right. All that happened seemed to fill again her brimming cup of bliss.

And still, in the back of her mind, there was the pear tree. It would be silver now, in the light of poor dear Eddie's moon, silver as Miss Fulton, who sat there turning a tangerine in her slender fingers that were so pale a light seemed to come from them.

What she simply couldn't make out—what was miraculous—was how she should have guessed Miss Fulton's mood so exactly and so instantly. For she never doubted for a moment that she was right, and yet what had she to go on? Less than nothing.

"I believe this does happen very, very rarely between women. Never between men," thought Bertha. "But while I am making the coffee in the drawing-room perhaps she will 'give a sign.'"

What she meant by that she did not know, and what would happen after that she could not imagine.

While she thought like this she saw herself talking and laughing. She had to talk because of her desire to laugh.

"I must laugh or die."

But when she noticed Face's funny little habit of tucking something down the front of her bodice—as if she kept a tiny, secret hoard of nuts there, too—Bertha had to dig her nails into her hands—so as not to laugh too much.

It was over at last. And: "Come and see my new coffee machine," said Bertha.

"We only have a new coffee machine once a fortnight," said Harry. Face took her arm this time; Miss Fulton bent her head and followed after.

The fire had died down in the drawing-room to a red, flickering "nest of baby phœnixes," said Face.

"Don't turn up the light for a moment. It is so lovely." And down she crouched by the fire again. She was always cold . . . "without her little red flannel jacket, of course," thought Bertha.

At that moment Miss Fulton "gave the sign."

"Have you a garden?" said the cool, sleepy voice.

This was so exquisite on her part that all Bertha could do was to obey. She crossed the room, pulled the curtains apart, and opened those long windows.

"There!" she breathed.

And the two women stood side by side looking at the slender, flowering tree. Although it was so still it seemed, like the flame of a candle, to stretch up, to point, to quiver in the bright air, to grow taller and taller as they gazed—almost to touch the rim of the round, silver moon.

How long did they stand there? Both, as it were, caught in that circle of unearthly light, understanding each other perfectly, creatures of another world, and wondering what they were to do in this one with all this blissful treasure that burned in their bosoms and dropped, in silver flowers, from their hair and hands?

For ever—for a moment? And did Miss Fulton murmur: "Yes. Just *that*." Or did Bertha dream it?

Then the light was snapped on and Face made the coffee and Harry said: "My dear Mrs. Knight, don't ask me about my baby. I never see her. I shan't feel the slightest interest in her until she has a lover," and Mug took his eye out of the conservatory for a moment and then put it under glass again and Eddie Warren drank his coffee and set down the cup with a face of anguish as though he had drunk and seen the spider.

"What I want to do is to give the young men a show. I believe London is simply teeming with first-chop, unwritten plays. What I want to say to 'em is: 'Here's the theatre. Fire ahead.'"

"You know, my dear, I am going to decorate a room for the Jacob Nathans. Oh, I am so tempted to do a fried-fish scheme, with the backs of the chairs shaped like frying pans and lovely chip potatoes embroidered all over the curtains."

"The trouble with our young writing men is that they are still too romantic. You can't put out to sea without being seasick and wanting a basin. Well, why won't they have the courage of those basins?"

"A *dreadful* poem about a *girl* who was *violated* by a beggar *without* a nose in a lit-tle wood. . . ."

Miss Fulton sank into the lowest, deepest chair and Harry handed round the cigarettes.

From the way he stood in front of her shaking the silver box and saying abruptly: "Egyptian? Turkish? Virginian? They're all mixed up," Bertha realized that she not only bored him; he really disliked her. And she decided from the way Miss Fulton said: "No, thank you, I won't smoke," that she felt it, too, and was hurt.

"Oh, Harry, don't dislike her. You are quite wrong about her. She's wonderful, wonderful. And, besides, how can you feel so differently about someone who means so much to me. I shall try to tell you when we are in bed to-night what has been happening. What she and I have shared."

At those last words something strange and almost terrifying darted into Bertha's mind. And this something blind and smiling whispered to her: "Soon these people will go. The house will be quiet—quiet. The lights will be out. And you and he will be alone together in the dark room—the warm bed. . . ."

She jumped up from her chair and ran over to the piano.

"What a pity someone does not play!" she cried. "What a pity some-body does not play."

For the first time in her life Bertha Young desired her husband.

Oh, she'd loved him—she'd been in love with him, of course, in every other way, but just not in that way. And, equally, of course, she'd understood that he was different. They'd discussed it so often. It had worried her dreadfully at first to find that she was so cold, but after a time it had not seemed to matter. They were so frank with each other—such good pals. That was the best of being modern.

But now—ardently! ardently! The word ached in her ardent body! Was this what that feeling of bliss had been leading up to? But then then—

"My dear," said Mrs. Norman Knight, "you know our shame. We are the victims of time and train. We live in Hampstead. It's been so nice."

"I'll come with you into the hall," said Bertha. "I loved having you. But you must not miss the last train. That's so awful, isn't it?"

"Have a whisky, Knight, before you go?" called Harry.

"No, thanks, old chap."

Bertha squeezed his hand for that as she shook it.

"Good night, good-bye," she cried from the top steps, feeling that this self of hers was taking leave of them for ever.

When she got back into the drawing-room the others were on the move.

". . . Then you can come part of the way in my taxi."

"I shall be *so* thankful *not* to have to face *another* drive *alone* after my *dreadful* experience."

"You can get a taxi at the rank just at the end of the street. You won't have to walk more than a few yards."

"That's a comfort. I'll go and put on my coat."

Miss Fulton moved towards the hall and Bertha was following when Harry almost pushed past.

"Let me help you."

Bertha knew that he was repenting his rudeness—she let him go. What a boy he was in some ways—so impulsive—so—simple.

And Eddie and she were left by the fire.

"I *wonder* if you have seen Bilks' *new* poem called *Table d'Hôte*," said Eddie softly. "It's *so* wonderful. In the last Anthology. Have you got a copy? I'd *so* like to *show* it to you. It begins with an *incredibly* beautiful line: 'Why Must it Always be Tomato Soup?' "

"Yes," said Bertha. And she moved noiselessly to a table opposite the drawing-room door and Eddie glided noiselessly after her. She picked up the little book and gave it to him; they had not made a sound.

While he looked it up she turned her head towards the hall. And she saw . . . Harry with Miss Fulton's coat in his arms and Miss Fulton with her back turned to him and her head bent. He tossed the coat away, put his hands on her shoulders and turned her violently to him. His lips said: "I adore you," and Miss Fulton laid her moonbeam fingers on his cheeks and smiled her sleepy smile. Harry's nostrils quivered; his lips curled back in a hideous grin while he whispered: "To-morrow," and with her eyelids Miss Fulton said: "Yes."

"Here it is," said Eddie. " 'Why Must it Always be Tomato Soup?' It's so *deeply* true, don't you feel? Tomato soup is so *dreadfully* eternal."

"If you prefer," said Harry's voice, very loud, from the hall, "I can phone you a cab to come to the door."

"Oh, no. It's not necessary," said Miss Fulton, and she came up to Bertha and gave her the slender fingers to hold.

"Good-bye. Thank you so much."

"Good-bye," said Bertha.

Miss Fulton held her hand a moment longer.

"Your lovely pear tree!" she murmured.

And then she was gone, with Eddie following, like the black cat following the grey cat.

"I'll shut up shop," said Harry, extravagantly cool and collected.

"Your lovely pear tree—pear tree—pear tree!"

Bertha simply ran over to the long windows.

"Oh, what is going to happen now?" she cried.

But the pear tree was as lovely as ever and as full of flower and as still.

Bibliography

The date of initial publication appears after the author's name; if I used a later edition, its date is listed at the end of the entry. The numbers in abbreviated entries refer to other parts of the bibliography ("3.2" designating chapter 3, section 2, etc.). There are entries for some works not cited in the text but relevant to the topics discussed.

Chapter 1. *Introduction*

    1.0   *Bibliographies of Twentieth-Century Theories of Narrative*

There is no adequate bibliography, but the following treat aspects of the subject.

Booth, Wayne. 1961. *The Rhetoric of Fiction*. Chicago: University of Chicago Press. Booth's annotated bibliography (399–434) is a history in miniature of twentieth-century theories. It includes important Continental criticism overlooked by other American critics. The second edition, 1983, contains a useful supplementary bibliography for the years 1961–82 (495–520).
Holbek, Bengt. 1977. "Formal and Structural Studies of Oral Narrative: A Bibliography." *Unifol: Årsberetning 1977* : 149–94.
Mathieu, Michel. 1977. "Analyse du récit." *Poétique* 30:226–59. A useful, extensively annotated bibliography emphasizing formalist, structuralist, and semiotic approaches. Includes, among others, sections on major critics; narrative types (folklore, biblical narrative, popular fiction); description, temporal ordering, and point of view (*vision*) in narrative.
Pabst, W. 1960. "Literatur zur Theorie des Romans." *Deutsche Vierteljahrschaft* 34:264–89.
Stevick. See 1.1.

1.1 *Theories of the Novel, 1945–1960*

Anthologies of critical writings on the novel published in the 1960s provide good introductions to twentieth-century theories; most of them are listed below.

Allen, Walter. 1955. *The English Novel.* New York: Dutton.

Auerbach. See 3.1.

Bowling, Lawrence. 1950. "What Is the Stream of Consciousness Technique?" Reprinted in Kumar and McKean (below).

Calderwood, James, and Harold Toliver, eds. 1968. *Perspectives on Fiction.* New York: Oxford University Press. Contains essays by Austin Warren ("The Nature and Modes of Narrative Fiction"), Ian Watt, Leslie Fiedler, Mark Schorer, Percy Lubbock, Wayne Booth, Robert Humphrey, and E. M. Forster, among others.

Crane, R. S. 1950. "The Concept of Plot and the Plot of *Tom Jones.*" In *Critics and Criticism,* ed. R. S. Crane. Chicago: University of Chicago Press, 1952.

Edel, Leon. 1955. *The Psychological Novel, 1900–1950.* New York: Lippincott.

Fiedler, Leslie. 1964. See Calderwood and Toliver 1968 (above).

Frank, Joseph. 1945. "Spatial Form in Modern Literature." In *The Widening Gyre,* 3–62. Bloomington: Indiana University Press, 1963. See also *Spatial Form in Narrative,* ed. Jeffrey Smitten and Ann Daghistany (Ithaca: Cornell University Press, 1982).

Friedman, Melvin. 1955. *Stream of Consciousness: A Study in Literary Method.* New Haven: Yale University Press.

Girard, René. 1976. "French Theories of Fiction: 1947–1974." *Bucknell Review* 22.1:117–26.

Halperin, John, ed. 1974. *The Theory of the Novel: New Essays.* New York: Oxford University Press. The introduction is a brief history of English theories of the novel before James.

Howe, Irving. 1959. "Mass Society and Post-modern Fiction." See Klein; Scholes (below).

Humphrey, Robert. 1954. *Stream of Consciousness in the Modern Novel.* Berkeley: University of California Press.

Klein, Marcus, ed. 1969. *The American Novel since World War II.* Greenwich, Conn.: Fawcett. The essays by William Barrett, Philip Rahv, Lionel Trilling, Alfred Kazin, and Irving Howe exemplify the commitment to realism and opposition to postwar trends in the novel discussed in this chapter; those by John Hawkes, William Gass, and John Barth show how convincingly contemporary novelists defend their methods.

Kumar, Shiv, and Keith McKean, eds. 1965. *Critical Approaches to Fiction.* New York: McGraw-Hill. Includes essays on plot, character, language, theme, setting, and technique (Schorer, Bowling, Booth's "Distance and Point-of-View," Rahv's "Fiction and the Criticism of Fiction").

Leavis, F. R. 1948. *The Great Tradition.* London: Stewart.

Levin, Harry. 1963. *The Gates of Horn.* New York: Oxford University Press.

Lukács. See 3.1.

O'Connor, William Van, ed. 1948. *Forms of Modern Fiction*. Minneapolis: University of Minnesota Press; rpt., Bloomington: Indiana University Press, 1959. Contains Schorer's "Technique as Discovery."

Rahv, Philip. 1956. See Kumar and McKean (above).

Scholes, Robert, ed. 1961. *Approaches to the Novel*. San Francisco: Chandler. An excellent selection of twentieth-century essays on narrative modes and forms (Northrop Frye, Watt), point of view (Lubbock, Norman Friedman), plot (Forster, R. S. Crane), structure (Edwin Muir, Austin Warren), and social and technical issues (Trilling, Howe, and Schorer). The second edition, 1966, adds essays on realism by Harry Levin, and on distance and point of view by Booth.

Schorer, Mark. 1947. "Technique as Discovery." Reprinted in Calderwood and Toliver; Kumar and McKean; O'Connor; Scholes; and Stevick.

Stevick, Philip, ed. 1967. *The Theory of the Novel*. New York: Macmillan. Essays and extracts on the novel as a genre, technique (Henry James and Schorer), point of view (Booth and Norman Friedman), plot, style, character, etc. Selections from novelists, seventeenth century to the present, on the relationship between life and art. Contains a useful, lightly annotated bibliography of twentieth-century theoretical writings on the novel (407–28).

Trilling, Lionel. 1948. "Manners, Morals, and the Novel" (1947; reprinted in Scholes) and "Art and Fortune" (1948; reprinted in Klein) both appear in his best-known book, *The Liberal Imagination* (New York: Viking, 1950); my quotations are from the latter essay.

Watt, Ian. 1957. *The Rise of the Novel*. Berkeley: University of California Press. Chapters of this standard work are reprinted in Scholes and by Calderwood and Toliver. See also Watt's "Serious Reflections on *The Rise of the Novel*," *Novel* 1 (1968): 205–18, an informative discussion of critical attitudes in the 1950s and 1960s.

1.2   *Theories of the Novel in the Early Twentieth Century*

In addition to the authors mentioned in the text, the following list includes some of the books on which my general statements concerning early twentieth-century criticism are based.

Baker, Ernest. 1924–39. *The History of the English Novel*. 10 vols. London: Witherby.

Beach, Joseph Warren. 1932. *The Twentieth Century Novel: Studies in Technique*. New York: Appleton-Century. One of the best American studies of technique in the novel.

Booth, Bradford. 1958. "The Novel." In *Contemporary Literary Scholarship*, ed. Lewis Leary, 259–88. New York: Appleton–Century–Crofts. A concise survey of trends during the preceding three decades.

Cross, Wilbur L. 1899. *The Development of the English Novel*. New York: Macmillan.

Edel, Leon, and Gordon Ray, eds. 1958. *Henry James and H. G. Wells: A Record of Their Friendship, Their Debate on the Art of Fiction, and Their Quarrel*. Urbana: University of Illinois Press.

Forster, E. M. 1927. *Aspects of the Novel*. London: Arnold.

Friedman, Norman. 1976. "Anglo–American Fiction Theory 1947–1972." *Studies in the Novel* 8:199–209.

Hamilton, Clayton. 1908. *Materials and Methods of Fiction*. New York: Baker and Taylor. For several decades, a standard text (later editions were entitled *A Manual of the Art of Fiction* and *The Art of Fiction*); deserves the attention of those who think that the study of narrative technique is a recent phenomenon. "A thoroughgoing 'rhetoric of fiction'" (Booth).

James, Henry. See Edel and Ray (above).

Jameson. See 3.1.

Lubbock, Percy. 1921. *The Craft of Fiction*. London: Cape.

Lukács. See 3.1.

Martin, Wallace. 1967. "The Realistic Novel." In *"The New Age" under Orage*, 81–107. Manchester: Manchester University Press. Arnold Bennett, Joseph Conrad, James, and Wells on realism and technique in the novel.

Perry, Bliss. 1902. *A Study of Prose Fiction*. Boston: Houghton Mifflin.

Phelps, William Lyon. 1916. *The Advance of the English Novel*. New York: Dodd, Mead.

Saintsbury, George. 1913. *The English Novel*. London: Dent.

Wells, H. G. See Edel and Ray (above).

1.3 *Theories of Narrative: Frye, Booth, and French Structuralism*

The works here listed contain surveys of structuralist and formalist theories of narrative. It is difficult to separate this topic from the general principles on which these movements are based, but the latter are not here the subject of discussion. Entries for particular critics and specific issues appear in the bibliographies of other chapters (esp. 4–6 for Barthes, Genette, Greimas, and Todorov). See also the entry for Mathieu, 1977, 1.0.

Booth. See 1.0.

Budniakiewicz, Therese. 1978. "A Conceptual Survey of Narrative Semiotics." *Dispositio* 3.7–8:189–217. A concise account of French structuralist theories.

Culler, Jonathan. 1975. *Structuralist Poetics*. Ithaca: Cornell University Press. An excellent survey; see esp. the chapter on "Poetics of the Novel." The bibliography lists English translations available in 1975.

Frye 1957. See 2.1.

Hamon, Philippe. 1972. "Mise au point sur les problèmes de l'analyse du récit." *Le Français moderne* 40:200–221.

Lévi-Strauss, Claude. 1967. *Structural Anthropology*. New York: Anchor. Chs. 2 and 3 remain among the best introductions to the use of linguistic models in anthropology and other disciplines; ch. 9, "The Structural Study of Myth" (1955), is Lévi-Strauss's best-known contribution to the theory of narrative.

Scholes, Robert. 1974. *Structuralism in Literature*. New Haven: Yale University Press. Chs. 4 and 5 contain concise summaries and commentaries on the theories of V. Propp, Lévi-Strauss, Tzvetan Todorov, Roland Barthes, and Gérard Genette, and a good introduction to Russian formalism. Useful annotated bibliography.

Striedter, Jurij. 1977. "The Russian Formalist Theory of Prose." *PTL* 2:429–70. A reliable account by a leading Slavic scholar.

Todorov, Tzvetan. 1968. *Introduction to Poetics*. Minneapolis: University of Minnesota Press, 1981. Ch. 2, "Analysis of the Literary Text," explains many of the terms used by structuralists in narrative analysis.

———. *The Poetics of Prose*. 1971. Ithaca: Cornell University Press, 1977. Contains "The Methodological Heritage of Russian Formalism," an informed survey of the movement, and several essays exemplifying how structuralists use linguistic models.

1.4   *Recent Trends*

Most of the works relevant to this section are listed in other chapters. For studies of narrative in other disciplines, see the bibliographies for chs. 3 (history and psychoanalysis) and 8 (philosophy); for communication models of narrative, see ch. 7. The following works not discussed later also repay attention:

Douglas, Mary. 1966. *Purity and Danger: An Analysis of Concepts of Pollution and Taboo*. London: Routledge & Kegan Paul. An English example of structural analysis in anthropology, illustrating as well as any other source the methodology of structuralism.

Dressler, Wolfgang, ed. 1978. *Current Trends in Textlinguistics*. New York: Walter de Gruyter. The contributions by Teun van Dijk and Walter Kintsch, Joseph Grimes, Götz Wienold, and Ernst Grosse concern formal analysis of narrative; Grosse is especially helpful in describing and providing a bibliography of trends in France to 1976. The highly technical methods discussed in this volume will not be treated in the following chapters.

Dundes, Alan, ed. 1965. *The Study of Folklore*. Englewood Cliffs, N.J.: Prentice-Hall. The essays by Axel Olrik, Lord Raglan, Clyde Kluckhohn, and Alan Dundes show the relevance of the study of folklore to literary criticism.

Gombrich, E. H. *Art and Illusion*. 1968. London: Phaidon. Gombrich's demonstration that "realistic" pictorial representation is highly conventionalized led many critics to realize that the same is true of literary realism. For his later views on this issue, see 3.5.

Labov, William. 1972. "The Transformation of Experience in Narrative Syntax." In *The Social Stratification of English in New York City*. University Park: University of Pennsylvania Press; London: Routledge & Kegan Paul.

Labov, William, and Joshua Waletzky. 1967. "Narrative Analysis: Oral Versions of Personal Experience." In *Essays on the Verbal and Visual Arts*, 12–45. Seattle: University of Washington Press.

Lord, Albert. 1960. *The Singer of Tales*. Cambridge, Mass.: Harvard University Press. A standard work on the formulaic structure of orally transmitted epics. On this subject, see also Parry (below).

Miranda, Elli Köngäs, and Pierre Miranda. 1971. *Structural Models in Folklore and Transformational Essays*. The Hague: Mouton. Shows how various forms of Lévi-Strauss's narrative formula can be applied to folklore.

Parry, Milman. 1971. *The Making of Homeric Verse*. Oxford: Clarendon.

Santillana, Giorgio de, and Hertha von Dechend. 1969. *Hamlet's Mill*. Boston: Gambit. A brilliant argument connecting mythical narratives with archaic cosmologies; Hamlet's melancholy is traced back to Indian myths.

Chapter 2. *From Novel to Narrative*

2.1 *Kinds of Narrative*

The discussion of oral narratives in this section is drawn from Scholes and Kellogg, who rely in part on Milman Parry and Alfred Lord (cf. 1.4). For a recent survey of this topic, see Foley. Additional works on classical narratives are listed in 2.5.

Arrathoon, Leigh, ed. 1984. *The Craft of Fiction: Essays in Medieval Poetics*. Rochester, Mich.: Solaris. Paul Zumthor, Peter Haidu, and B. Roberts discuss the differences between oral and written narratives; Tony Hunt, Douglas Kelley, and Eren Branch treat aspects of medieval narrative structure.

Dorfman, Eugene. 1969. *The Narreme in the Medieval Romance Epic: An Introduction to Narrative Structures*. Toronto: University of Toronto Press.

Foley, John. 1981. "The Oral Theory in Context." In *Oral Tradition in Literature: A Festschrift for Albert Bates Lord*, 27–122. Columbus, Ohio: Slavica Publishers.

Frye, Northrop. 1957. *Anatomy of Criticism*. Princeton: Princeton University Press. Page references in the text are to this work; the following two entries supplement his account of narrative genres.

——. 1963. "Myth, Fiction, and Displacement." In *Fables of Identity*, 21–38. New York: Harcourt, Brace & World.

——. 1976. *The Secular Scripture: A Study of Romance*. Cambridge: Harvard University Press.

Nichols, Stephen G. 1961. *Formulaic Diction and Thematic Composition in the "Chanson de Roland."* Chapel Hill: University of North Carolina Press.

Scholes, Robert, and Robert Kellogg. 1966. *The Nature of Narrative*. New York: Oxford University Press.
Vinaver, Eugène. 1971. *The Rise of Romance*. Oxford: Clarendon.

2.2 The Romance-Novel Matrix: History, Psychology, and Stories of Life

Freud, Sigmund. "Creative Writers and Daydreaming" (1908) and "Family Romances" (1909). In *The Standard Edition of the Complete Psychological Works of Sigmund Freud*, 9:143–53, 9:237–41. London: Hogarth, 1953–73.
Girard, René. 1961. *Deceit, Desire, and the Novel: Self and Other in Literary Structure*. Baltimore: Johns Hopkins University Press, 1965.
Robert, Marthe. 1971. *Origins of the Novel*. Bloomington: Indiana University Press, 1980.

2.3 Does "the Novel" Exist?

The essays by Freedman and Kern contain helpful historical surveys of attempts to define the novel. Together with Mylne and Showalter, they provide useful corrections to accounts of the origins of the novel based exclusively on English sources. Eighteenth-century statements on this tangled topic are conveniently collected in the volumes edited by Lynch and Williams. For English fiction from 1400 to 1740, see also Schlauch and Morgan (the latter contains a useful primary bibliography); on Elizabethan fiction, see Nelson (2.4) and Walter Davis (3.3).

Adams, Percy. 1983. *Travel Literature and the Evolution of the Novel*. Lexington: University Press of Kentucky.
Blair, Hugh. 1762. "On Fictitious History." See Williams (below), 247–51.
Blanckenburg, Friedrich von. 1774. *Versuch über den Roman*. Rpt., Stuttgart: Metzlersche Verlagsbuchhandlung, 1965.
Chandler, Frank. 1907. *The Literature of Roguery*. Boston: Houghton Mifflin.
Congreve, William. 1691. Preface to *Incognita*. See Williams (below), 27.
Diderot, Denis. 1761. "Eloge de Richardson." See Lynch (below), 121.
Freedman, Ralph. 1968. "The Possibility of a Theory of the Novel." In *The Disciplines of Criticism*, ed. Peter Demetz et al., 57–77. New Haven: Yale University Press.
Kern, Edith. 1968. "The Romance of the Novel/Novella." In *The Disciplines of Criticism* (see preceding entry), 511–30.
Lynch, Lawrence. 1979. *Eighteenth Century French Novelists and the Novel*. York, S.C.: French Literature Publications.
Morgan, Charlotte E. 1911. *The Rise of the Novel of Manners: A Study of English Prose Fiction between 1600 and 1740*. New York: Columbia University Press.
Mylne, Vivienne. 1981. *The Eighteenth-Century French Novel: Techniques of Illusion*. Cambridge: Cambridge University Press.

Reeve, Clara. 1785. *The Progress of Romance, through Times, Countries, Manners.*
. . . New York: Facsimile Text Society, 1930.

Richardson, Samuel. Preface to *Clarissa Harlowe.* See Williams (below), 167.

Schlauch, Margaret. 1963. *Antecedents of the English Novel, 1400–1600: From Chaucer to Deloney.* Warsaw: Polish Scientific Pubs.

Segrais, Jean Regnault de. 1656. See Showalter (below), 23.

Showalter, English. 1972. *The Evolution of the French Novel, 1641–1782.* Princeton: Princeton University Press.

Williams, Ioan. 1970. *Novel and Romance, 1700–1800: A Documentary Record.* New York: Barnes & Noble.

Wolff, S. L. 1912. *The Greek Romance in Elizabethan Prose Fiction.* New York: Columbia University Press.

2.4 *The Novel as Oppositional Discourse*

Damrosch, Leopold. 1985. *God's Plot & Man's Stories: Studies in the Fictional Imagination from Milton to Fielding.* Chicago: University of Chicago Press.

Davis, Lennard. 1983. *Factual Fictions: The Origins of the English Novel.* New York: Columbia University Press.

May, Georges. 1963. *Le Dilemme du roman au XVIIIe siècle.* New Haven: Yale University Press.

Nelson, William. 1973. *Fact or Fiction: The Dilemma of the Renaissance Storyteller.* Cambridge: Harvard University Press.

Reed, Walter L. 1981. *An Exemplary History of the Novel: The Quixotic Versus the Picaresque.* Chicago: University of Chicago Press.

Richetti, John. 1969. *Popular Fiction before Richardson: Narrative Patterns 1700–1739.* Oxford: Clarendon Press.

2.5 *Formalist and Semiotic Theories of Narrative Kinds*

Many of Shklovsky's writings have not appeared in English. My account of him is based in part on unpublished translations kindly provided by Richard Sheldon. Todorov's discussion of Bakhtin, cited below, is very helpful. In his discussion of Greek narratives, Bakhtin was indebted to Erwin Rohde, *Der griechische Roman und seine Vorläufer* (1876). The entries for Hägg, Heiserman, and Perry below provide synopses and analyses of this material in English.

Bakhtin, M. M. 1981. *The Dialogic Imagination.* Trans. Caryl Emerson and Michael Holquist. Austin: University of Texas Press, 1981.

Hägg, Tomas. 1983. *The Novel in Antiquity.* Berkeley: University of California Press.

Heiserman, Arthur. 1977. *The Novel before the Novel: Essays and Discussions about the Beginnings of Prose Fiction in the West.* Chicago: University of Chicago Press.

Perry, Ben Edwin. 1967. *The Ancient Romances: A Literary–Historical Account of Their Origins*. Berkeley: University of California Press.

Shklovsky, Victor. 1917. "Art as Technique." In *Russian Formalist Criticism: Four Essays*, trans. Lee Lemon and Marion Reis, 5–24. Lincoln: University of Nebraska Press, 1965.

———. 1919. "On the Connection between Devices of *Syuzhet* Construction and General Stylistic Devices." In *Russian Formalism*, ed. S. Bann and J. E. Bowlt, 48–72. New York: Barnes and Noble, 1973.

———. 1923. "Literatur und Kinematograph." In *Formalismus, Strukturalismus und Geschichte*, 22–41. Kronberg: Scriptor, 1974.

———. 1925. "La construction de la nouvelle et du roman." In *Théorie de la littérature*, trans. Tzvetan Todorov, 170–96. Paris: Seuil, 1965.

Todorov, Tzvetan. 1981. *Mikhail Bakhtine: le principe dialogique*. Paris: Seuil. English translation, Minneapolis: University of Minnesota Press, 1984.

Tynjanov, Juri. 1927. "On Literary Evolution." In *Readings in Russian Poetics*, ed. Ladislav Matejka and Krystyna Pomorska, 66–78. Ann Arbor: Michigan Slavic Publications, 1978.

2.5 *Summary*

Jameson. See 3.1.

Chapter 3. *From Realism to Convention*

3.1 *Characteristics of Realism*

Becker's anthology provides a useful selection of statements on realism and a short bibliography (599–603). For a concise bibliographic survey of twentieth-century discussions, see Lucente. Loofbourow's essays suggest ways to integrate the divergent conceptions of realism discussed in this section.

Auerbach, Erich. 1946. *Mimesis: The Representation of Reality in Western Literature*. Garden City, N.Y.: Doubleday, 1957.

Bakhtin. See 2.5.

Becker, George. 1963. Introduction to *Documents of Modern Literary Realism*, 3–38. Princeton: Princeton University Press.

Booth. See 1.0.

Brown, Marshall. 1981. "The Logic of Realism: A Hegelian Approach." *PMLA* 96:224–41.

Diderot. See 2.3.

Ermarth, Elizabeth Deeds. 1983. *Realism and Consensus in the English Novel*. Princeton: Princeton University Press. Ermarth's theory of the social and perceptual evolution of "realism" bears comparison with the philosophical evolution proposed by Hans Blumenberg, "The Concept of Reality and the

Possibility of the Novel," in *New Perspectives in German Literary Criticism* (Princeton: Princeton University Press, 1979), 29–48.

James, Henry. 1883. "Anthony Trollope." In *The Future of the Novel: Essays on the Art of Fiction*, ed. Leon Edel, 248. New York: Vintage, 1956.

Jameson, Fredric. 1981. *The Political Unconscious: Narrative as a Socially Symbolic Act*. Ithaca: Cornell University Press.

Levin, Harry. 1963. *The Gates of Horn* (see 1.1), 32. For Levin's conception of realism, see "What Is Realism?" in *Contexts of Criticism* (New York: Atheneum, 1963), 67–75.

Levine, George. 1981. *The Realistic Imagination: English Fiction from Frankenstein to Lady Chatterly*. Chicago: University of Chicago Press.

Loofbourow, John. 1970. "Literary Realism Redefined." *Thought* 45:433–43.

——. 1974. "Realism in the Anglo-American Novel: The Pastoral Myth." In Halperin (see 1.1), 257–70.

Lucente, Gregory. 1981. *The Narrative of Realism and Myth: Verga, Lawrence, Faulkner, Pavese*. Baltimore: Johns Hopkins University Press. Bibliographic note, 162–64.

Lukács, Georg. 1935–39. *Studies in European Realism*. New York: Grosset & Dunlap, 1964.

——. 1936. "Narrate or Describe?" In *Writer and Critic* (below). Elsewhere this essay has been translated with the title "Idea and Form in Literature."

——. 1938. "Realism in the Balance." In *Aesthetics and Politics*, ed. Ronald Taylor, 28–59. London: New Left Books, 1977. See also Brecht's reply in the same volume, 68–85.

——. 1958. *Realism in Our Time*. New York: Harper & Row, 1964.

——. 1971. *Writer and Critic, and Other Essays*. New York: Grosset & Dunlap.

Richardson, Samuel. Quoted in Nelson 1973 (see 2.4), 111–12.

Tolstoy, Leo. See Shklovsky 1919, 2.5.

Watt, Ian. See 1.1.

Wellek, René. 1960. "The Concept of Realism in Literary Scholarship." In *Concepts of Criticism*, 222–55. New Haven: Yale University Press, 1963.

3.2 *Realism Viewed as a Convention*

Hawthorne, Stevenson, Virginia Woolf, and other novelists who have used non-realistic methods defend their positions in excerpts conveniently collected in Allott, 41–84. For a survey of formalist and structuralist approaches to realism, see Hamon.

Allott, Miriam. 1959. *Novelists on the Novel*. New York: Columbia University Press.

Barthes, Roland. 1968. "The Reality Effect." In *French Literary Theory Today*, ed. Tzvetan Todorov, 11–17. Cambridge: Cambridge University Press, 1982.

Brown. See 3.1.

Culler. See 1.3.

Eigner, Edwin. 1978. *The Metaphysical Novel in England and America*. Berkeley: University of California Press.

Frye 1957. See 2.1.

Genette, Gérard. 1969. "Vraisemblance et motivation." In *Figures II*, 71–99. Paris: Seuil.

Gombrich. See 1.4.

Guerard, Albert. 1976. *The Triumph of the Novel: Dickens, Dostoievsky, Faulkner*. New York: Oxford University Press.

Hamon, Philippe. 1973. "Un discours contraint." *Poétique* 16:411–45.

Jakobson, Roman. 1921. "On Realism in Art." In *Readings in Russian Poetics: Formalist and Structuralist Views*, ed. Ladislav Matejka and Krystyna Pomorska, 38–46. Ann Arbor: Michigan Slavic Publications, 1978.

Schank, Roger, and Robert Abelson. 1977. *Scripts, Plans, Goals and Understanding: An Inquiry into Human Knowledge Structures*. Hillsdale, N.J.: Erlbaum.

Schank, Roger, and Peter Childers. 1984. *The Cognitive Computer*. Reading, Mass.: Addison-Wesley. See "Tale-Spin," 81–87.

Shklovsky 1925. See 2.5.

Tomashevsky, Boris. 1925. "Thematics." In *Russian Formalist Criticism: Four Essays*, ed. Lee Lemon and Marion Reis, 61–95. Lincoln: University of Nebraska Press, 1965.

3.3 *Narrative Conventions in History*

The best summaries of recent writings on narrative and historiography are those of Ricoeur and White (1984). For a bibliography of the subject, see *The Writing of History*, 151–58 (listed below under Mink 1978). The contributions of Croce, Collingwood, Morton White, and Gallie to the analysis of history as narrative are summarized by Mandelbaum (1967), Mink (1970), and Dray. Mandelbaum is among those who oppose this view of history. For a persuasive defense of his distinction between factual and fictional narrative, see Ricoeur.

Braudy, Leo. 1970. *Narrative Form in History and Fiction: Hume, Fielding and Gibbon*. Princeton: Princeton University Press.

Danto, Arthur. 1965. *Analytical Philosophy of History*. Cambridge: Cambridge University Press.

Davis, Walter. 1969. *Idea and Act in Elizabethan Fiction*. Princeton: Princeton University Press.

Dray, W. H. 1971. "On the Nature and Role of Narrative in Historiography." *History and Theory* 10:153–71.

Gallie, W. B. 1964. *Philosophy and Historical Understanding*. London: Chatto & Windus.

Gossman, Lionel. 1978. "History and Literature: Reproduction or Signification." In *The Writing of History* (see Mink 1978, below), 3–23.

Hempel, Carl. 1942. "The Function of General Laws in History." *The Journal of Philosophy* 39:35–48.

Mandelbaum, Maurice. 1967. "A Note on History as Narrative." *History and Theory* 6:413–19. Replies to this article appeared in the same journal, vol. 8 (1969): 275–94.

——. 1977. *The Anatomy of Historical Knowledge*. Baltimore: Johns Hopkins University Press.

Mink, Louis. 1970. "History and Fiction as Modes of Comprehension." *New Literary History* 1:541–58.

——. 1978. "Narrative Form as a Cognitive Instrument." In *The Writing of History: Literary Form and Historical Understanding*, ed. Robert Canary and Henry Kozicki, 129–49. Madison: University of Wisconsin Press. All quotations in my text are from this essay.

Nelson. See 2.4.

Ricoeur, Paul. 1983. *Time and Narrative*, vol. 1. Chicago: University of Chicago Press, 1984. Chs. 4–6 provide an excellent survey of recent theories concerning the narrative as a mode of historical explanation.

von Wright, Georg H. 1971. *Explanation and Understanding*. London: Routledge.

White, Hayden. 1973. *Metahistory: The Historical Imagination in Nineteenth-Century Europe*. Baltimore: Johns Hopkins University Press.

——. 1980. "The Value of Narrativity in the Representation of Reality." *Critical Inquiry* 7:5–27. All quotations in the text are from this essay.

——. 1984. "The Question of Narrative in Contemporary Historical Theory." *History and Theory* 23:1–33. A concise review of recent theories.

3.4 *Narrative in Autobiography and Psychoanalysis*

On aspects of autobiography I have not treated, see the essays by Starobinski and Renza in Olney. Paul de Man explores subtler aspects of autobiography as narrative in essays on Rousseau.

Brooks, Peter. 1984. *Reading for the Plot: Design and Intention in Narrative*. New York: Knopf. Chs. 1, 4, and 8 are especially relevant to the relation between plot and psychoanalysis; ch. 10 is the most pertinent to my citation in the text.

Culler, Jonathan. 1981. "Story and Discourse in the Analysis of Narrative." In *The Pursuit of Signs: Semiotics, Literature, Deconstruction*, 169–87. Ithaca: Cornell University Press.

de Man, Paul. 1979. *Allegories of Reading*. New Haven: Yale University Press.

Gusdorf, Georges. 1956. "Conditions and Limits of Autobiography." In Olney (below), 28–48.

Laplanche, Jean. 1970. *Life and Death in Psychoanlaysis*. Baltimore: Johns Hopkins University Press, 1976.

Olney, James, ed. 1980. *Autobiography: Essays Theoretical and Critical.* Princeton: Princeton University Press.

Pascal, Roy. 1960. *Design and Truth in Autobiography.* Cambridge: Harvard University Press.

Ricoeur. See 3.3.

Schafer, Roy. 1981. *Narrative Actions in Psychoanalysis.* Worcester, Mass.: Clark University Press. A valuable account of the differences between mechanistic and interpretive/narrative explanation in psychoanalysis.

Spacks, Patricia Meyer. 1976. *Imagining a Self: Autobiography and Novel in Eighteenth-Century England.* Cambridge: Harvard University Press.

Spence, Donald. 1982. *Narrative Truth and Historical Truth: Meaning and Interpretation in Psychoanalysis.* New York: Norton.

3.5 *Conventions and Reality*

Brinker, Menachem. 1983. "Verisimilitude, Conventions, and Beliefs." *New Literary History* 14:253–67.

Ermarth. See 3.1.

Gombrich, E. H. 1984. "Representation and Misrepresentation." *Critical Inquiry* 11:195–201. Comments on widespread misunderstandings of his position concerning the conventional nature of representation.

Goodman, Nelson, 1983. "Realism, Relativism, and Reality," *New Literary History* 14:269–72.

Littérature. 1985. Special issue on "Logiques de la représentation," no. 57 (February).

Lodge, David. 1977. *The Modes of Modern Writing.* Ithaca: Cornell University Press, 1977.

Margolis, Joseph, ed. 1978. "Representation in Art." In *Philosophy Looks at the Arts,* 223–88. Philadelphia: Temple University Press. The essays by Nelson Goodman, Richard Wolheim, and Patrick Maynard help clarify the issues discussed in this section.

Putnam, Hilary. 1981. "Convention: A Theme in Philosophy." *New Literary History* 13:1–14.

Chapter 4. *Narrative Structure: Preliminary Problems*

The introductory passage from "Lost in the Funhouse" can be found in John Barth, *Lost in the Funhouse* (Garden City, N.Y.: Doubleday, 1968). For E. M. Forster, see 1.2; for Claude Lévi-Strauss, see 1.3; for Vladimir Propp, see 4.2.

4.1 *"Open Form" and Its Predecessors*

Barthes 1970. See 7.3.

Forster. See 1.2.

Freytag, Gustav. 1863. *Freytag's Technique of the Drama*. Chicago: Griggs, 1895.
Friedman, Alan. 1966. *The Turn of the Novel*. New York: Oxford University Press.
Kermode, Frank. 1978. "Sensing Endings." *Nineteenth-Century Fiction*, 33:144–58.
Miller, D. A. 1981. *Narrative and Its Discontents: Problems of Closure in the Traditional Novel*. Princeton: Princeton University Press.
Miller, J. Hillis. 1978. "The Problematic of Ending in Narrative." *Nineteenth-Century Fiction* 33:3–7.
Shklovsky 1925. See 2.5.
Torgovnick, Marianna. 1981. *Closure in the Novel*. Princeton: Princeton University Press.
Vinaver. See 2.1.

4.2   *Endings and Beginnings in Life, Literature, and Myth*

Campbell, Joseph. 1949. *The Hero with a Thousand Faces*. New York: Pantheon.
Cornford, F. M. 1914. *The Origin of Attic Comedy*. Cambridge: Cambridge University Press.
Forster. See 1.2.
Frye 1957. See 2.1.
Kermode, Frank. 1967. *The Sense of an Ending: Studies in the Theory of Fiction*. New York: Oxford University Press.
Miller, D. A. See 4.1.
Miller, J. Hillis. 1974. "Narrative and History." *ELH* 41:455–73.
Propp, V. 1928. *Morphology of the Folktale*. Trans. Laurence Scott. 2d. ed. Austin: University of Texas Press, 1968.
———. 1928–68. *Theory and History of Folklore*. Trans. Ariadna Martin and Richard Martin. Minneapolis: University of Minnesota Press, 1984. A valuable supplement to his better-known book.
Lord Raglan. 1936. *The Hero: A Study in Tradition, Myth, and Drama*. New York: Vintage, 1956.
Said, Edward. 1975. *Beginnings: Intention and Method*. New York: Basic Books.
Tobin, Patricia. 1978. *Time and the Novel: The Genealogical Imperative*. Princeton: Princeton University Press.
Weston, Jessie. 1920. *From Ritual to Romance*. Cambridge: Cambridge University Press.

4.3   *Structural Analysis of Narrative Sequences*

Apo, Satu. 1980. "The Structural Schemes of a Repertoire of Fairy Tales. A Structural Analysis . . . Using Propp's Model." In *Genre, Structure and Reproduction in Oral Literature*, ed. Lauri Honko and Vilmos Voight, 147–58. Budapest: Akadémiai Kiadó.

Barthes, Roland. 1971. "Action Sequences." In *Patterns of Literary Style*, ed. Joseph P. Strelka, 5–14. University Park: Penn State University Press.

Bremond, Claude. 1970. "Morphology of the Folktale." *Semiotica* 2:251.

——. 1980. "The Logic of Narrative Possibilities." *New Literary History* 11:387–411. A translation of a 1966 essay, with a "postface" concerning the development of the theory since then.

——. 1982. "A Critique of the Motif." In *French Literary Theory Today*, ed. Tzvetan Todorov, 125–46. Cambridge: Cambridge University Press.

Bremond, Claude, and Jean Verrier. 1984. "Afanasiev and Propp." *Style* 18:177–95.

Budniakiewicz 1978. See 1.3.

Campbell. See 4.2.

Chomsky, Noam. 1957. *Syntactic Structures*. The Hague: Mouton.

Colby, B. N. 1973. "A Partial Grammar of Eskimo Folktales." *American Anthropologist* 75:645–62.

Culler 1975. See 1.3.

Doležel, Lubomír. 1976a. "Narrative Modalities." *Journal of Literary Semantics* 5:5–14.

Greimas, A.-J. 1971. "Narrative Grammar: Units and Levels." *MLN* 86:793–806.

Hendricks, William. 1973. *Essays on Semiolinguistics and Verbal Art*. The Hague: Mouton.

Labov. See 1.4.

Lévi-Strauss, Claude. 1955. "The Structural Study of Myth." In *Structural Anthropology* (see 1.3), 202–28.

——. 1960. "Structure and Form. Reflections on a Work by Vladimir Propp." In *Structural Anthropology*, vol. 2, 115–45. New York: Basic Books, 1976. See also Propp, 1966 (below).

Liberman, Anatoly. 1984. Introduction to Propp 1928–68 (see 4.2).

Martin, Wallace, and Nick Conrad. 1981. "Formal Analysis of Traditional Fictions." *Papers on Language and Literature* 17.1:3–22.

Prince, Gerald. 1973a. *A Grammar of Stories*. The Hague: Mouton.

——. 1980. "Aspects of a Grammar of Narrative." *Poetics Today* 3.1:49–63. A concise, updated summary of the theory presented in the preceding entry.

Propp 1928. See 4.2.

Propp, V. 1946. *Historical Roots of the Wondertale*. Two chapters of this book have been translated in *Theory and History of Folklore* (see 4.2).

——. 1966. "The Structural and Historical Study of the Wondertale" (his reply to Lévi-Strauss 1960, above). In *Theory and History of Folklore* (see 4.2), which also contains the Lévi-Strauss essay.

Rummelhart, David. 1975. "Notes on a Schema for Stories." In *Representation and Understanding*, ed. Daniel Bobrow and A. Collins, 211–36. New York: Academic Press.

Scholes 1974. See 1.3.

Smith, Barbara Herrnstein. 1980. "Narrative Versions, Narrative Theories." *Critical Inquiry* 7:213–36.

Stewart, Ann Harleman. Forthcoming. "Models of Narrative Structure." *Semiotica*. An excellent summary, upon which I rely heavily.

Todorov, Tzvetan. 1969. *Grammaire du Décaméron*. The Hague: Mouton.

van Dijk, Teun. 1975. "Action, Action Description, and Narrative." *New Literary History* 6:273–94. A concise introduction to the subject; for a more recent and detailed discussion, see his *Macrostructures* (Hillsdale, N.J.: Erlbaum, 1980).

4.4 *Uses and Abuses of Structural Analysis*

Campbell. See 4.2.

Holloway, John. 1979. *Narrative and Structure*. Cambridge: Cambridge University Press.

Hymes, Dell. 1967. "The 'Wife' Who 'Goes Out' like a Man: Reinterpretation of a Clackamas Chinook Myth." *Social Science Information* 7:173–99.

Kermode, Frank. 1969. "The Structures of Fiction." *MLN* 84:891–915.

Lévi-Strauss. See 4.3.

Popper, Karl. 1935. *The Logic of Scientific Discovery*. New York: Harper & Row, 1965.

Propp 1966. See 4.3.

Ramsey, Jarold W. 1977. "The Wife Who Goes Out like a Man, Comes Back as a Hero: The Art of Two Oregon Indian Narratives." *PMLA* 92:9–18.

Revzin, I. I., and O. G. Revzina. 1976. "Toward a Formal Analysis of Plot Construction." In *Semiotics and Structuralism: Readings from the Soviet Union*, ed. Henryk Baran, 244–56. White Plains, N.Y.: Arts & Sciences.

Shklovsky. See 2.5.

Chapter 5. *Narrative Structure: A Comparison of Methods*

5.1 *Varieties of Narrative Theory*

Barthes, Roland. 1966. "Introduction to the Structural Analysis of Narratives." In *Image—Music—Text*, 79–124. London: Collins, 1977.

Benveniste, Emile. 1966. *Problems in General Linguistics*, 205–15. Coral Gables: University of Miami Press, 1971.

Blanckenburg 1774. See 2.3.

Booth 1961. See 1.0.

Chatman, Seymour. 1969. "New Ways of Analyzing Narrative Structure." *Language and Style* 2:3–36.

——— . 1978. *Story and Discourse: Narrative Structure in Fiction and Film*. Ithaca: Cornell University Press.

Culler 1975. See 1.3.

Genette, Gérard. 1972. *Narrative Discourse: An Essay in Method*. Ithaca: Cornell University Press, 1980.

———. 1983. *Nouveau discours du récit.* Paris: Seuil. A clarification of the concepts presented in *Narrative Discourse* in light of more recent theories. Contains a useful bibliography for 1972–83.

Rimmon-Kenan, Shlomith. 1983. *Narrative Fiction: Contemporary Poetics.* London: Methuen.

Scholes, Robert. 1982. *Semiotics and Interpretation.* New Haven: Yale University Press. Ch. 6 concerns Joyce's "Eveline."

Smith 1980. See 4.3.

Todorov, Tzvetan. 1973. "Some Approaches to Russian Formalism." In *Russian Formalism*, ed. Stephen Bann and John Bowlt, 6–19. New York: Barnes & Noble.

Tomashevsky 1925. See 3.2.

5.2   *Functional and Thematic Synthesis in Tomashevsky and Barthes*

Barthes 1966. See 5.1.

Chatman 1978. See 5.1.

Culler 1975. See 1.3.

Doležel, Lubomír. 1980a. "Narrative Semantics and Motif Theory." In *Studia Poetica*, 2, ed. Karol Csúri, 32–43. Szeged: Jozsef Attila Tudomanyegyetem. A valuable exploration of how the theories of Propp and Tomashevsky might be modified, in light of more recent theories, to create "an integrated semantic theory of narrative texts."

Tomashevsky. See 3.2.

5.3   *Functions and Motifs*

Barthes. See 5.1.

Holloway. See 4.4.

Tomashevsky. See 3.2.

5.4   *The Composition of Character*

Barthes. See 5.1.

Benjamin, Walter. 1936. "The Storyteller." In *Illuminations*, 83–109. New York: Schocken, 1969.

Brooks 1984. See 3.4.

Chatman 1978. See 5.1.

Docherty, Thomas. 1983. *Reading (Absent) Character: Towards a Theory of Characterization in Fiction.* Oxford: Clarendon. Contains a useful bibliography, 270–84.

Genette 1972. See 5.1.

Greimas, A.-J., and J. Courtès. 1976. "The Cognitive Dimension of Narrative Discourse." *New Literary History* 7:433–47.

Honeywell, J. Arthur. 1968. "Plot in the Modern Novel." In Kumar and McKean (see 1.1, 45–55).

Jameson 1981. See 3.1.

Josipovici. See 8.1.

Lacan, Jacques. I think Lacan is best approached through secondary sources. Elizabeth Wright's *Psychoanalytic Criticism* (London: Methuen, 1984) is helpful; *Interpreting Lacan*, ed. Joseph Smith and William Kerrigan (New Haven: Yale University Press, 1983) contains excellent introductions to his work. See also *Lacan and Narration*, ed. Robert Con Davis (Baltimore: Johns Hopkins University Press, 1983).

New Literary History. 1974. Special issue on "Changing Views of Character," vol. 5.2.

O'Grady, Walter. 1965. "On Plot in Modern Fiction: Hardy, James, and Conrad." *Modern Fiction Studies* 11:107–15. Reprinted in Kumar and McKean (see 1.1), 57–65.

Price, Martin. 1983. *Forms of Life: Character and Moral Imagination in the Novel*. New Haven: Yale University Press.

Rimmon-Kenan 1983. See 5.1.

Spilka, Mark, ed. 1978. "Character as a Lost Cause." *Novel* 11:197–219. Comments by Martin Price, Julian Moynahan, and Arnold Weinstein.

Tomashevsky. See 3.2.

5.5   *Indices, Informants, and Static Motifs*

Bland, D. S. 1961. "Endangering the Reader's Neck: Background Description in the Novel." *Criticism* 3:121–39.

Genette, Gérard. 1966. "Frontiers of Narrative." In *Figures of Literary Discourse*, 127–44. New York: Columbia University Press, 1982.

Hamon, Philippe. 1981. *Introduction à l'analyse du descriptif*. Paris: Hachette. The first chapter is a historical survey of critical conceptions of description.

——— . 1972. "What Is a Description?" In *French Literary Theory Today*, ed. Tzvetan Todorov, 147–78. Cambridge: Cambridge University Press, 1982.

Hoffman, Gerhard. 1978. *Raum, Situation, erzählte Wirklichkeit*. Stuttgart: Metzler.

James, Henry. 1900. "The Art of Fiction." In *The Future of the Novel: Essays on the Art of Fiction*, ed. Leon Edel, 15. New York: Vintage, 1956.

Kittay, Jeffrey. 1981. "Descriptive Limits." See *Yale French Studies* 1981 (below), 225.

Klaus, Peter. 1982. "Description and Event in Narrative." *Orbis Litterarum* 37:211–16.

Liddell, Robert. 1947. *Robert Liddell on the Novel*, 100–18. Chicago: University of Chicago Press, 1969.

Littérature. 1980. Special issue on "Le décrit," no. 38 (May).

Sternberg, Meir. 1981. "Ordering/Unordered; Time, Space, and Descriptive Coherence." *Yale French Studies* 1981 (below), 73.

Yale French Studies. 1981. Special issue "Towards a Theory of Description," vol. 61. In addition to the articles listed above, see those by Michel Beaujour and Michael Riffaterre.

5.6 Narrative Temporality

The following works supplement Genette's treatment of the subject in *Narrative Discourse* (1972; see 5.1), which served as the basis of my own discussion.

Doležel, Lubomír. 1976b. "A Scheme of Narrative Time." In *Semiotics of Art: Prague School Contributions,* ed. Ladislav Matejka and Irwin Titunik, 209–17. Cambridge: MIT Press.
Holloway. See 4.4.
Lämmert, Eberhard. 1955. *Bauformen des Erzählens.* Stuttgart: Metzler, 1967. Contains informative discussions of what Genette calls "order" and "duration."
Miel, Jan. 1969. "Temporal Form in the Novel." *MLN* 84:916–30.
Sternberg, Meir. 1978. *Expositional Modes and Temporal Ordering in Fiction.* Baltimore: Johns Hopkins University Press.
Weinrich, Harald. 1964. *Tempus: Besprochene und erzählte Welt.* Stuttgart: Kohlhammer. Paul Ricoeur (1985) provides a summary of Weinrich's book (see 8.4).

5.7 Syuzhet, Theme, and Narration

Barthes. See 5.1.
Culler. See 3.4.
Greimas. See 4.3.

Chapter 6. *Points of View on Point of View*

6.0 Comprehensive Theories of Point of View

Among the taxonomies of narrative methods produced during the past twenty years, those of Chatman, Doležel, Genette, and Stanzel have been most influential. Unable to compare them within the limits of this chapter, I have listed primary and secondary sources below in the hope that readers will consult them to supplement my discussion. The most useful comparisons of the theoretical positions involved can be found in Cohn 1981; Cohn and Genette 1985; Genette 1983; and Stanzel 1984, 46–66.

Barbauld, Anna. 1804. "A Biographical Account of Samuel Richardson." See Allott, 3.2.
Chatman 1978. See 5.1. Pp. 146–253 treat methods of narration in a linear progression from "nonnarrated stories" to "covert" and then "overt" narrators.

Cohn, Dorrit. 1978. *Transparent Minds: Narrative Modes for Presenting Consciousness in Fiction*. Princeton: Princeton University Press. While not claiming to present a comprehensive taxonomy, Cohn comes close to doing so (see the tabular summaries, 138–40, 184).

———. 1981. "The Encirclement of Narrative: On Franz Stanzel's *Theorie des Erzählens*." *Poetics Today* 2.2:157–82. A description of Stanzel's theory, comparing it with Genette's, with helpful diagrams.

Cohn, Dorrit, and Gérard Genette. 1985. "Nouveaux nouveaux discours du récit." *Poétique* 61:101–9. Cohn responds to Genette's comments on her work in *Nouveau discours du récit* (1983; see 5.1), and Genette replies. A concise account of many terminological differences.

Doležel, Lubomír. 1967. "The Typology of the Narrator: Point of View in Fiction." In *To Honor Roman Jakobson*, 1:541–52. The Hague: Mouton. A fuller account of the taxonomy in the following entry.

———. 1973. *Narrative Modes in Czech Literature*. Toronto: University of Toronto Press. The introduction contains a complete and cogent taxonomy of narrative modes that combines a verbal model (grammatical person, type of discourse) with a functional model (objective, rhetorical, or subjective presentation).

Genette 1972. See 5.1. The relevant chapters are those on "Mood" and "Voice." See Mosher and Rimmon (below) for convenient summaries, and Bal 1977 and 1983 (6.3) for a penetrating critique.

———. 1983. See 5.1. Replies to critics of the theory presented in *Narrative Discourse* and comments on other theories. Contains a useful bibliography for the years 1972–83.

Mosher, Harold F. 1980. "A New Synthesis of Narratology." *Poetics Today* 1.3:171–86. Compares Chatman with Genette.

Rimmon, Shlomith. 1976. "A Comprehensive Theory of Narrative: Genette's *Figures III* and the Structuralist Study of Fiction." *PTL* 1:33–62. A tabular summary of the theory appears on page 61.

Stanzel, Franz. 1979. *A Theory of Narrative*. Cambridge: Cambridge University Press, 1984. Stanzel uses three axes (person, similar to the first- or third-person distinction; perspective, which is internal or external; and mode, corresponding roughly to the showing-telling distinction) for a classification which, in circular form, allows for gradations between narrative modes. Cohn 1981 (above) presents a simplified version of the resultant diagram, the original version of which is reproduced opposite p. 1 of Stanzel's book.

6.1 *Point of View in American and English Criticism*

For a more complete bibliography of this subject, see 1.1.

Beach 1932. See 1.2.
Booth. See 1.0.
Cohn 1978. See 6.0.

Friedman, Melvin. See 1.1.
Friedman, Norman. 1955. "Point of View in Fiction: The Development of a Critical Concept." *PMLA* 70:1160–84.
Genette 1972. See 5.1.
Humphrey 1954. See 1.1.
Lubbock. See 1.2.
Spielhagen, Friedrich. 1883. *Beiträge zur Theorie und Technik des Romans.* Leipzig: Staackmann.
Stanzel. See 6.0.
Uspensky. See 6.2.

6.2 The Grammar of Narration

Bakhtin. See 6.4.
Banfield, Ann. 1982. *Unspeakable Sentences: Narration and Representation in the Language of Fiction.* London: Routledge.
Bickerton, Derek. 1967. "Modes of Interior Monologue: A Formal Definition." *Modern Language Quarterly* 28:229–39.
Bronzwaer, W. J. M. 1971. *Tense in the Novel.* Groningen: Wolters— Noordhoff.
Cohn, Dorrit. 1966. "Narrated Monologue: Definition of a Fictional Style." *Comparative Literature* 18:97–112.
—— 1978. See 6.0.
Doležel 1973. See 6.0.
Głowiński, Michałł. 1973. "On the First-Person Novel." *New Literary History* 9 (1977): 103–14.
Hamburger, Käte. 1957. *The Logic of Literature.* Bloomington: Indiana University Press, 1973.
Hernadi, Paul. 1971. "Verbal Worlds Between Action and Vision: A Theory of the Modes of Poetic Discourse." *College English* 33:18–31.
McHale, Brian. 1978. "Free Indirect Discourse: A Survey of Recent Accounts." *PTL* 3:249–87.
Martínez-Bonati, Félix. 1960. *Fictive Discourse and the Structures of Literature: A Phenomenological Approach.* Ithaca: Cornell University Press, 1981.
Pascal, Roy. 1977. *The Dual Voice: Free Indirect Speech and Its Functioning in the Nineteenth-century European Novel.* Manchester: Manchester University Press.
Vološinov, V. N. 1930. *Marxism and the Philosophy of Language.* Trans. Ladislav Matejka and I. R. Titunik. New York: Seminar, 1973.

6.3 Structures of Narrative Representation: Focus

Bal, Mieke. 1977. *Narratologie: Essais sur la signification narrative dans quatre romans modernes.* Paris: Klincksieck.

——— . 1983. "The Narrating and the Focalizing: A Theory of the Agents in Narrative." *Style* 17:234–69. Translation of the first chapter of the preceding entry, containing the essentials of her theory.

Brooks, Cleanth, and Robert Penn Warren. 1943. *Understanding Fiction*. New York: Crofts.

Genette 1972. See 5.1.

Uspensky, Boris. 1970. *A Poetics of Composition*. Berkeley: University of California Press, 1973.

Vitoux, Pierre. 1982. "Le jeu de la focalisation." *Poétique* 51:359–68.

6.4 The Languages and Ideologies of Narration

Bakhtin, M. M. 1929. *Problems of Dostoevsky's Poetics*. Minneapolis: University of Minnesota Press, 1984.

——— . 1934–35. "Discourse in the Novel." In *The Dialogic Imagination* (see 2.5).

Cohn 1978. See 6.0.

Uspensky. See 6.3.

Vološinov. See 6.2.

Chapter 7. From Writer to Reader: Communication and Interpretation

Critics discussed in this chapter have occasionally published interpretations of the same novel, thus providing opportunities for a more detailed comparison of their theories. For readers interested in pursuing such comparisons, I have provided a few citations in section 7.4, below. The introductory pages of the chapter cite Booth 1961 (see 1.0) and Booth 1984, his Introduction to Bakhtin 1929 (see 6.4).

7.1 The Communication Model

Booth, Wayne C. 1979. *Critical Understanding: The Powers and Limits of Pluralism*, 268–72. Chicago: University of Chicago Press.

Eco. See 7.2.

Gibson. See 7.2.

Jakobson, Roman. 1960. "Closing Statement: Linguistics and Poetics." In *Style in Language,* ed. Thomas Sebeok, 350–77. Cambridge: M.I.T. Press.

Lanser, Susan Sniader. 1981. *The Narrative Act: Point of View in Prose Fiction*. Princeton: Princeton University Press.

Ohmann, Richard. 1973. "Literature as Act." In *Approaches to Poetics,* ed. Seymour Chatman, 81–107. New York: Columbia University Press.

Pratt, Mary Louise. 1977. *Toward a Speech Act Theory of Literary Discourse*. Bloomington: Indiana University Press.

Prince. See 7.2.
Rabinowitz. See 7.2.

7.2 *Kinds of Readers*

The anthologies of reader-response criticism edited by Suleiman and Crosman and by Tompkins provide excellent general introductions to the subject.

Bellow, Saul. In Booth 1961 (see 1.0).
Bleich, David. 1978. *Subjective Criticism.* Baltimore: Johns Hopkins University Press.
Booth 1961. See 1.0.
Culler, Jonathan. 1980. "Prolegomena to a Theory of Reading." In Suleiman and Crosman (below), 46–66. A survey of recent theories from a semiotic perspective.
———. 1982. *On Deconstruction: Theory and Criticism after Structuralism.* Ithaca: Cornell University Press.
Docherty. See 5.4.
Eco, Umberto. 1979. *The Role of the Reader: Explorations in the Semiotics of Texts.* Bloomington: Indiana University Press.
Gibson, Walker. 1950. "Authors, Speakers, Readers, and Mock Readers." In Tompkins (below) 1–6.
Holland, Norman. 1980. "Unity Identity Text Self." In Tompkins (below), 118–33. See Tompkins's annotated bibliography for Holland's other writings on reader response.
Holub, Robert C. 1984. *Reception Theory: A Critical Introduction.* London: Methuen. Contains useful discussions of Wolfgang Iser and Hans Robert Jauss. Annotated bibliography, 173–84.
Iser, Wolfgang. 1976. *The Act of Reading: A Theory of Aesthetic Response.* Baltimore: Johns Hopkins University Press, 1978. For conveniently brief expositions of Iser's theory, published before and after this book, see "The Reading Process: A Phenomenological Approach" in Tompkins (below), 50–69; and "Interaction between Text and Reader," in Suleiman and Crosman (below), 106–19.
Jameson. See 3.1.
Jauss, Hans Robert, 1977. *Aesthetic Experience and Literary Hermeneutics.* Minneapolis: University of Minnesota Press, 1982.
———. 1982. *Toward an Aesthetic of Reception.* Minneapolis: University of Minnesota Press.
Mailloux, Steven. 1982. *Interpretive Conventions: The Reader in the Study of American Fiction.* Ithaca: Cornell University Press. A useful survey of reader-response theories.
Prince, Gerald. 1973b. "Introduction to the Study of the Narratee." In Tompkins (below), 7–25.

Rabinowitz, Peter J. 1977. "Truth in Fiction: A Reexamination of Audiences." *Critical Inquiry* 4:121–41.
Sartre, Jean-Paul. 1947. *What Is Literature?* New York: Harper & Row, 1965.
Suleiman, Susan R., and Inge Crosman, eds. 1980. *The Reader in the Text: Essays on Audience and Interpretation.* Princeton: Princeton University Press. Annotated bibliography, 401–24.
Tompkins, Jane P., ed. 1980. *Reader-Response Criticism: From Formalism to Post-Structuralism.* Baltimore: Johns Hopkins University Press. Annotated bibliography, 233–72.
Wolff, Erwin. 1971. "Der intendierte Leser." *Poetica* 4:141–66.

7.3 Reading

Barthes, Roland. 1970. *S/Z.* New York: Hill & Wang, 1974.
———. 1973. "Textual Analysis of Poe's 'Valdemar.'" In *Untying the Text,* ed. Robert Young, 133–61. London: Routledge, 1981.
Chatman 1969. For his analysis of "Eveline," see 5.1.
Culler 1982. See 7.2.
Dillon, George. 1978. *Language Processing and the Reading of Literature: Towards a Model of Comprehension.* Bloomington: Indiana University Press.
Kermode, Frank. 1975. *The Classic: Literary Images of Permanence and Change.* Cambridge: Harvard University Press, 1983.
———. 1979. *The Genesis of Secrecy: On the Interpretation of Narrative.* Cambridge: Harvard University Press.
———. 1983. *The Art of Telling: Essays on Fiction.* Cambridge: Harvard University Press.
Miller, J. Hillis. 1982. *Fiction and Repetition: Seven English Novels.* Cambridge: Harvard University Press.
Ray, William. 1984. *Literary Meaning: From Phenomenology to Deconstruction.* London: Basil Blackwell. A survey that treats from a philosophical point of view many of the theories I discuss.
Scholes 1982. For his application of Barthes's theory to "Eveline," see 5.1.

7.4 Interpretation: Theory and Practice

Henry James, "The Figure in the Carpet"

Chambers, Ross. 1984a. "Not for the Vulgar? The Question of Readership in 'The Figure in the Carpet.'" In *Story and Situation* (see 8.1), 151–80.
Iser 1976. See 7.2, 3–10.
Miller, J. Hillis. 1980a. "The Figure in the Carpet." *Poetics Today* 1.3:107–18.
———. 1980b. "A Guest in the House: Reply to Shlomith Rimmon-Kenan's Reply." *Poetics Today* 1.3:189–91.
Rimmon, Shlomith. 1973. "Barthes's 'Hermeneutic Code' and Henry James's

Literary Detective: Plot and Composition in 'The Figure in the Carpet.'"
Hartford Studies in Literature 1:183–207

Rimmon-Kenan, Shlomith. 1980. "Deconstructive Reflections on Deconstruction: In Reply to J. Hillis Miller." *Poetics Today* 2.1b: 185–88.

Todorov, Tzvetan. *The Poetics of Prose*. Ithaca: Cornell University Press, 1977, 144–49.

Emily Bronte, *Wuthering Heights*

Jacobs, Carol. 1979. "*Wuthering Heights:* At the Threshold of Interpretation." *Boundary 2*, 7.3:49–71.

Kermode 1975. See 7.3, 117–34.

Miller, J. Hillis. See 7.3, 42–72.

Joseph Conrad, *Lord Jim*

Jameson. See 3.1, 206–80.

Miller, J. Hillis. See 7.3, 22–41.

Chapter 8. *Frames of Reference: Metafiction, Fiction, and Narrative*

The quotation from Shklovsky in the introductory section is taken from "*Evgeny Onegin* (Pushkin and Sterne)," in *Ocherki po poetike Pushkina* (Berlin, 1923), 199–220, translated by Richard Sheldon (unpublished).

8.1   *Crossing Theoretical Borders: Models of Misreading*

Chambers, Ross. 1984b. *Story and Situation: Narrative Seduction and the Power of Fiction*. Minneapolis. University of Minnesota Press.

Culler 1982. See 7.2.

de Man, Paul. 1969. "The Rhetoric of Temporality." In *Blindness and Insight*, 2d ed., 187–228. Minneapolis: University of Minnesota Press, 1983.

——— . 1979. *Allegories of Reading: Figural Language in Rousseau, Nietzsche, Rilke, and Proust*. New Haven: Yale University Press.

Johnson, Barbara. 1980. "Melville's Fist: The Execution of *Billy Budd*." In *The Critical Difference: Essays in the Contemporary Rhetoric of Reading*. Baltimore: Johns Hopkins University Press.

——— . 1984. "Rigorous Unreliability." *Critical Inquiry* 11:278–85. On Paul de Man.

Josipovici, Gabriel. 1971. *The World and the Book: A Study of Modern Fiction*. London: Macmillan.

8.2.   *Irony, Parody, and Metafiction*

Hutcheon, Linda. 1980. *Narcissistic Narrative: The Metafictional Paradox*. Waterloo, Ont.: Wilfrid Laurier University Press.

Lotman, Jurij. 1977. *The Structure of the Artistic Text*. Ann Arbor: Dept. of Slavic Languages, University of Michigan.

Poetics Today. 1983. A special issue (vol. 4) on "The Ironic Discourse," with sections on irony in literature and language, philosophy, sociology, and psycholinguistics.

Rose, Margaret. 1979. *Parody/Meta-fiction: An Analysis of Parody as a Critical Mirror to the Writing and Reception of Fiction*. London: Croom Helm.

Scholes, Robert. 1967. *The Fabulators*. New York: Oxford University Press.

Tynjanov, Juri. 1921. "Dostoevskij and Gogol (Zur Theorie der Parodie)." In *Russischer Formalismus*, ed. and trans. Jurij Striedter, 301–71. Munich: Fink, 1971.

8.3   What Is Fiction?

Altieri, Charles. 1981. *Act and Quality: A Theory of Literary Meaning and Humanistic Understanding*. Amherst: University of Massachusetts Press.

Austin, J. L. 1962. *How to Do Things with Words*. Cambridge: Harvard University Press.

Bateson, Gregory. 1972. "A Theory of Play and Fantasy." In *Steps to an Ecology of Mind*, 177–93. New York: Ballantine.

Cebik, L. B. 1984. *Fictional Narrative and Truth: An Epistemic Analysis*. Lanham, Md.: University Press of America, 1984.

Culler, Jonathan. 1984. "Problems in the Theory of Fiction." *Diacritics* 14.1:2–11.

Derrida, Jacques. 1975. "Economimesis." *Diacritics* 11.2 (1981):3–25.

Doležel, Lubomír. 1980b. "Truth and Authenticity in Narrative." *Poetics Today* 1.3:5–25.

Hutchison, Chris. 1984. "The Act of Narration: A Critical Survey of Some Speech-Act Theories of Narrative Discourse." *Journal of Literary Semantics* 13:3–35.

Margolis, Joseph. 1983. "The Logic and Structures of Fictional Narrative." *Philosophy and Literature* 7:162–81.

Martínez-Bonati 1981. See 6.2.

———. 1983. "Towards a Formal Ontology of Fictional Worlds." *Philosophy and Literature* 7:182–95.

Ohmann. See 7.1.

Pavel, Thomas G. 1976. "'Possible Worlds' in Literary Semantics." *Journal of Aesthetics and Art Criticism* 34:165–76.

———. 1981. "Ontological Issues in Poetics: Speech Acts and Fictional Worlds." *Journal of Aesthetics and Art Criticism* 40:167–78.

———. 1981–82. "Fiction and the Ontological Landscape." *Studies in Twentieth Century Literature* 6:149–63.

———. 1983. "Incomplete Worlds, Ritual Emotions." *Philosophy and Literature* 7:48–57.

Prado, C. G. 1984. *Making Believe: Philosophical Reflections on Fiction*. Westport, Conn.: Greenwood Press.

Pratt. See 7.1.

Rorty, Richard. 1979. "Is There a Problem about Fictional Discourse?" In *Consequences of Pragmatism (Essays: 1972–1980)*, 110–38. Minneapolis: University of Minnesota Press, 1982.

Searle, John. 1979. "The Logical Status of Fictional Discourse." In *Expression and Meaning: Studies in the Theory of Speech Acts*, 58–75. Cambridge: Cambridge University Press.

Smith, Barbara Herrnstein. 1979. *On the Margins of Discourse: The Relation of Literature to Language*. Chicago: University of Chicago Press.

Strawson, P. F. For his analysis of presuppositions, see Cebik (above), 136–43.

Waugh, Patricia. 1984. *Metafiction: The Theory and Practice of Self-Conscious Fiction*. London: Methuen.

8.4   *What Is Narrative?*

Altieri. See 8.3.

Anscombe, G. E. M. 1957. *Intention*. Oxford: Blackwell.

Cebik. See 8.3.

Dray. See 3.3.

Goffman, Erving. 1974. *Frame Analysis: An Essay on the Organization of Experience*. New York: Harper.

Jones, Peter. 1975. *Philosophy and the Novel*. New York: Oxford University Press.

Prado. See 8.3.

Ricoeur 1983. See 3.3.

———. 1984. *Time and Narrative, vol. 2*. Chicago: University of Chicago Press, 1985. The first three chapters treat the topics I have discussed in chapters 2–6, in the same order. Ricoeur's book appeared after I had completed my manuscript; thus I was unable to refer to his insights in my text.

Schafer. See 3.4.

Spence. See 3.4.

Turner, Victor. 1980. "Social Dramas and Stories about Them." *Critical Inquiry* 7:141–68.

von Wright 1971. See 3.3.

———. 1974. *Causality and Determinism*. New York: Columbia University Press.

Index

239

Index

Index

recognition, 117
Reed, Walter, 44–45
referential code, 163
repetition, 168
representation. *See* Realism
represented discourse, 138
represented speech and thought, 138–40
reversal, 117
Richardson, Samuel, 43–44, 58
Ricoeur, Paul, 76, 190
Robert, Marthe, 41
role model, 40
roman, 43
roman à clef, 43
romance, 21–22, 33, 36, 42–43, 64
roman fleuve, 84
Rorty, Richard, 184
Rose, Margaret, 179–80

Said, Edward, 87
Sartre, Jean-Paul, 158
satellites, narrative, 113
satire, 179–80
scene, 124–26, 131–34
Schlegel, Friedrich, 53
Scholes, Robert, 35–38
Schorer, Mark, 16
scripts, 67–68, 157
Searle, John, 186–87
self, 41, 75–78, 121, 141, 157–58; linguistic basis of, 148–50
semic code, 163–64
sequence, narrative, 112–13, 126
setting, 122–23
Shklovsky, Victor, 25, 47–50
showing, 124
skaz, 142
Smith, Barbara Herrnstein, 90–91, 183
speech-act theory, 182–84
Stanzel, Franz, 134–35, 231
Stewart, Ann Harleman, 95–97

story: distinguished from discourse, 108–9
stream of consciousness, 17, 134, 140
stretch, 124
structuralism, 23–26, 119–20
style, 148–50; low, 62
style indirect libre, 138
stylistic contagion, 149–50
subjectivity, 157–58
summary, 124–26, 131–34
surface structure, 99, 103
symbolic code, 164
syuzhet, 107–8, 115, 126

telling, 124
tense, grammatical: in narration, 131–34, 136–40
theme, 126–29, 188
theories: limits of, 173–74; nature of, 15, 23, 30; scientific, 174
time: in narrative, 74–76, 86–87, 123–29, 136–39
Todorov, Tzvetan, 26
Tolstoy, Leo, 65
Tomashevsky, Boris, 112–18
tree structures, 95–97
Trilling, Lionel, 18
truth, 182, 186–87
Twain, Mark: *The Adventures of Huckleberry Finn*, 54–55, 68–70, 126

Uspensky, Boris, 136, 146

voice, 124, 131, 135
vraisemblance, 64, 67–68, 73

Wellek, René, 59–61
Wells, H. G., 20
White, Hayden, 72–74
writable text, 83
writing, 28–29

Library of Congress Cataloging-in-Publication Data

Martin, Wallace.
   Recent theories of narrative.

   Bibliography: p.
   Includes index.
   1. Narration (Rhetoric) I. Title.
PN212.M37   1986   808.3   85-22401
ISBN 0-8014-1771-6 (alk. paper)
ISBN 0-8014-9355-2 (pbk. : alk. paper)